VCP

VMware Certified Professional

Elias Khnaser

VCP Exam Cram, VMware Certified Professional

ISBN-13: 978-0-7897-3805-9
ISBN-10: 0-7897-3805-8

Library of Congress Cataloging-in-Publication Data

Khnaser, Elias N.

  VCP exam cram : VMware certified professional / Elias Khnaser.— 1st ed.

    p. cm.

  ISBN 978-0-7897-3805-9 (pbk. w/cd)

  1. Electronic data processing personnel—Certification. 2. Virtual computer systems—Examinations—Study guides. 3. VMware. I. Title.

  QA76.3.K498 2009

  005.4'3—dc22

                          2008044885

Printed in the United States of America

Second Printing: February 2009

Trademarks

Warning and Disclaimer

Bulk Sales

Que Publishing offers excellent discounts on this book when ordered in quantity for bulk purchases or special sales. For more information, please contact

> **U.S. Corporate and Government Sales**
> **1-800-382-3419**
> **corpsales@pearsontechgroup.com**

For sales outside of the U.S., please contact

> **International Sales**
> **+1-317-581-3793**
> **international@pearsontechgroup.com**

Associate Publisher
David Dusthimer

Acquisitions Editor
Betsy Brown

Development Editor
Andrew Cupp

Managing Editor
Patrick Kanouse

Senior Project Editor
Tonya Simpson

Copy Editor
Chuck Hutchinson

Indexer
Ken Johnson

Proofreader
Water Crest Publishing

Technical Editors
Chris Huss

Joseph Noga

Thomas Reich

Publishing Coordinator
Vanessa Evans

Book Designer
Gary Adair

Composition
Gina Rexrode

Contents at a Glance

Table of Contents

About the Author

Elias Khnaser is an author, speaker, and IT consultant specializing in Microsoft, Citrix, and VMware technologies. He has more than 12 years of experience in administration, engineering, and architecture and has written many books and articles on the subjects. Elias has designed and deployed some of the largest Citrix implementations in the world, including 14,000 users with Rush University Medical Center in Chicago. Elias has also been designing and deploying some of the largest VMware ESX deployments, helping companies consolidate servers and build scalable environments. With the need for DR and BC, Elias has helped numerous companies design, deploy, and test viable DR and BC plans. Elias has been involved in the build-out of numerous data centers, including Rush University; General Growth Properties, the second largest owner and operator of shopping malls in the world; TransMarket group, a Futures Trading firm with offices worldwide; Huron Consulting Group; and many more.

Elias' publications and accomplishments:

- *VMware Certified Professional Exam Cram* by Que Publishing
  ISBN: 0-7897-3805-8 (June 2008)
- VMware VI3: ESX Server 3.5 & Virtual Center 2.5 Training DVD by EliasKhnaser.com (April 2008)
- "VMware ESX Server 3.0 CBT" by EliasKhnaser.com
- "Citrix MetaFrame XP CBT" by CBTnuggets.com

Co-author of three published books:

- *Citrix CCA MetaFrame Presentation Server 3.0 and 4.0* (Exams 223/256) (Exam Cram) by Que Publishing
- *MCSE Designing Security for a Windows Server 2003 Network: Exam 70-298 Study Guide and DVD Training System* by Syngress Publishing
- *Citrix MetaFrame XP Including Feature Release 1* by Syngress Publishing

Contributing author at:

- *WindowsITPro Magazine*
- Techrepublic.com
- Certcities.com
- Cramsession.com
- Dabcc.com

About the Contributing Author

Warren E. Wyrostek is the owner of Warren E. Wyrostek, M.Ed. (a Novell Authorized Partner) and 3WsCertification.com (a portal dedicated to Novell Training and Support). He holds a master's degree in Vocational-Technical Education from Valdosta State College, a master's in Divinity from New York's Union Theological Seminary, and is devoted to technical education as reflected by his list certifications. He currently holds 25 Novell certifications, including the CNI, MCNE, and CDE. Warren has been teaching more than 20 years and has taught at the college and secondary school levels. He has taught Novell authorized courses since 1996. Professionally, his main joy comes from being a freelance writer, course developer, and contract trainer for various technologies that revolve around integrated networking. He has been the technical editor for more than 20 certification titles in the past few years. At heart, he is a teacher who loves what technical education offers. Many of Warren's certification articles can be found on Informit.com, including "Now What? A Career Changer's Odyssey." You can reach Warren at wyrostekw@msn.com.

Dedication

To "Princess" Maya and "Batman" Peter, my gorgeous niece and nephew, may you grow up under the Lord and your parents' watchful eyes to become fantastic people that light up the sky like a flame. To my gorgeous sister, Aida, and my brothers, Zach, Eddie, and Danny, for being there when it matters.

Acknowledgments

No book would ever come to fruition without the incredible work done by everyone behind the scenes, and as such, I must extend a huge "thank you" to all the people at Que for their amazing work. To Dave Dusthimer, associate publisher, for his immediate interest and excitement about this book, thank you for trusting me on this one. To Betsy Brown, acquisitions editor extraordinaire, thank you so much for your promptness and patience. I'm very thankful to have had you on this project (honestly, it's true!). You're a pleasure to work with. To Drew Cupp, development editor, I can only imagine what you had to put up with to get this done. To Chuck Hutchinson, thanks for correcting my shoddy grammar, pointing out the obvious mistakes, and tirelessly ensuring that I'm actually saying what I think I'm saying. Special thanks to all the production staff who silently (at least silently from my perspective) work to put everything together. As always, it looks fantastic! And finally, thanks to the great work of our technical editors, Joe Noga, Thomas Reich, and Chris Huss, who provided excellent insight, suggestions, and corrections to my work. Of course, any errors or omissions are strictly my doing. These guys can't be expected to find everything!

And special thanks to the friends and family who had to once again endure the pressures and pains of book writing. They'll get used to it someday...

Happy reading and good luck!

We Want to Hear from You!

As the reader of this book, *you* are our most important critic and commentator. We value your opinion and want to know what we're doing right, what we could do better, what areas you'd like to see us publish in, and any other words of wisdom you're willing to pass our way.

As an associate publisher for Que Publishing, I welcome your comments. You can email or write me directly to let me know what you did or didn't like about this book—as well as what we can do to make our books better.

Please note that I cannot help you with technical problems related to the topic of this book. We do have a User Services group, however, where I will forward specific technical questions related to the book.

When you write, please be sure to include this book's title and author as well as your name, email address, and phone number. I will carefully review your comments and share them with the author and editors who worked on the book.

Email: feedback@quepublishing.com

Mail: David Dusthimer
         Que Publishing
         800 East 96th Street
         Indianapolis, IN 46240 USA

Reader Services

Visit our website and register this book at informit.com/register for convenient access to any updates, downloads, or errata that might be available for this book.

Preface

Virtualization is one of the hottest topics in the tech industry today. The leader in the virtualization space at the present time is without a doubt VMware with its virtual infrastructure offering. As VMware software began to take its place in the data center and demand respect in the industry, the need for a certification path became clear. Such a certification separates those who have studied the technology and can apply it at a professional level from those who have just installed it and started messing with it. I am a big believer that there is no alternative to studying a technology thoroughly. There is only so much you can learn from installing it and using it in only a few specific circumstances, because that exposes you only to limited features and obscures you from harnessing the full potential of the software by leveraging features you probably never knew existed. For this reason and many more, I am a strong believer that you should study the software, learn it, and then use it hands on as much as possible. It is by doing this that you truly master the software.

When you have studied and understand a software, taking a certification exam becomes relatively easy. For example, if you've thoroughly studied, you know that the maximum amount of physical memory that ESX 3.5 supports is 256GB. However, someone who just installs the software and starts using it may not know this because the software installation does not require this knowledge at the time of installation.

This book aims to present the information you need to recap and reinforce your existing knowledge of VMware Infrastructure 3 and properly prepare you to confidently take the VCP-310 exam. The book is structured in a way to help you with your final exam preparation and contains enough information to make it a true test preparation book, but in a concise manner.

Introduction

Welcome to the *VCP Exam Cram*. The purpose of this book is to properly prepare you and equip you with the needed knowledge to successfully sit and pass the VCP-310 exam. Here, we provide a general overview of the VMware certification program and discuss how this *Exam Cram* book will help you reach your goals of becoming certified.

This book, as with its predecessors in the *Exam Cram* family of certification books, concentrates on reinforcing your knowledge of the subject matter at hand and preparing you to sit the exam. That being said, this book will not teach you everything there is to know about the technology because this is not its primary purpose. We instead concentrate on the material that is most likely to appear on the test.

Before you dive in head first into the information provided, we recommend you take the self-assessment that immediately follows this introduction. This self-assessment will help you evaluate your knowledge of the VMware material both in the real world and under ideal exam circumstances.

Based on the results of the self-assessment, you may feel that additional education is necessary. Numerous resources are available, including

- ▶ Official VMware-authorized training. VMware Infrastructure 3: Install & Configure V3.5 is the ideal course for the VCP exam.

- ▶ VMware product documentation and technical white papers are available at http://www.vmware.com.

- ▶ VMware VI3: ESX Server 3.5 & VC 2.5 Training DVD by Elias Khnaser goes in depth on the subject matter and is a great way to learn again and again at your own pace. See http://www.eliaskhnaser.com.

- ▶ Other books, including *Mastering VMware Infrastructure 3* by Chris McCain, are also excellent resources on the subject.

Although reading a book is an excellent way of learning, we strongly recommend that you take the knowledge you acquire from book learning and use it to install and configure VMware ESX Server and VirtualCenter. Hands-on experience is imperative not only to your successful completion of the exam, but also to your successful endeavors in properly implementing and maintaining an ESX environment.

About the VMware VCP Program

The VMware VCP program was designed to allow candidates to demonstrate their expertise with the software by completing certain requirements and passing an exam. The program is open to any individuals who complete the requirements. There are many advantages to becoming VCP certified. For some, it will be for career advancement; for others, it will be to become VMware partners, and so on.

The requirements set forth by VMware on becoming a VCP are as follows:

- Attend a VMware authorized course. These instructor-led courses provide a great learning method and hands-on exposure to the product.

- Gain hands-on experience with the product.

- Sit and pass the VCP-310 exam to demonstrate your expertise on the matter.

VMware also provides various documents on its website that help you gain a better understanding of the topics that you will be challenged on during the exam. I would like to single out the VI3 Exam blueprint as a great reference for the exam.

Taking a VMware Certification Exam

As of this writing, VMware Education requires you to attend a VMware-authorized training class to fulfill your eligibility on becoming a VMware Certified Professional (VCP). After you have attended the VMware-authorized class and have completed your preparations for taking the exam, you need to register at a VMware testing center in your area. Currently, all VMware certification exams are administered by Pearson VUE. You can register online at http://www.pearsonvue.com/vmware or by calling 1-800-676-2797 in the United States and Canada. Outside the Americas, please consult the Pearson VUE website for contact information in your region of the world.

The VCP-310 exam costs $175 USD and must be booked at least 24 hours in advance. You may reschedule your exam up to 24 hours before the date you intend on taking it. Cancellation may be subject to a fee, so please consult the Pearson VUE website for more details on the policy.

When scheduling the exam, you need to provide personal identification to validate your identity, the name and number of the exam you want to take, and a method of payment. Online registration requires the creation of a personal account with Pearson VUE; this account will track all the exams you have taken, with the result of the exam in the form of a pass/fail. Your account will also be used for all future tests you want to take that are administered by Pearson VUE. On the day of the exam, you must provide appropriate identification to verify your identity. Typically, two forms of identification are required, with one of them being a photo ID.

Plan to arrive at the exam location at least 10 to 15 minutes early so that you can fill out any last-minute forms, be seated, relax, and prepare prior to the start of the exam. All VMware exams are completely closed book. No study aids—or anything else for that matter—are permitted into the testing area. This includes coats, bags, or purses, all of which must be left with the administrator before entering the room. The best advice is to bring as little as possible with you to the test facility.

In the test room, the administrator logs you in to your exam, verifying that your user ID and exam number are correct. After you review the introduction information, the exam begins.

The VCP-310 VMware Certification exam has 75 questions, and native English speakers have 105 minutes to complete the exam. Non-English speakers have an additional 30 minutes, for a total of 135 minutes. The testing application is Windows based and presents a single question per screen. On the top right, you will find the time and number of questions remaining.

Questions are typically multiple choice, and the difficulty level varies from question to question. You can expect the following:

▶ **Select the correct answer:** With these types of multiple-choice questions, you are asked to choose the one correct answer that most appropriately answers the given question. In some situations, different answers may be correct under slightly different configurations, so make sure you read the question carefully and answer it according to what is asked in the specific question.

▶ **Select all that apply (or don't apply):** These types of questions ask you to select all the answers listed that correctly apply to the question given. None of the answers to all of them may apply, so be sure to read these types of questions carefully. In many cases, subtle wording has been purposely used to trip up those who aren't paying attention. Partial credit is not given for these types of questions. Unless the correct answer is given, you receive no credit for the question.

▶ **True or False:** These types of questions present you with the option to agree with the statement in the question or refuse it. Read the question carefully and choose true or false.

When your test is scored, no added penalty is given for a wrong answer compared to a giving no answer at all, so answering every question asked is worthwhile even if you are not sure and must guess. To the best of its ability, VMware has attempted to make the questions as fair as possible and to ensure that all questions have a single correct answer. Of course, mistakes do happen, and a "poor" question may find its way onto your test, presenting you with a poorly worded or ambiguous question that may not have a clearly correct answer.

In this situation, the best thing to do is to answer the question to the best of your knowledge. You are not allowed to leave the test area with any written exam questions or notes or any kind of information, so you are not able to write down the question for later review. Clearly, you can contact VMware regarding a particular ambiguous question so that it may be corrected on future tests, but you should not expect that your exam will be rescored because of a single question. If you have properly and adequately prepared for the exam, a single question will have no bearing on whether you pass or fail.

After you complete the exam, the testing software responds with your score after a few seconds and informs you whether you have passed or failed. The VCP-310 exam requires a minimum score of 75% to pass the exam.

If you don't pass the exam, the key point is not to become discouraged. We have all had days when things just didn't quite go as well as we had hoped. Take some time after the exam to review areas where you struggled during the test. Maybe a particular area caught you by surprise, or you felt you had a stronger handle on it than you actually did. The best method in this situation is to return as soon as possible to the study process and brush up on your weak areas in preparation for another exam attempt.

You can reschedule a new test through Pearson VUE as soon as available if you so choose. We recommend that you schedule time sooner rather than later so that material that you have already studied is still fresh in your mind. You are required to pay the full fee to take the test again.

How to Prepare for the Exam

Preparing for the VCP exam, as with any other technical exam, requires that you dedicate time to both acquiring and studying directly related material to the VCP-310 exam. To pass this exam, you are expected to know the different components and technologies that make up the VMWare Infrastructure 3 suite, which includes intimate knowledge of both ESX Server 3.5 and VirtualCenter 2.5.

> **NOTE**
>
> There is significant information to absorb and go through that is required for you to pass the VCP-310 exam. Therefore, if your plan is to study the night before or a few days before the exam, don't expect to be fully prepared on the day of the exam.

The following is a general list of material that can be helpful in preparing you for the VCP-310 exam:

- ▶ This *Exam Cram* book, which provides you with a concise and thorough review of the material considered vital to your exam-taking success. This book serves as a supplement to reinforce your knowledge of the technology.

- ▶ VMware ESX Server 3.5 and VirtualCenter 2.5 evaluation kits from VMware. By acquiring an evaluation of the software, installing it, and getting intimately familiar with it, you are training yourself hands on, and this knowledge is extremely valuable as you learn better as you do things. This step also takes you from the theoretical to the practical.

- ▶ VMware-authorized training course. The instructor-led four-day class enables you to focus your training on a mixture of lecture and hands-on labs. The instructor-led class is filled with valuable information and helpful labs and is sure to prime you for the VCP exam in addition to its being a requirement for fulfilling the VCP requirements.

- ▶ VMware Infrastructure 3 Training DVD from http://www.eliaskhnaser.com is a great way to learn, reinforce existing knowledge, or simply have handy as a reference any time you need it. The DVD is filled with information and goes beyond the VCP-310 requirements. It is a study-at-your-own-pace training course.

- ▶ Exam preparation tests from respectable vendors. Getting accustomed to the types of questions that are asked on the VCP exam is extremely helpful; you will find that VMware has some sample questions on its website. You may also find certification exam vendors that sell respectable preparation tests.

What This Book Will Do

This book is designed to be read as a pointer to the areas of knowledge you will be tested on. In other words, you might want to read the book one time just to get insight into how comprehensive your knowledge of this topic is. The book is also designed to be read shortly before you go for the actual test. We think you can use this book to get a sense of the underlying context of any topic in the chapters or to skim-read for Exam Alerts, bulleted points, summaries, and topic headings.

We have drawn on material from VMware's own listing of knowledge requirements, from other preparation guides, and from the exams themselves. We have also drawn from a battery of technical websites, as well as from our own experience with VMware ESX Server and the exam. Our aim is to walk you through the knowledge you will need.

What This Book Will Not Do

This book will *not* teach you everything you need to know about VMware Infrastructure 3 and ESX Server 3.5. The scope of the book is exam preparation. The book is intended to ramp you up and give you confidence heading into the exam. This book reviews what you need to know before you take the test, with its fundamental purpose dedicated to reviewing the information needed on the VMware certification exam.

This book uses a variety of teaching and memorization techniques to analyze the exam-related topics and to provide you with everything you need to know to pass the test.

About This Book

We suggest that you read this book from front to back. You will not be wasting your time because nothing we have written is a guess about an unknown exam. We have had to explain certain underlying information on such a regular basis that we have included those explanations here.

After you have read the book, you can brush up on a certain area by using the index or the table of contents to go straight to the topics and questions you want to re-examine. We have tried to use the headings and subheadings to provide outline information about each given topic. After you have been certified, we think you will find this book useful as a tightly focused reference and an essential foundation of VMware Infrastructure 3 configuration and management.

How to Use This Book

Each *Exam Cram* chapter follows a regular structure, along with graphical cues about especially important or useful material. The structure of a typical chapter is as follows:

▶ **Opening hotlists:** Each chapter begins with lists of the terms you need to understand and concepts you need to master before you can be fully conversant in the chapter's subject matter. We follow the hotlists with a few introductory paragraphs, setting the stage for the rest of the chapter.

▶ **Topical coverage:** After the opening hotlists, each chapter covers the topics related to the chapter's subject.

▶ **Exam Alerts:** Throughout the text, we highlight material most likely to appear on the exam by using a special Exam Alert that looks like this:

EXAM ALERT

This is what an Exam Alert looks like. An Exam Alert stresses concepts, terms, or best practices that will most likely appear in one or more certification exam questions. For that reason, we think any information presented in an Exam Alert is worthy of unusual attentiveness on your part.

Even if material is not flagged as an Exam Alert, *all* the content in this book is associated in some way with test-related material. What appears in the chapter content is critical knowledge.

▶ **Notes:** This book is an overall examination of ESX Server configuration, management, and troubleshooting. As such, we delve into many aspects of computer networks. Where a body of knowledge is deeper than the scope of the book, we use notes to indicate areas of concern.

NOTE

Cramming for an exam will get you through a test, but it will not make you a competent professional. Although you can memorize just the facts you need to become certified, your daily work in the field will rapidly put you in water over your head if you do not know the underlying principles.

▶ **Tips:** We provide tips that will help you to build a better foundation of knowledge or to focus your attention on an important concept that reappears later in the book. Tips provide a helpful way to remind you of the context surrounding a particular area of a topic under discussion.

> **TIP**
>
> This is how tips are formatted. Keep your eyes open for these, and you'll become an ESX Server guru in no time!

▶ **Practice questions:** This section presents a short list of test questions related to the specific chapter topic. Following the questions are explanations of both correct and incorrect answers. The practice questions highlight the areas we found to be most important on the exam.

The bulk of the book follows this chapter structure, but we would like to point out a few other elements:

▶ **Practice Exams:** The book has two practice exams so you can practice on all the exam topics.

▶ **Practice Exam Answer Explanations:** Each practice exam is followed by an answer key that includes thorough explanations to each question so you know why you got it wrong or right.

▶ **Glossary:** Near the back of the book is an extensive glossary of important terms used in this book.

▶ **Cram Sheet:** This feature appears as a tear-away sheet inside the front cover of this *Exam Cram* book. It is a valuable tool that represents a collection of the most difficult-to-remember facts and numbers we think you should memorize before taking the test. Remember, you can dump this information out of your head onto a piece of paper as soon as you enter the testing room. These are usually facts that we have found require brute-force memorization. You need to remember this information only long enough to write it down when you walk into the test room. Be advised that you will be asked to surrender all personal belongings other than pencils before you enter the exam room itself.

You might want to look at the Cram Sheet in your car or in the lobby of the testing center just before you walk into the testing center. The Cram Sheet is divided under headings, so you can review the appropriate parts just before each test.

▶ **CD:** The CD features an innovative practice test engine so you can practice taking the exam electronically. See Appendix B, "What's on the CD-ROM?," for more details.

Self-Assessment

Before you attempt to take the VCP-310 exam and try to become a VMware Certified Professional (VCP), it is imperative that you know considerable information about VMware Infrastructure 3 and all its suite components. There is so much breadth to this exam that we felt it necessary to include a Self-Assessment within this book to help you evaluate your exam readiness. Within this portion of the book, take a look at what is needed to pass the exam and assess your preparedness.

VCP in the Real World

To complete the VCP certification, you have to be a very well-rounded ESX Server-aware individual. The VCP certification is meaningful and maps closely to the everyday virtualization work environment found in the real world. With that said, you will also likely find this particular exam quite challenging to complete successfully.

The exam requires you to have at least a base level of knowledge about the entire VMware Infrastructure suite. You need to know how ESX Server 3.5 networking works, including the concept of virtual networking within a virtual infrastructure. You need to be intimately familiar with storage in an ESX environment, including what types of storage are supported and how to best configure this storage for optimal performance of the virtual machines. Backup is no small task in any environment, and knowing how to safeguard your VMs and recover them when necessary is crucial to VCP certification. Monitoring and resource management are other areas where you will be tested, without a doubt. And all these text topics are certainly not to dismiss VirtualCenter in all its intricacies.

Increasing numbers of people are becoming VCPs, so the goal is within reach. If you're willing to tackle the process seriously and do what it takes to obtain the necessary experience and knowledge, you can take—and pass—the exam involved in obtaining a VCP certification.

The Ideal VCP Candidate

Just to give you some idea of what an ideal candidate is like, here is some relevant information about the background and experience such an individual should have:

▶ Training or significant on-the-job experience in network theory, concepts, and operations is helpful. This includes everything from networking media and transmission techniques through network operating systems, services, and applications.

▶ Experience with any UNIX operating system is a plus to any candidate. Because the Service Console operating system is Linux based, knowing Linux in particular or UNIX in general will help you navigate better and use common UNIX commands in daily tasks.

▶ Training or significant on-the-job experience in storage technologies including Fiber Channel and iSCSI is a huge plus, but this book covers these concepts to the extent they are tested on the VCP exam. However, knowledge of these technologies will make you more comfortable with the material.

▶ A thorough understanding of how to install operating systems is required because these virtual machines require an OS installation.

Put Yourself to the Test

The following series of questions and observations are designed to help you figure out how much work you'll face in pursuing the VCP certification and what kinds of resources you can consult on your quest. Be absolutely honest in your answers; otherwise, you'll end up wasting money on an exam you're not ready to take. There are no right or wrong answers—only steps along the path to certification. Only you can decide when you are ready.

Two things should be clear from the outset, however:

▶ Even a modest background in computer science is helpful.

▶ Hands-on experience with ESX Server and its technologies is an essential ingredient for success.

Educational Background

1. Have you ever taken any computer-related classes?

    If Yes, proceed to question 2; if No, proceed to question 4.

2. Have you taken any classes on computer operating systems?

    If Yes, you will probably be able to handle ESX's architecture and system component discussions. If you're rusty, brush up on basic operating system concepts.

    If No, consider some basic reading in this area. We strongly recommend a good general operating systems book such as *Operating Systems Concepts*, 7th edition (ISBN: 0471694665), by Abraham Silberschatz.

3. Have you taken any networking concepts or technologies classes?

    If Yes, you will probably be able to handle ESX's networking terminology, concepts, and technologies (brace yourself for frequent departures from normal usage). If you're rusty, brush up on basic networking concepts and terminology, especially networking media, transmission type, and networking technologies such as Ethernet.

    If No, you might want to read one or two books in this topic area. The two best books that we know of are *Computer Networks*, 4th edition (Prentice-Hall, 2002, ISBN: 0-13-066102-3), by Andrew S. Tanenbaum and *Computer Networks and Internets with Internet Applications*, 4th edition (Prentice-Hall, 2004, ISBN: 0-13-143351-2), by Douglas E. Comer.

    Skip to the next section, "Hands-On Experience."

4. Have you done any signification reading or self-directed study on operating systems?

    If Yes, you will probably be able to handle ESX's architecture and system component discussions. If you're rusty, brush up on basic operating system concepts.

    If No, consider some basic reading in this area. We strongly recommend a good general operating systems book such as *Operating Systems Concepts*, 7th edition (ISBN: 0471694665), by Abraham Silberschatz.

5. Have you done any signification reading or self-directed study on computer networking?

If Yes, you will probably be able to handle ESX's networking terminology, concepts, and technologies (brace yourself for frequent departures from normal usage). If you're rusty, brush up on basic networking concepts and terminology, especially networking media, transmission type, and networking technologies such as Ethernet.

If No, you might want to read one or two books in this topic area. The two best books that we know of are *Computer Networks*, 4th edition (Prentice-Hall, 2002, ISBN: 0-13-066102-3), by Andrew S. Tanenbaum and *Computer Networks and Internets with Internet Applications*, 4th edition (Prentice-Hall, 2004, ISBN: 0-13-143351-2), by Douglas E. Comer.

Hands-On Experience

Perhaps the most important key to success on any certification exam is hands-on experience, especially with ESX Server, plus the many add-on services and components like VMotion, Storage VMotion, and others. If you leave with only one realization after taking this self-assessment, it should be that there's no substitute for time spent installing, configuring, and using the various VMware Infrastructure components on which you'll be tested repeatedly and in depth.

Have you installed, configured, and worked with ESX 3.5?

▶ If yes, make sure you have a good understanding of virtual networking, storage, resource management, and the entire VI suite.

You can download objectives, practice exams, and other data about the VCP exam from the VMware Certification page at http://mylearn1.vmware.com/portals/certification/. Use the exam blueprint link to obtain specific exam information.

▶ If you haven't worked with ESX 3.5, you must obtain one or two machines and a copy of the software. Then learn the software and any other components on which you'll also be tested. You can download an evaluation copy of ESX, which is good for 60 days.

TIP

Taking an instructor-led class has many benefits. Aside from being a requirement for fulfilling your VCP certification, the class also is particularly important for those just starting out or with limited knowledge or access to state-of-the-art computer systems. VMware has designed good courses available to be taken in most communities. In addition, the course includes trial versions of the software that is the focus of your course.

Testing Your Exam Readiness

Whether you attend a formal class on a specific topic to get ready for an exam or use written materials to study on your own, some preparation for the certification exams is essential. You pay for your exam attempts pass or fail, so you want to do everything you can to pass on your first try.

This book includes several practice exam questions for each chapter and two sample tests. If you don't score well on the chapter questions, study more and then tackle the sample tests at the end of the book. Use the questions to identify areas of deficiency.

Have you taken a VCP practice exam and scored well?

▶ If yes and you scored 90% or better, you're probably ready to tackle the real thing. Make sure you can score this regularly.

▶ If you haven't taken any practice exams or your score isn't above that crucial 90% threshold, use the practice exams in this book and on the CD to keep at it until you break that barrier. Make note on the topics you struggle with most. Go back and study in your areas of deficiency, and repeat the practice tests. Keep at it until you can comfortably break the 90% threshold.

> **TIP**
>
> There is no better way to assess your test readiness than to take a good-quality practice exam and pass with a score of 90% or better. When we're preparing, we shoot for 95+%, just to leave room for the "weirdness factor" that sometimes shows up on exams.

Onward, Through the Fog!

After you've assessed your readiness, undertaken the right background studies, obtained the hands-on experience that will help you understand the products and technologies at work, and reviewed the many sources of information to help you prepare for a test, you'll be ready to take a round of practice tests. When your scores come back positive enough to get you through the exam, you're ready to go after the real thing. If you follow this regimen, you'll know not only what you need to study, but also when you're ready to take the exam. Good luck!

CHAPTER ONE

Introducing VMware Infrastructure 3

Terms you'll need to understand:

- ✓ VMkernel
- ✓ Service Console (SC)
- ✓ VMware Infrastructure
- ✓ Virtual Machine (VM)
- ✓ VMware Symmetric Multi-Processing (SMP)
- ✓ VMotion
- ✓ Distributed Resource Scheduler (DRS)
- ✓ Virtual Machine File System (VMFS)
- ✓ VMware Consolidated Backup (VCB)
- ✓ High Availability (HA)

Concepts and techniques you'll need to master:

- ✓ What virtualization is and how VMware Infrastructure 3 (VI3) delivers enterprise class virtualization
- ✓ The relationship between the Service Console and the ESX Server Host
- ✓ The different components that make up the VI3 family and what they do
- ✓ The different types of virtualization available and which category VI3 falls under

This chapter digs in and starts talking about virtualization in general and progresses to a discussion of VMware Infrastructure 3 specifically. The word *virtualization* gets thrown around a lot these days, and in most cases it's used to imply server virtualization. But because virtualization is so much more than just server virtualization, this chapter discusses the different types of virtualization technologies that are at your disposal today.

It will be imperative that you, as a virtualization professional, can identify and distinguish between types of virtualization solutions. After you have reinforced your knowledge of the types of virtualization, this chapter moves on to a virtual machine overview and provides an understanding of the different components of a *virtual machine (VM)* and how a VM compares to a physical machine.

The chapter wraps up with an introduction to VMware Infrastructure 3, which is the subject of this book and the topic of your exam. This chapter breaks down the main components of the VI3 suite—identifying and explaining its main architectural features.

What Is Virtualization?

When you think of the concept of virtualization and realize that it has been around for quite some time now, you might ask what happened to suddenly make this technology so attractive that it has penetrated every data center in the world one way or another and even requires its own professional certification. Virtualization in its purest form is the separation of the physical hardware from the software that is installed on it by adding a layer of software between them. This layer is known as the *hypervisor* and is typically installed on bare metal.

The hypervisor allows you to install multiple instances of the same or different operating systems on the same physical machine. It virtualizes the hardware components of the machine it is installed on and presents virtual hardware to the operating system to facilitate the installation. The hypervisor then acts as the "maestro," or the regulator, that organizes how these operating system instances (referred to as virtual machines) have access to the hardware.

Why You Need Virtualization

To understand why you need virtualization, first take a quick look at the data center today without virtualization. The first things you will notice in any data center are siloed servers and applications; in other words, there is a one-to-one relationship between the server and the application that resides on it. Examples include servers that are dedicated for Microsoft Exchange or SQL or Internet Information Services (IIS) or Citrix; there are servers that are just domain controllers, domain name system (DNS) servers, or print servers. This practice leaves servers that are underutilized as far as resources are concerned. So if you have a dual-socket, dual-core server acting as a domain controller or an IIS server, for example, a closer look at these servers will reveal that their resource utilization as far as CPU is concerned is probably no more than 15–20%.

So underutilized hardware and crowded data centers that require a lot of cooling and power are the main denominators at any data center. This is where virtualization shines. By virtualizing, you are taking advantage of the best of both worlds: You can have multiple server instances on the same hardware, preserving the one-to-one, server-to-application siloing you have been accustomed to for stability and separation reasons, while now taking better advantage of resources and reducing the amount of cooling and power needed. As the amount of physical hardware shrinks, this allows for more efficient usage of energy, leading to "Green IT."

Types of Virtualization

There are different types of virtualization. The most common and most popular as of this writing is operating system virtualization, which is what VMware Infrastructure 3 is. Server virtualization is the process of separating the physical hardware from the operating system software.

The different forms of virtualization can be categorized as follows:

▶ *Bare metal* is what ESX 3.5 and ESXi are. This type of operating system virtualization installs a thin layer of software known as the hypervisor, or the virtualization layer, on bare metal.

▶ In *host-based virtualization* you have an underlying operating system loaded on the physical machine and then you install software that allows virtual machines to be created and run. Examples include VMware Workstation, VMware Server, Microsoft Virtual PC, and Microsoft Virtual Servers. This type of virtualization is less efficient because it carries the additional resource burden of an underlying operating system and also relies on this operating system to remain stable for the VM loaded on it to function properly.

EXAM ALERT

As a VMware Certified Professional, you are expected to know the difference between host-based and bare metal hypervisors. The exam will surely touch on this subject.

▶ *Application virtualization* is the process of separating the application from being installed on the operating system. What you end up with here are a bunch of files that make up the virtual application. The virtual application is then run on the operating system as if it were installed on it but without actually installing. This eliminates any potential for application conflicts and shared DLL problems because the application is not installed and is not sharing the Registry or the DLLs. All the files and Registry settings it needs to run are encapsulated within the files of the virtual application.

▶ *Storage virtualization* is the process of presenting virtual storage to the hosts. This virtual storage can be a combination of different physical technologies and can reside in different places on the network, but is presented to the host as a single storage capacity.

Virtual Machine Overview

Virtual machines are similar to physical machines in terms of what they are made up of and what constitutes them. The only difference is that physical machines obviously use physical hardware, whereas virtual machines use virtual hardware. In virtual machines, you find all the usual components that make up a physical machine, such as a virtual CPU, virtual memory, virtual hard drive, and a virtual network interface card (NIC). Similar to physical machines where you can add additional physical components like small computer system interface (SCSI) adapters or serial ports, virtual machines enable you to add virtual components on the fly, whether they are SCSI adapters, serial ports, or parallel ports.

In essence, a virtual machine creates an x86 or x64 platform that allocates all the needed virtual components to allow for an operating system installation. Virtual machines are also very portable because they are made up of a collection of files, which means at any given time you can back up these files, move them, copy them to your USB drive, and take them anywhere.

Virtual machines using VMware technology have two different file extensions:

▸ .vmx: This file contains all the configurations that make up a particular VM, such as how many virtual processors are allocated, how much memory is reserved, the path to the hard drive, and any additional components that are configured for this VM.

▸ .vmdk: This file is the physical hard drive equivalent. It holds the file system, the operating system, and any applications or software loaded on this VM.

Virtual machine benefits are numerous, but the following are the fundamental benefits:

▸ **Isolation:** Because virtual machines run independently of one another and are not dependent on one another to function, the failure of one VM is completely isolated to that VM and in no way affects other VMs running on the same ESX host.

▸ **Encapsulation:** Virtual machines are encapsulated in a series of files and are thus very portable and easy to work with.

▸ **Hardware independence:** Virtual machines running on ESX hosts are unaware of the underlying hardware and don't care about it. They interact with physical hardware resources through the virtualization layer.

▸ **Compatibility:** All virtual machines are presented with a standard x86 or x64 hardware architecture, thereby ensuring proper compatibility and stability between the virtualized hardware and the operating system.

Simulation and Emulation

A common mistake that people not familiar with virtualization make is that they think virtualization is similar to emulation or simulation. The fact of the matter is virtualization is neither emulation nor simulation, because with virtualization you install the actual operating system on virtual hardware. You go through the same steps, and the operating system itself does not know that it is being installed on virtualized hardware. Furthermore, virtualization requires no custom development or programming of any sort, whereas simulation and emulation do.

That being said, it's important to understand what simulation and emulation are so you have a clearer understanding of why they are not virtualization. A simulation is a preconfigured environment in which limited functionality is available, and as such you are limited to this preconfigured environment. For example, you can develop a fighting simulation based on certain rules and programming languages to mimic real conflict, without there being actual fighting. You do this for training purposes mainly. A flight simulator is a common example of using a simulator for training—computers can mimic the complications of flight without the trainee having to take the risk of flight.

Emulation, on the other hand, is the process of taking a piece of hardware and trying to port it to software. For example, to emulate a router (hardware), you need to create software that performs the functions of the router. You basically need to program the commands that you want to emulate and make sure they respond the same way they would on the real hardware.

In both simulation and emulation, there is a significant programming and development process that takes place to re-create something, whereas that is not the case with virtualization.

> **EXAM ALERT**
>
> Part of VMware's virtualization marketing strategy is to emphasize that virtualization is not simulation or emulation. It would be a safe assumption that this topic will be covered on the exam.

Virtual and Physical Machine Comparison

One of the main advantages to using VMs over physical machines is that VMs use what is known as "ideal hardware," and what we mean by that is VMs will always run on the same type of virtual motherboard with all the same components. Whether you are loading Linux or Windows, the VM sees the same ideal hardware. This capability is great because if you are running your ESX host on an HP and decide to move your VMs to an IBM or Dell, they are not affected because they don't know the difference and in no way rely on the underlying hardware of the host.

They all see the same x86 ideal hardware presented to them. This capability is critical for the stability of the system; historically, blue screens and other instability factors were in most cases related to hardware and software not coexisting—incompatible drivers, firmware issues, and so on. However, by standardizing the virtual hardware, you have now stabilized the system and chopped off a significant factor that used to lead to instability.

Physical machines have the following limitations compared to virtual machines:

- ▶ Underutilize resources

- ▶ Are bound to the hardware

- ▶ Require complicated process to be copied, cloned, or moved

On the other hand, virtual machines have the following benefits:

- ▶ No binding to a particular set of hardware

- ▶ Standard x86 architecture

- ▶ Collection of files can be easily moved around, copied, or backed up

EXAM ALERT

Because one of the main reasons to virtualize is to replace physical machines with virtual machines, this topic will surely make the VCP exam.

Why VMware Infrastructure 3?

Virtualization has been around for many years. The reason it is now one of the most needed and most sought after solutions on the market is that VMware developed this technology with the enterprise in mind. You can now do virtualization on an enterprise level. VI3 has many features that make it attractive—all of which are discussed in different chapters in this book. These features include *VMotion*, which allows you to move a virtual machine from one host to another without powering it down, and *Distributed Resource Scheduler (DRS)*, which automatically moves virtual machines from one host to another if it determines that a host is running low on resources where another host has plenty available.

VI3 has made the provisioning of a server a quick and easy process, as well as a portable process. You can now have your entire data center on a USB hard drive that you can move wherever you want.

VMware Infrastructure 3 Suite

VMware Infrastructure 3 is a suite of applications that collectively make enterprise class virtualization possible. The VI3 components are organized as follows:

- ▶ **VMware ESX 3.5 or ESXi:** The platform upon which VMs run. The main difference between ESX 3.5 and 3i is that 3.5 uses a *Service Console (SC)* as its management arm, whereas 3i has no Service Console and has a smaller footprint of just 32MB. We will discuss this in broader detail in later chapters.

▶ **VMware Virtual Symmetric Multi-Processing (SMP):** The VMware-developed technology that allows virtual machines to have more than one virtual CPU (vCPU). SMP allows VMs to have up to 4 vCPUs and thus be able to virtualize those applications that are resource hungry.

▶ **VMware Virtual Center 2.5:** A Windows-based application that centrally manages your enterprise deployment of ESX Servers. From Virtual Center, you can control all your ESX hosts, configure resource optimization, and take advantage of all the enterprise-class tools available with ESX.

▶ **VMotion:** The technology that allows you to move VMs between hosts without interruption to the user or loss of data. It moves VMs while they are online.

▶ **Storage VMotion:** A new feature introduced with Virtual Center 2.5 that allows you to migrate the virtual machine files from one shared storage to another with no interruption to the user or loss of data.

▶ **Update Manager:** A feature that allows for the automatic download and patching of ESX Server and its Windows and Linux VMs. Think of it as the Windows Update equivalent.

▶ **VMware Converter:** The tool that allows you to convert physical machines to virtual machines, a process otherwise known as P2V. It also allows you to convert non-ESX VMs to ESX-compatible VMs, a process otherwise known as V2V.

▶ **High Availability (HA):** A technology that allows you to restart VMs on a different ESX host in the event that the original ESX host should experience any problems. HA ensures the VMs are brought back online as quickly as possible.

▶ **Distributed Resource Scheduler (DRS):** A technology that allows for the balancing of ESX host resources. In the event that an ESX host is running low on system resources like CPU or memory, DRS will migrate VMs from this host to another ESX host that is not experiencing a lack of resource allocation.

▶ **VMware Consolidated Backup (VCB):** A backup framework that allows third-party backup software to plug in and back up VMs in a centralized fashion.

You might have noticed how feature rich the VI3 suite is, and what makes it even more compelling and powerful is the fact that it is self-contained. You can run a *virtual infrastructure* without needing any other tools. This is not to say that you will not need third-party tools that can render many tasks easier and less complicated, but in the final analysis, the VI3 suite can run on its own. VMware recognized that the suite it is offering will need an optimal environment to run in and therefore created the Virtual Machine Files System, the VI3 suite's playground.

What Is VMFS?

Virtual Machine File System (VMFS) is a VMware-developed file system designed solely to run virtual machines. VMFS is a lightweight file system in that it does not have all the overhead that the other file systems have, making it an ideal environment for VMs to run in. The only structure you can create on VMFS volumes is directories to organize the VM files.

The VMkernel

The *VMkernel*, also known as the hypervisor, is the software that is installed on the bare metal hardware and thus creates the virtualization layer. The VMkernel is the regulator that manages access to the physical hardware.

It is imperative to note that the VMkernel is a proprietary kernel that was developed by VMware. (See the "Is VMware ESX Server Based on UNIX or Linux?" sidebar.)

EXAM ALERT

It is highly possible that one of the questions on the exam will ask whether VMkernel is a proprietary kernel developed by VMware.

Is VMware ESX Server Based on UNIX or Linux?

Many people are confused about whether VMware ESX Server is based on UNIX or Linux and the reason is simple: They see Linux in the commands, in the drivers, and in the boot process; therefore, they automatically conclude that ESX is just another modified version of Linux. The VMkernel itself is proprietary, and VMware makes that point very clear, so there should be no confusion here. The confusion comes into play with the relationship the Service Console has with the VMkernel. Many people believe that because the SC facilitates the ESX boot process, it is relying on Linux and cannot boot on its own

(continues)

(continued)

and thus is derived in some form from Linux. VMware clearly answers those arguments with the introduction of ESX Server 3i, which does not rely on the SC for booting, and as such the VMkernel boots on its own and is not a modified version of Linux or UNIX. It does, however, use BusyBox, which is a modified version of Linux. It uses BusyBox as its command-line interface with some useful tools.

Furthermore, for those interested in the origins of VMkernel, check out the biographies of the founders of VMware—people like Dr. Mendel Rosenblum, chief scientist; Edouard Bugnion; and Scott Devine, principal engineer—and you will notice that they all worked together at Stanford University and developed the Hive operating system, the SimOS machine simulator, and the Disco virtual machine monitor. So it would be safe to assume that ESX Server is based on the latter.

The Service Console

Think of the Service Console as the first VM on the ESX host. It is used to manage ESX Server, but it is also used to help the VMkernel during its boot process. The Service Console operating system is a modified version of Red Hat Linux Enterprise 3 Update 9. The Service Console also provides the following services:

- Apache Tomcat Web Server
- Firewall
- Secure Shell (SSH) access
- SNMP agents

EXAM ALERT

As of the release of ESX 3.5 Update 2, the SC console operating system is now based on Red Hat Linux Enterprise 3 Update 9, as opposed to Red Hat Linux Enterprise 3 Update 6, which was the case prior to ESX 3.5 Update 2. Watch out for this on the exam.

The VI Client

The Virtual Infrastructure (VI) client is a Windows-based application that is used to provide a GUI to connect to either an ESX host directly or to Virtual Center. Using the VI client, you can configure different features on the ESX host or via Virtual Center. As of this writing, the VI client is supported only on 32-bit operating systems. Although you can hack it and get the VI client to install and function on a 64-bit system, you should keep in mind that this is unsupported by VMware.

Exam Prep Questions

1. One of the benefits of virtual machines is that if one of them crashes, it does not affect the others. What is the correct term for this benefit?

   - ○ **A.** Hardware independence
   - ○ **B.** Compatibility
   - ○ **C.** Isolation
   - ○ **D.** Encapsulation

2. Which VMware product is used to migrate physical machines to virtual machines with Virtual Center 2.5?

   - ○ **A.** VMware P2V Assistant
   - ○ **B.** VMware Converter
   - ○ **C.** Virtual Center Clone
   - ○ **D.** VMware Migrator

3. Which file system does VMware ESX server use to run virtual machines?

   - ○ **A.** EXT3
   - ○ **B.** VFS
   - ○ **C.** VMFS
   - ○ **D.** VMDK

4. Select three benefits of virtual machines.

   - ○ **A.** Isolation
   - ○ **B.** Encapsulation
   - ○ **C.** Hardware Bound
   - ○ **D.** Compatibility

5. Which feature of the VMware Infrastructure 3 family allows a running virtual machine to be migrated to another host without interruption?

   - ○ **A.** Distributed Resource Scheduler (DRS)
   - ○ **B.** Storage VMotion
   - ○ **C.** VMotion
   - ○ **D.** VMware Converter

6. Which Virtual Infrastructure technology allows VMs to have more than one virtual CPU?

   ○ **A.** High Availability

   ○ **B.** Symmetric Multi-Processing

   ○ **C.** Virtualization Technology (VT)

   ○ **D.** Virtual Center

7. What is the maximum number of virtual processors you can allocate to a virtual machine?

   ○ **A.** 4

   ○ **B.** 6

   ○ **C.** 8

   ○ **D.** 2

8. True or false: VMware ESX 3.5 is an application that gets installed on top of an existing operating system such as Microsoft Windows or Linux.

   ○ **A.** True

   ○ **B.** False

9. True or false: VMware ESX 3.5 allows virtual machines to have direct access to physical resources.

   ○ **A.** True

   ○ **B.** False

10. The Service Console operating system is based on which version of Red Hat Linux?

    ○ **A.** Enterprise 3 Update 9

    ○ **B.** Enterprise 6 Update 9

    ○ **C.** Enterprise 3 Update 6

    ○ **D.** Enterprise 6 Update 3

Answers to Exam Prep Questions

1. Answer **C** is correct. Although hardware independence, compatibility, and encapsulation are all benefits of VMs, isolation is the correct answer here. With isolation, if a VM crashes, it has no effect on other VMs. Hardware independence means that VMs do not detect and are not aware of the actual physical hardware. Encapsulation means that VMs are a collection of files. Compatibility means they share ideal hardware based on x86 standard architecture.

2. Answer **B** is correct. Although P2V Assistant is a correct answer for earlier versions, the question is which product to use with Virtual Center 2.5. In this case, the only correct answer is VMware Converter.

3. Answer **C** is correct. EXT3 is a Linux file system, VFS does not exist, and VMDK is the file extension given to the files that hold the VM virtual hard drive.

4. Answers **A**, **B**, and **D** are correct. Virtual machines are not hardware bound; they are actually hardware independent. That is one of the advantages of VMs because they use "ideal hardware."

5. Answer **C** is correct. DRS is a feature that distributes the resource load between ESX hosts and organizes resource pools. Storage VMotion moves a running VM's files from one shared storage to another. VMware Converter converts a physical machine into a virtual machine or converts a virtual machine into another virtual machine. VMotion is the technology that moves a running VM between ESX hosts with no interruption.

6. Answer **B** is correct. High Availability is a feature that allows VMs from a failed host to be started on another host and does not allow for multiprocessing on VMs. VT is an Intel technology that is enabled in the BIOS of a system. Virtual Center is an enterprise management tool.

7. Answer **A** is correct. VMware SMP currently supports a maximum of four vCPUs per VM.

8. Answer **B**, False, is correct. VMware ESX Server is a bare metal install that does not rely on an underlying operating system to run.

9. Answer **B**, False, is correct. VMware ESX 3.5 does not allow VMs direct access to physical resources. ESX installs the virtualization layer that regulates VM access to hardware resources.

10. Answer **C** is correct. As of ESX 3.5 Update 2, the service console is now based on Red Hat Linux Enterprise 3 Update 9.

CHAPTER TWO

Planning, Installing, and Configuring ESX 3.5

Terms you'll need to understand:

- ✓ Graphical mode
- ✓ Diagnostic data
- ✓ Text mode
- ✓ Secure Shell (SSH)
- ✓ Network Time Protocol (NTP)

Concepts and techniques you'll need to master:

- ✓ Installing ESX 3.5
- ✓ ESX 3.5 post-installation configurations
- ✓ Troubleshooting ESX Server issues that may arise after a fresh install

One of the basic tasks you need to perform as a VMware Certified Professional is properly installing ESX 3.5 and also knowing the different methods that are available for installing it. In this chapter, we look at the prerequisites and different methodologies of installing ESX Server.

ESX 3.5 Minimum Hardware Requirements

Before we dig deep into the steps of installing ESX 3.5, let's look at the minimum hardware requirements needed to install the software. Keep in mind, this is the minimum you need to install the software. This is by no means a recommended hardware configuration. ESX servers in the real world are beefy servers, which is what allows them to host so many virtual machines. The requirements are as follows:

- ▶ 2 Intel or AMD x86 processors with clock speeds of 1500 MHz or higher

- ▶ 1GB of physical memory or RAM

- ▶ 1 network interface card (NIC)

- ▶ 1 RAID LUN, Fiber Channel LUN, SCSI LUN, or SCSI disk with at least 4GB of free space

With ESX 3.5 you can install and boot from the following disks:

- ▶ SCSI disk

- ▶ IDE disk

- ▶ SATA disk

- ▶ Storage Area Networks (SANs)

TIP

Before purchasing or installing ESX 3.5, consult "Systems Compatibility Guide for ESX Server 3.5 and ESX Server 3i" at http://blogs.vmware.com/compatibilityguides/.

NOTE

ESX 3.5 supports 10GB ethernet cards; make sure you check the compatibility guides for the models supported and the vendors.

Disk Partitioning ESX 3.5

As with any operating system deployment, disk partitioning is critical with ESX 3.5. Knowing how to partition the disk to best fit the operating system is just as important. Now because ESX 3.5 has a console operating system based on Red Hat Linux, familiarity with the Linux file system is necessary.

The Linux file system is a single hierarchy file system where everything is mounted under the root represented by /. This means that if you were adding a new partition, this partition would show up in a directory under the root and is known as a *mount point*. This differs from a typical Windows file system where every new partition is its own root represented by a letter, for example, C:\ or D:\. With Windows, every drive letter is the equivalent of the root in Linux. Figure 2.1 shows a comparison between a Windows file system and a Linux file system hierarchy.

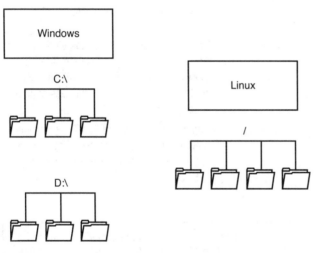

FIGURE 2.1
Windows and Linux file systems.

Also note here that an x86 disk can have a total of four primary partitions, which is a limitation because you need more partitions to satisfy the different operating system architecture. That being said, if you take the fourth partition and make it into an extended partition rather than a primary, you now have more partitions and are no longer limited. You do this at no sacrifice to performance. It is also important to note here that IDE disks can have a maximum of 63 partitions, whereas SCSI disks can have a maximum of 15 partitions.

Table 2.1 lists the different partition configurations, their types, and what they do.

Table 2.1 ESX Disk Partitions

Mount Point	Type	Size	Function
/boot	ext3	100MB	This is the place where ESX Server stores all the files it needs to boot.
/	ext3	5GB	This is the root of the Service Console operating system.
none	swap	544MB	This is the swap file of the Service Console. It is allocated 544MB by default because the Service Console is allocated 272MB by default, which means the swap file is twice the size of the Service Console memory allocation.
/var/log	ext3	2GB	This is the place where all the logs are stored. It is also used to patch management. The default size is 2GB, but best practice calls for an increase in disk space allocation.
none	VMFS-3	Varies	This is the place where all the VMs will live; you can also store images here. The size varies here, but by default VMFS-3 is equal to the disk size minus all the sizes of all the other partitions.
none	vmkcore	100MB	This is the place where ESX Server writes its dump information in the event of a system crash or a Purple Screen of Death (PSOD).

> **NOTE**
>
> The Service Console can be allocated a maximum of 800MB of memory. Therefore, the swap partition should not be allocated more than 1600MB of disk space. Otherwise, you would be wasting disk space. The swap file is calculated based on the Service Console memory allocation. If the SC can be allocated only 800MB, the swap file should not exceed 1600MB.

Installing ESX 3.5 Using a CD-ROM

To kick-start this installation, you need to configure the server to boot from a CD-ROM. Pop in the VMware ESX 3.5 CD, and the first screen should look similar to the one in Figure 2.2.

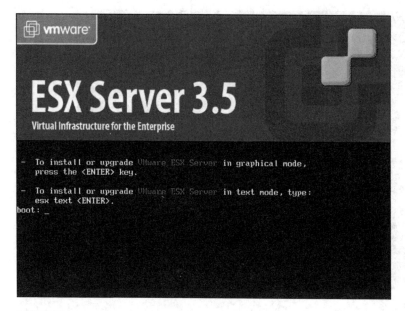

FIGURE 2.2
Installation mode.

The first choice you need to make is one of the following:

- ► *Graphical mode*, as its name suggests, guides you through the installation with a graphical user interface in which you can use your mouse. This is the default mode.

- ► *Text mode* is a lightweight installation method that skips on the rich and colorful graphics and relies solely on a text-based installation, which also means you will not have the use of the mouse. This method is ideal for ESX installations over slow networks.

For the purposes of this demonstration, choose the graphical mode. Up next, you are presented with a screen similar to that shown in Figure 2.3 that will prompt you to validate the installation media from which you are attempting this install. Your options here are to either test the media for errors or skip the test and continue with the installation.

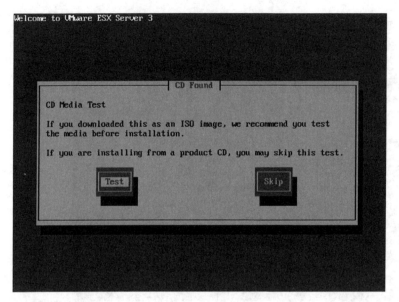

FIGURE 2.3
Media validation.

TIP

If this is your first time installing ESX 3.5 from this media or you are unsure of the media, we recommend you run the test to validate it.

As we have used our media CD many times while preparing for this example, we will go ahead and select Skip and continue with the installation. The next two screens will prompt you to select the type of keyboard and mouse that you have. We elect to stay with the default selection for these prompts.

The next screen, as shown in Figure 2.4, prompts you to initialize the device that will hold the partitions to be used to install ESX Server. This step is important because you have to be cautious not to initialize a device that might hold data. This means that if you have more than one device connected to the server, such as a SAN LUN, you should select No for this prompt. Otherwise, you will lose all data on this device.

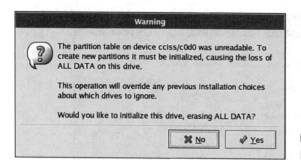

FIGURE 2.4
Disk initialization.

For the purposes of this example, click Yes and continue the installation.

CAUTION

VMware best practice recommends that you disconnect any devices or LUNs prior to starting the setup of ESX 3.5 to minimize the potential for loss of data.

Before moving on with the installation, you need to accept the terms of the license agreement and then click Next to continue. As you can see in Figure 2.5, you are now tasked with partitioning the disk. You can choose Recommended or Advanced. Choosing Advanced forces you to manually create all the partitions, so instead select Recommended. In the next step, the setup wizard allows you to make any changes necessary to the partition tables before they are committed. By doing this, you let setup do all the work for you and then you can make final tweaks as you see fit. Before you move on to the next screen, we strongly recommend you select the check box next to Keep Virtual Machines and the VMFS (Virtual Machine File System) That Contains Them. This setting preserves any VMFS from damage or loss. Now you are ready to proceed, so choose Next.

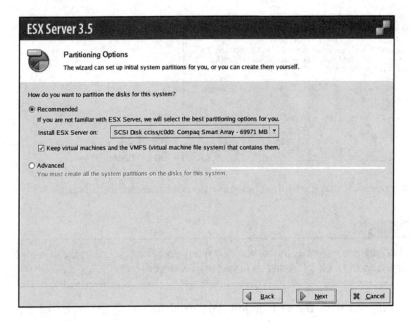

FIGURE 2.5
Disk partitioning.

The next screen, as shown in Figure 2.6, is a warning screen informing you that setup is about to wipe out any partitions on this device with the exception of VMFS. Click Yes to proceed.

FIGURE 2.6
Existing partition deletion warning.

Up next is a critical part of the installation, as shown in Figure 2.7. You are now presented with a blueprint of how setup intends on partitioning the disk. It is in this step that you make any final modifications before you commit the changes. For example, if you want to increase the swap space to 1600MB, this would be the time. You can highlight the swap partition, select Edit, and input the number you desire. Choose Next to continue.

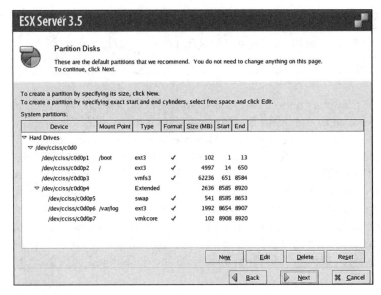

FIGURE 2.7
Partitions blueprint.

As the installation moves on, as shown in Figure 2.8, you are now prompted to select the boot configuration. Make sure that the setup wizard has elected to boot from the same drive as the one you chose to partition in earlier steps.

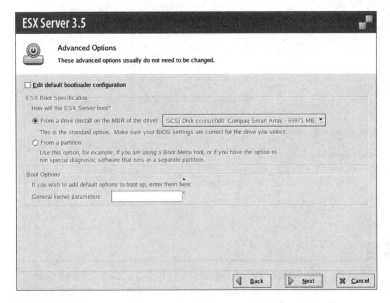

FIGURE 2.8
Bootable device selection.

> **CAUTION**
>
> The Master Boot Record (MBR) must always be configured on the same drive as the Service Console.

The setup now prompts you to assign the server network settings, as shown in Figure 2.9. You need to supply an IP address, a subnet mask, a default gateway, primary and secondary DNS entries, and a hostname in the form of a fully qualified domain name (FQDN) for this server. You also have the option to configure a VLAN ID for this server. By default, a check box is selected next to Create a Default Network for Virtual Machines. This means that the NIC that you have configured will be shared between the Service Console and virtual machines. Best practice calls for the separation of the Service Console NIC from that of the virtual machines. This option can be modified at any time after the installation has been completed. Therefore, keep the default and click Next to continue.

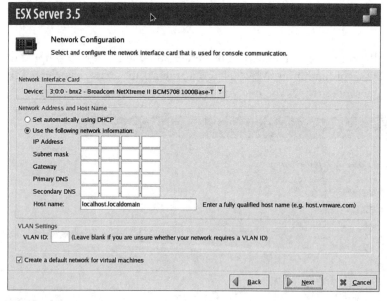

FIGURE 2.9

Network settings.

> **TIP**
>
> If you want to select the first physical NIC on the server, as in NIC 0, click the drop-down menu next to Device and choose the lowest decimal number. That is the first physical NIC on your server and is shown as vmnic0 on the ESX Server.

CAUTION

Selecting the wrong physical NIC will result in your server being inaccessible, so make sure that the device you select is the correct one that you want to use for the Service Console.

Time zone selection is next. Make sure you choose the time zone in which your server resides and click Next to continue. As you can see in Figure 2.10, you are now prompted to enter a password for the root account, which is the administrator account on the ESX Server. Enter a strong password and click Next to continue.

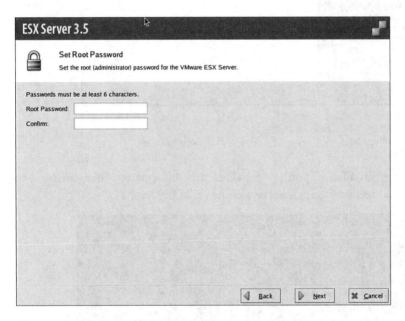

FIGURE 2.10
Root password.

NOTE

The root password must be a minimum of six characters.

You are one step away from the end of the journey. This is the place where you are provided with a summary of all the settings you chose during the setup wizard's run to the install. Go over the settings one last time, and if all looks correct, click Next to continue. This kicks off the installation of ESX 3.5.

When the installation is complete, a screen similar to the one shown in Figure 2.11 is displayed. Click Finish to restart ESX 3.5.

FIGURE 2.11
Installation complete.

After the server reboots, you are provided with information that you need to remotely connect to the ESX Server, as shown in Figure 2.12.

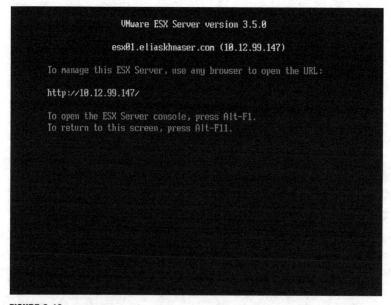

FIGURE 2.12
ESX Server console screen.

ESX 3.5 Post-Installation Configurations

When ESX 3.5 is up and running, you need to complete a few post-installation configurations before you begin further advanced configurations or prior to putting the server in full production. We cover the following:

- ▶ Accessing ESX Server using the VI client
- ▶ Accessing ESX Server using SSH
- ▶ Modifying Service Console memory allocation
- ▶ Configuring NTP Client on ESX Server

Accessing ESX Using the VI Client

You can download the Virtual Infrastructure (VI) client from any ESX Server by opening a supported Internet browser such as Internet Explorer or Firefox and pointing to the IP address or FQDN of the server. This leads you to a screen similar to the one shown in Figure 2.13. From here, you can click Download VMware Infrastructure Client. This prompts you to download or run the setup package. Go ahead and install it now.

> **EXAM ALERT**
>
> At the time of this writing, the VI client is a 32-bit application. Make sure you double-check this point prior to taking the exam just in case VMware releases a 64-bit version and happens to put a question on the exam in this regard.

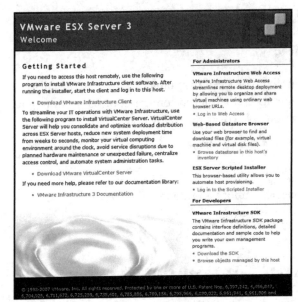

FIGURE 2.13
ESX Server Web interface.

After you install the VI client, you can run it, which brings you to a screen similar to the one shown in Figure 2.14. Enter the IP address or FQDN of your ESX Server host. Enter root for username and the password you assigned during setup. Click Login.

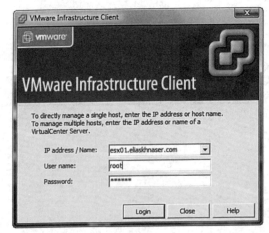

FIGURE 2.14
Virtual Infrastructure client.

The VI client is your graphical user interface into ESX Server's hardware and software configuration.

Accessing ESX Server Using SSH

Secure Shell (SSH) access allows you to remotely access your ESX Server and configure and manage it from a command line. You will find this type of access useful in many circumstances in which you need advanced configurations that the VI client does not provide or it would be much easier to accomplish using SSH.

By default, ESX 3.5 denies SSH access to the root user. This is done in accordance with security best practices. It is recommended that you create a generic account that you use to log in to the server using SSH and then switch the user to root, thereby acquiring root permissions. That being said, some may want to bypass this step and login as root. Although we don't recommend this method, we demonstrate how you can configure it. The two options for SSH access are

▶ Create a user account that can access the server using SSH.

▶ Enable SSH root access.

Creating a User Account That Can Access the Server Using SSH

After the installation of ESX 3.5, you will notice that you cannot access the server using SSH even with the root account. This security best practice measure is enabled to deny hackers the ability to perform a brute force attack on the server. Because root does not have SSH access, you need to create a user account on the ESX host that does have SSH access to make administration of the box easier.

Creating a user account on the ESX Server is an easy task. Remember that the Service Console that manages ESX runs a modified version of Linux; therefore, ESX Server host user accounts are Linux accounts and can be created in the same manner as you would a Linux account. For the purposes of this example, use the VMware VI client to create the account, even though you can create it through the command line using Linux commands. The following steps show how to accomplish this:

1. Launch the VI client and log in.

2. Click the Users & Groups tab.

3. In the Users pane, right-click and select Add.

4. When the Add New User dialog is displayed, fill in the information.

5. Check Grant Shell Access to This User.

6. Click OK. The user you created should show up in the Users pane.

Enabling SSH Root Access

To enable SSH access using root, you need to have console access to the ESX Server and follow these steps:

1. Type **vi /etc/ssh/sshd_config**. This command launches the vi editor in Linux and allows you to edit the file sshd_config.

2. Change the parameter PermitRootLogin no to PermitRootLogin yes.

3. Press the Esc button, and then type **:wq**, so the command should look like Esc :wq, which saves the files and exits the editor.

4. At the command prompt, type **service sshd restart**, which restarts the SSHD service.

5. Using your SSH client, try logging in using root.

> **EXAM ALERT**
>
> It is highly possible that one of the questions on the exam will revolve around security best practices and why the root account is disabled. Make sure you are aware of this and are well prepared to answer it.

Modifying Service Console Memory Allocation

The Service Console is allocated 272MB of memory by default after the installation of ESX Server. Best practice calls for the increase of this memory, especially if you will be using third-party applications, because this will eat away from the 272MB dedicated to the SC. The maximum memory you can allocate to the SC is 800MB, and the minimum is 272. To modify the SC memory, follow these steps:

1. Launch the VI client and log in to the ESX Server.

2. In the right pane, select the Configuration tab.

3. Under the Hardware menu, select the Memory link.

4. Click Properties.

5. Enter a value between 272 and 800.

6. Click OK.

7. For your changes to take effect, you must restart your ESX Server.

Configuring NTP Client on ESX Server

Time is of the essence in ESX Server. It is a critical component to configure and should be a top priority because time synchronization issues can affect backups, authentication, performance charting, SSH key expiration, and more. To avoid all these nuisances, follow these steps to configure the Network Time Protocol (NTP) client:

1. Launch the VI client and log in to the ESX Server.

2. In the right pane, select the Configuration tab.

3. Click the Time Configuration link.

4. Click Properties.

5. Check NTP Client Enabled.

6. Click Options.

7. Select NTP Settings in the left pane.

8. Click Add and add the hostname or IP address of your NTP server.

9. Select the check box next to Restart NTP Service to apply the changes.

10. Click OK.

11. Verify the NTP Client is running and the correct NTP servers are configured.

EXAM ALERT

When you enable the NTP client, you are opening UDP port 123 on the SC firewall. The VCP loves to quiz you on port numbers, so keep this one in mind.

Troubleshooting ESX 3.5 Installation

The reality is that issues may come up with installation. Knowing how to properly deal with them and what tools are at your disposal makes the troubleshooting process a little bit easier. In this section we tackle common issues, covering what to look for and what to do in certain circumstances.

Hardware Issues and Misconfigurations

If this is a new ESX Server installation that is experiencing problems after installation, the most likely cause is hardware. Hardware can be a combination of things. Hardware issues include

▶ The hardware you are using is not compatible with ESX 3.5. Check the compatibility guide and make sure your hardware is compatible.

▶ Hardware problems can also be caused by a faulty CPU, for example, or a bad memory module, so make sure that the hardware you are using is healthy and is not faulting. Do so by testing the hardware and software configuration for a few days prior to putting the server in production.

Misconfigurations are also an issue that you need to examine carefully because they may cause problems. For example, if you did not properly configure the correct physical NIC during installation, the server will be rendered inaccessible because there will be no communication with it. Therefore, checking your existing configuration should be your second step.

Purple Screen of Death

Microsoft has its infamous Blue Screen of Death, and VMware has its Purple Screen of Death (PSOD). If a PSOD occurs, that is bad and the server console will go, as you might have guessed, purplish. Two of the most common reasons for PSOD are

▶ CPU problems

▶ Memory problems

When a PSOD occurs, information is dumped to a file after ESX Server reboots and is recorded in the vmkcore partition in binary format. This dump file, as with any other, can be sent to VMware support for analysis and advanced troubleshooting.

Diagnostic Data Collection

In the event of a server crash, you need to go through the normal steps of troubleshooting the problem. For example, determine if anything changed recently that could cause the server to crash. Variables can include hardware changes. Has anything changed in the environment where ESX is hosted, has the temperature changed, have you had a power loss? You also need to check whether any external devices such as LUNs have been disconnected and finally make sure you take a screen capture of any console errors that may appear because this will help VMware support staff as they troubleshoot the problem.

Finally, using the VI client, you can export *diagnostic data* that you can send to VMware support. To do this, follow these steps:

1. Launch and log in to the ESX Server.

2. From the File menu, select File > Export Diagnostic Data.

3. Choose a folder where you want to save the data.

4. The diagnostic data is stored in a folder called VMware VirtualCenter-support-*date@time* and contains the following:

   ▶ A folder named viclient-support-*date@time*.tgz, which contains VI Client's log files

   ▶ A file named esx-support-*date@time*.tgz, which contains ESX Server diagnostic data

---

TIP

You can generate the diagnostic data file by initiating the command vm-support from an SSH command prompt.

Exam Prep Questions

1. Choose the five partitions that are required for ESX Server installation.

   ○ **A.** /boot

   ○ **B.** /var

   ○ **C.** /etc

   ○ **D.** swap

   ○ **E.** /

   ○ **F.** vmfs

   ○ **G.** vmkcore

2. Choose the correct partition type of the swap partition.

   O **A.** none

   O **B.** ext3

   O **C.** vmfs

   O **D.** swap

3. True or false: The vmkcore partition has a mount point of /vmkcore.

   O **A.** True

   O **B.** False

4. What is the default size of the /var/log partition?

   O **A.** 500MB

   O **B.** 2,000MB

   O **C.** 5,000MB

   O **D.** Varies

5. True or false: By default, ESX Server's Service Console does not allow root access via an SSH client.

   O **A.** True

   O **B.** False

6. What is the default amount of memory allocated to the Service Console?

   O **A.** 256

   O **B.** 272

   O **C.** 800

   O **D.** 1600

7. What is the default size of the swap partition?

   O **A.** 544

   O **B.** 572

   O **C.** 574

   O **D.** 576

8. How many primary partitions can you have on an x86 disk?

- ○ **A.** 3
- ○ **B.** 4
- ○ **C.** 5
- ○ **D.** 6

9. What is the maximum number of partitions that you can have on a SCSI disk?

- ○ **A.** 15
- ○ **B.** 25
- ○ **C.** 45
- ○ **D.** 63

10. Why should the ESX log files be stored on a different partition?

- ○ **A.** For better performance
- ○ **B.** To prevent the / from being filled
- ○ **C.** Easier access to the files
- ○ **D.** Partition will be shared with other hosts

Answers to Exam Prep Questions

1. Answers **A**, **D**, **E**, **F**, and **G** are correct. /var and /etc are not required partitions for the installation of ESX 3.5.

2. Answer **D** is correct. In this case, none, ext3, and vmfs are not the correct partition type for swap.

3. Answer **B**, False, is correct. Vmkcore does not need a mount point.

4. Answer **B** is correct. By default, setup suggests that the /var/log partition have a 2,000MB size.

5. Answer **A**, True, is correct. By default, the Service Console does not allow root access via SSH.

6. Answer **B** is correct. The minimum amount of memory that can be allocated to the Service Console is 272. The maximum amount of memory that can be allocated is 800, so 1600 is incorrect.

7. Answer **A** is correct. The default size of the swap partition is twice the size of the default memory allocated to the SC. Because, by default, the SC is allocated 272, the correct size is 544.

8. Answer **B** is correct. You can house only four primary partitions on an x86 disk.

9. Answer **A** is correct. On a SCSI disk, you can have a total of 15 partitions. On an IDE drive, you can have a total of 63 partitions.

10. Answer **B** is correct. The logs are stored on a separate partition to prevent them from taking up all the disk space available for the root file system.

CHAPTER 3

Licensing VMware Infrastructure 3

Terms you'll need to understand:

✓ Per processor
✓ Per instance
✓ Host-based license file
✓ Server-based license file
✓ License server

Concepts and techniques you'll need to master:

✓ The difference between host-based and server-based licensing
✓ How per-processor licenses are calculated
✓ Behavior of the different components when the license server is lost
✓ How to install the license server

This chapter covers VMware Infrastructure 3 (VI3) licensing, including ESX Server and VirtualCenter licensing, how the license key functions, and the *license server*.

Licensing

As with any enterprise class technology, VMware Infrastructure 3 requires licensing so that you can enable or disable certain features based on the types of licenses you have purchased. Licensing is a great source of income for VMware, but it can be costly for you if you are not sure what types of licenses you need for your environment and how many licenses you need. Licensing can be a devious topic that we all wish we did not have to deal with; however, this chapter covers VMware licensing as clearly as possible to make it easy for you to understand.

VMware Infrastructure does not have an extremely complicated licensing realm, but it is enough to confuse if not understood properly. Therefore, we have dedicated this chapter to the discussion of licensing in the Virtual Infrastructure enterprise. VMware Infrastructure 3 has two components that require licensing. Those two components are the heart of the infrastructure suite:

- ESX 3.5

- VirtualCenter 2.5

ESX Server Licensing

ESX Server is the single most important component of the VMware Infrastructure 3 suite. VMware has released three versions of ESX Server that address various organization needs. Based on the ESX Server edition you purchased, certain features either are available or are considered add-ons that you may purchase at any time when you are ready for them.

The three available ESX Server editions are as follows:

- **Foundation:** Considered a starter edition and gives you access to basic features and none of the more enterprise-level features. This edition is recommended for smaller environments of maybe one or two ESX Servers.

- **Standard:** A bit more advanced version of ESX Server that gives you access to all the features that come with the Foundation edition plus High Availability (HA).

▶ **Enterprise:** The ultimate edition that incorporates all the features of the Standard edition plus all the enterprise-level technologies.

Table 3.1 outlines the three different editions of ESX 3.5 and the features that come with each.

Table 3.1   ESX 3.5 Editions

Feature	Foundation	Standard	Enterprise
VMFS	✓	✓	✓
Virtual SMP	✓	✓	✓
VirtualCenter Agent	✓	✓	✓
VMware HA		✓	✓
VMware DRS			✓
VMware DPM			✓
Update Manager	✓	✓	✓
Consolidated Backup	✓	✓	✓
VMotion			✓
Storage VMotion			✓
VirtualCenter Server			✓

NOTE

Another edition of ESX is available. ESXi, formerly known as ESX Server 3i, is the embedded version of ESX that has access to VMFS and Virtual SMP. If combined with VirtualCenter (VC), it then has access to VC features.

After you have decided on the edition of ESX 3.5 that you want to purchase, you are presented with a license file that enforces your edition of ESX Server. The license file is what determines which features are locked and which features are unlocked. There are two ways of making ESX 3.5 aware of the license file: host-based licensing and server-based licensing. You can open the License Sources panel from the VI client by going to Configuration, selecting Licensed Features, and clicking Edit. When you do so, you will notice that there are *actually* four modes in which you can license the host:

▶ Evaluation Mode

▶ Serial Number

▶ License Server (Server Based)

▶ Host License File (Host Based)

Figure 3.1 shows the License Sources panel with these four modes.

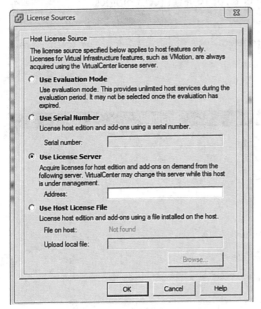

FIGURE 3.1
License Sources panel.

The following sections describe each mode in more detail and expand on their usability scenarios.

Evaluation Mode

As its name implies, the Evaluation Mode is used to evaluate ESX 3.5. After the successful installation of ESX, you may put the server in Evaluation Mode without a need to acquire a license file. You have full access to all the features and technologies for a period of 60 days, after which you need to purchase a license file to continue to use the software.

Serial Number

The Serial Number is actually not intended for use with ESX 3.5. It is added there for ESXi (formerly known as ESX Server 3i or ESX 3i). Therefore, you cannot take advantage of this mode in any way using ESX 3.5.

Host-Based Licensing

With *host-based licensing*, you upload the license file to the ESX Server host. This license file becomes attached to this ESX Server and only this ESX Server.

This type of licensing is well suited for smaller environments where there are not many ESX Servers and where you don't really care about having a pool of licenses available to ESX Servers. With host-based licensing, if the server goes down, the license file that is attached to it also goes down.

> **NOTE**
>
> Host-based licensing is most commonly used in small ESX shops where VirtualCenter is not deployed.

When you are using the host-based licensing model, the license files are stored in the following location on each ESX Server host:

```
/etc/vmware/vmware.lic
```

Server-Based Licensing

Server-based licensing takes advantage of a license server, which centralizes license management. In this scenario, you point all your ESX Server hosts to the license server. The license server then allocates a license to the ESX Servers from a pool of licenses at its disposal. In this scenario, if an ESX Server goes down and you bring a replacement server online, a license is allocated from the pool. This scenario is ideal for enterprise-level deployments.

When you are using a server-based licensing model, the license files are stored in the following location on the license server:

```
C:\Program Files\VMware\VMware License Server\Licenses
```

> **EXAM ALERT**
>
> The VCP exam is sure to quiz you on the difference between host-based licensing and server-based licensing. Make sure you review this section until you are comfortable with this topic.

> **NOTE**
>
> To use enterprise-level features such as VMotion, HA, or DRS, you need to have server-based licensing.

VirtualCenter Licensing

Similar to ESX Server, VirtualCenter also comes in different editions, as follows:

- **VirtualCenter Foundation:** This edition allows you to manage up to three ESX Server hosts.

- **VirtualCenter:** This enterprise-level edition allows you to manage up to 200 ESX Server hosts.

Upgrading from VirtualCenter Foundation to VirtualCenter is easy; you simply need to acquire a new license file and switch the editions. You do not need to reinstall VirtualCenter Server.

How the License Key Functions

The license key is constructed to enable or disable features of ESX Server and VirtualCenter. Currently, the license file is configured in two ways:

- Per Processor

- Per Instance

It is important for you to know which parts of the Virtual Infrastructure suite are ESX Server components and which are VirtualCenter components. Table 3.2 clearly defines this membership.

Table 3.2   VI Feature Membership

VI Member	ESX Server	VirtualCenter
ESX Server	✓	
Symmetric Multi-Processing (SMP)	✓	
Consolidated Backup	✓	
VirtualCenter		✓
VMotion		✓
Storage VMotion		✓
High Availability (HA)		✓
Distributed Resource Scheduler (DRS)		✓
Distributed Power Management (DPM)		✓

Per Processor

VMware Infrastructure 3 currently licenses its entire feature set *per processor* with the exception of VirtualCenter, which is licensed on a *per instance* basis. When you purchase licenses from VMware, they are sold in increments of two, and these licenses, if deployed on the license server (server-based licensing), can be used by any host that is pointing to the license server.

To make things simple, when you purchase a server, calculate the number of physical processors in it. Figure how many sockets you have in a server that can host a processor. If you purchased a dual socket processor server, you need two licenses. If you purchased a quad socket processor, you need four licenses.

EXAM ALERT

When you are purchasing licenses per processor, they are sold in increments of two. On the exam, you will more than likely be asked a licensing question. Do *not* take into consideration how VMware sells the licenses. Today they are in increments of two; tomorrow they may be in increments of four. As far as you are concerned, you calculate the number of sockets that host a processor, and that is the number of licenses you need.

NOTE

Many processors today have cores, so you might see dual processors dual cores, dual processors quad cores, quad processors dual cores, or any other combination. You should always count only how many sockets you have in your server.

The following products are licensed on a per processor basis:

- ESX Server
- VirtualCenter Agent
- VMotion
- Storage VMotion
- Consolidated Backup
- DRS
- DPM
- HA

As far as the features are concerned, if you bought VMotion licenses for four processors, that means you can use VMotion on two servers that each have two processors. You cannot use a four-license VMotion on a server that has four processors and also a server that has two processors. The reason is that you need a six-processor VMotion license to do that.

You cannot partially license a host. A quad processor server requires four licenses; you cannot use two license files and just license half of it. This also applies to the features.

Per Instance

Per instance licensing is simple and straightforward and falls within the realm of how licensing works traditionally. You buy the software, and it comes with a license. You can install the software on a server, regardless of the number of processors.

The only product of the VI suite that uses per instance licensing is VirtualCenter.

License Server

The license server is the central repository where license files are stored in a pool and assigned to ESX Server hosts as needed and when these ESX Servers point to the license server. The license server is typically installed on the same server as the VirtualCenter Server, but this is certainly not a requirement, and they can run independent of one another. In some cases, you may want to have your license server as a virtual machine, and as a result, it can take advantage of High Availability and becomes less prone to failure.

TIP

VMware best practice calls for installing the license server on the same server as your VirtualCenter Server. This ensures simplicity, visibility, and guaranteed communications between the license server and the VirtualCenter Server. Separate these two components only if there is a legitimate need.

Installing the License Server

To start the installation of the license server, you need access to the VMware Infrastructure Installation media files. The following steps guide you through the installation process:

1. If you are using a CD and the autorun screen pops up, close out of it and browse to the \vpx folder.

2. Locate and double-click the VMware-licenseserver.exe file.

3. When the install wizard starts, click Next to continue.

4. The License Agreement is up next. Unless you have a problem with it, select I Accept the Terms in the License Agreement and click Next to continue.

5. Folder selection is up next. If you don't want to use the default location, now is the time to make that change. Make your selection and click Next.

6. You are now prompted to upload a license file. Browse to the location of this file and click Next.

7. Click Install to start the installation process.

8. Click Finish to complete the installation.

> **TIP**
>
> Make sure you place the license files in a location accessible by the license server.

> **NOTE**
>
> The license server is supported only under a Windows platform. You cannot deploy the license server on any other operating system.

Working with the License Server

After the license server has been installed, adding licenses becomes easy. Just drop the license files in the following directory on the license server:

```
C:\Program Files\VMware\VMware License Server\Licenses
```

Then restart the License Server Windows Service to allow the license server to rescan the directory and capture the file. To restart the License Server service, open the Services console in Windows and restart VMware license server.

> **NOTE**
>
> You no longer have to edit the license files and copy and paste them into a single file to consolidate them so that the license server can read a single file. With ESX 3.5, you only need to put all your licenses in the specified directory, and the license server can read them all.

If you need to change the location where the license files are stored, follow these steps to change the default location:

1. On the license server, click Start > Programs > VMware > VMware License Server > VMware License Server Tools.

2. Click the Config Services tab.

3. Click the Browse button next to Path to License File to specify its location, or you can simply type in the new path to the directory where you want to store your license files.

4. Click the Start/Stop/Reread tab.

5. Click Stop and then click Start.

6. Click the ReRead License File button to scan and reload the new license files from the new location.

The license server has two main processes that listen on two different TCP ports. It is important when troubleshooting to make sure that the license server is listening on these ports. These two processes are

▶ lmgrd.exe: Listens on TCP port 27000.

▶ VMWARELM.exe: Listens on TCP port 27010.

To verify that the license server is actually listening, open a command prompt and type **netstat -ab**.

> **TIP**
>
> You can also check the status of the license server by opening VMware License Server Tools and clicking the Server Status tab. You can then click the Perform Status Inquiry button, which queries the server.

Losing the License Server

Because the license server presents a single point of failure, it is very important to know what happens in the event that the license server goes offline. One of the measures you can take to protect against a single point of failure scenario for the license server is to make it into a virtual machine so that it can take advantage of High Availability. As such, if the host where it is located goes offline, another host in the cluster automatically restarts the license server. Now this, of course, does not protect against operating system failures.

In the event that the license server does go down for whatever reason, you have a grace period of 14 days to bring it back online. This amount of time should be more than ample to resolve whatever issue caused that server outage. Table 3.3 outlines what tasks you can perform when the license server is unavailable both within and after the 14-day grace period.

Table 3.3   License Server Outage Allowed/Disallowed Behavior

Task	Within Grace Period	After Grace Period
ESX Server:		
Configure ESX Server	✓	✓
Power on and off	✓	✓
Modify license type; Add or Remove license file	✓	✓
Server continues to operate	✓	✓
VM powers on after a failed host	✓	X
VirtualCenter:		
Add ESX Server	X	X
Remove ESX Server	✓	✓
Remove ESX Server from VMotion, DRS, and HA cluster	X	X
Add ESX Server to a VMotion, DRS, and HA cluster	X	X
Connect/reconnect ESX Server	✓	✓
VMotion between existing ESX Servers	✓	X
Add/remove license keys	X	X
DRS continues normal operations	✓	X
Migrate a powered-off VM between ESX Servers	✓	✓

Table 3.3   Continued

Task	Within Grace Period	After Grace Period
Virtual Machine:		
Power on	✓	X
Suspend and resume	✓	✓
Create and delete	✓	✓
All Components:		
Upgrade	X	X

EXAM ALERT

It is inevitable that the VCP exam will quiz you about the operations that you can and cannot perform during and after the grace period. As an administrator, you are expected to know what actions can and cannot be performed, and therefore, you can be sure there will be a few questions on this subject.

Table 3.3 shows that VirtualCenter features are not affected by the license server outage. Therefore, if you lose the license server, features that rely on VirtualCenter such as VMotion, Storage VMotion, and DRS continue to work with no time restrictions. The reason is that the VirtualCenter Server relies on a cached version of the license server as it was before the outage. You obviously cannot make any modifications, but you can use all the features as they were when the server was still online. Any modifications will need the server to be online so that they can be checked in and out, as per Table 3.3.

Exam Prep Questions

1. How many ESX Server hosts can be managed using a single VirtualCenter Server instance?

   ○ **A.** 10

   ○ **B.** 100

   ○ **C.** 200

   ○ **D.** Unlimited

2. On which two TCP ports does the VMware license server listen?

    ◯ **A.** 27010

    ◯ **B.** 27001

    ◯ **C.** 27000

    ◯ **D.** 27100

3. Select the two processes that make up the license server?

    ◯ **A.** vmwarels.exe

    ◯ **B.** vmwarelm.exe

    ◯ **C.** lmgrd.exe

    ◯ **D.** lmmgr.exe

4. If the license server experiences an outage, what is the grace period?

    ◯ **A.** 14 days

    ◯ **B.** 30 days

    ◯ **C.** 16 days

    ◯ **D.** 36 days

5. Given a server with a quad processor quad core, how many licenses do you need for this server?

    ◯ **A.** 2

    ◯ **B.** 4

    ◯ **C.** 8

    ◯ **D.** 16

6. Given a server with a dual processor quad core, how many VMotion licenses do you need?

    ◯ **A.** 1

    ◯ **B.** 2

    ◯ **C.** 4

    ◯ **D.** 6

7. Select two features that are ESX Server host specific.

    ○ **A.** VMware Consolidated Backup (VCB)

    ○ **B.** VMware Update Manager

    ○ **C.** VMware Storage VMotion

    ○ **D.** VMware Virtual SMP

8. True or false: The VMware license server can be installed on a dedicated server apart from VirtualCenter Server.

    ○ **A.** True

    ○ **B.** False

9. True or false: VMware ESX 3.5 can be licensed on a per instance basis at a higher cost.

    ○ **A.** True

    ○ **B.** False

10. Which two modes of licensing are supported by ESX 3.5 and VirtualCenter?

    ○ **A.** Host Based

    ○ **B.** Client Based

    ○ **C.** Server Based

    ○ **D.** Serial number

Answers to Exam Prep Questions

1. Answer **C** is correct. With VirtualCenter Server, you can manage a maximum of 200 ESX Server hosts; with VirtualCenter Foundation, you can manage up to 3 ESX Server hosts.

2. Answers **A** and **C** are correct. The VMware license server listens on TCP ports 27000 and 27010.

3. Answers **B** and **C** are correct. The two processes that make up the VMware license server are vmwarelm.exe and lmgrd.exe. Answers A and D are incorrect because these two processes do not exist.

4. Answer **A** is correct. In the event of a license server outage, you are given a 14-day grace period in which everything continues to function as of the last known state of the license server.

5. Answer **B** is correct. When calculating licenses, you should not take into account a processor's cores; you should calculate only the number of sockets that are in the server. Based on the question, this is a quad processor server, which means you need four licenses, one for each processor.

6. Answer **B** is correct. When calculating VirtualCenter features such as VMotion, you should calculate only the number of sockets in the server, disregarding the number of cores because they are irrelevant for licensing purposes. Because you have a dual processor server, you need two licenses.

7. Answers **A** and **D** are correct. VMware Virtual SMP and VMware Consolidated Backup (VCB) are two features that are ESX Server specific.

8. Answer **A**, True, is correct. While VMware best practice does not recommend you separate the license server from the VirtualCenter Server for guaranteed communications between LS and VC, it is possible to install the two separate from each other.

9. Answer **B**, False, is correct. VMware ESX 3.5 cannot be licensed on a per instance basis; it is licensed on a per processor basis. Only VirtualCenter is licensed on a per instance basis.

10. Answers **A** and **C** are correct. The two modes supported by ESX 3.5 and VirtualCenter are Host Based and Server Based. Serial number is an option supported by ESXi (formerly ESX Server 3i).

CHAPTER FOUR

Virtual Networking Operations

Terms you'll need to understand:

✓ Route Based on the Originating Virtual Port ID
✓ Route Based on Source MAC Hash
✓ Notify Switches
✓ Promiscuous Mode
✓ Port Trunking
✓ 802.1Q VLAN Tagging
✓ Link Status
✓ Beacon Probing
✓ Traffic Shaping
✓ NIC Teaming

Concepts and techniques you'll need to master:

✓ Understanding port groups and policies
✓ Understanding virtual switch security policies
✓ Understanding how NIC teaming works
✓ Understanding how failover works

Just as physical machines connect to physical networks, virtual machines connect to virtual networks. In turn, virtual networks connect to the physical network. Virtual networking is the bridge by which physical connectivity is made possible to virtual machines. Similar to physical machines that require an entire networking infrastructure and framework to connect different devices and create different environments, virtual networking mimics physical networking by creating a virtual environment and a virtual framework for virtual machines.

In this chapter, we discuss all the components that make up virtual networking and how it facilitates communications for virtual machines.

What Are Virtual Switches?

Virtual switches (vSwitches) are the inevitable route that all communications inbound to or outbound from an ESX host must go through. Virtual switches make up the IP networking backbone of an ESX deployment. Whether you are seeking to implement IP storage or simply connect virtual machines to virtual machines, communications must pass through a virtual switch. Similarly, when the Service Console, which is the management interface of ESX, wants to access the ESX host, it too goes through a virtual switch.

You can quickly see how virtual switches are the beating heart of the infrastructure, and it is by leveraging them that you are able to create different scenarios. For example, you could create an isolated environment where VMs can communicate only with other VMs on the same ESX host, you could create a DMZ-like environment, or you could provide fault tolerance and High Availability through virtual switches. Virtual switches have the following characteristics:

▶ Virtual switches are software objects that reside on the VMkernel of every ESX host.

▶ Virtual switches in ESX 3.5 can have a minimum of 8 ports and a maximum of 1,016 ports. Similar to physical switches that have available ports on them for physical devices to connect to, virtual switches also have that functionality. The advantage with virtual switches is the port density is much higher, and you can customize your virtual switches with the port capacity you need. With physical switches, that is not an easy task to do; you would have to swap out the switch for another. Virtual switches give you the flexibility to add or remove ports as you need.

▶ Virtual switches can be serviced by one or more physical NICs. More NICs provide fault tolerance, High Availability, and more, as you will see throughout this chapter.

▶ Virtual NICs that connect to virtual switches have unique MAC addresses just like every physical network interface card (NIC) connecting to a physical switch has its own unique MAC address.

▶ Virtual switches support 802.1q (known as VLAN Tagging), which allows VMs connected to a virtual switch to communicate with different VLANs in your network infrastructure. This topic is covered in greater detail in the "VLANs in Virtual Networking" section in this chapter.

▶ Virtual switches also support different port groups or connection types that outline the communication of this virtual switch, such as Service Console, VMkernel, or virtual machine communications.

EXAM ALERT

By default, when you are creating a virtual switch, and unless you manually change it, the virtual switch is created with 56 ports.

NOTE

Virtual switches operate at layer 2 of the OSI model and are capable of providing segregation, security, and checksums.

Comparing Physical and Virtual Switches

Virtual switches are to virtual machines what physical switches are to physical devices. The virtual switches concept was created in the image of physical switches, so they share many similarities. However, they do differ somewhat in functionality and capability. Let's start off by examining the similarities between physical and virtual switches:

▶ They both maintain MAC address tables.

▶ They both check each frame's MAC address destination upon receiving it.

▶ They both forward frames to one or more ports.

▶ They both avoid unnecessary deliveries.

Now that you recognize the similarities, let's outline the differences:

- ▶ Virtual switches do not require or support the Spanning Tree Protocol.

- ▶ Virtual switches cannot be connected to one another the same way physical switches can be. You can connect VMs to a virtual switch, but you cannot connect another virtual switch.

- ▶ A virtual switch's forwarding data table is unique to each virtual switch.

- ▶ Virtual switch isolation prevents loops in the switch configuration.

EXAM ALERT

As VMware makes the case for virtualization, you can be assured that the VCP exam will challenge your knowledge of the advantages and disadvantages of virtual versus physical switches.

Types of Virtual Switches

There are three different types of virtual switches that you can configure, depending on the case or scenario that you need to implement. Within the framework of these three virtual switch types, you can create isolated environments, a DMZ, fault tolerance, High Availability, and you can maximize throughput for optimal performance and for those bandwidth-hungry applications. In the following sections, we discuss the following three virtual switch types and their usage scenarios:

- ▶ Internal virtual switch

- ▶ Single adapter virtual switch

- ▶ Multiple adapter virtual switch, also known as NIC teaming

Internal Virtual Switch

An internal virtual switch is used to provide communication to virtual machines that are on a single ESX host. In other words, when you deploy an internal virtual switch, virtual machines on the ESX host can communicate with one another but are completely isolated from the rest of the network and are unable to communicate with other VMs on other ESX hosts or any other devices on the network. Figure 4.1 shows a sample of this configuration. A possible usage scenario for this type of virtual switch is isolating a single application for testing purposes where you build a series of VMs on a single ESX host that are required by this application, and then you test against this application before allowing to communicate with the rest of the production network.

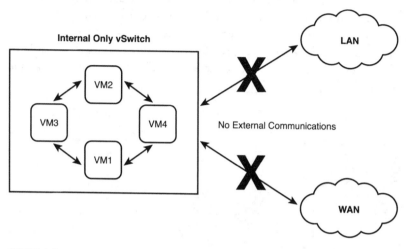

FIGURE 4.1
Internal only vSwitch.

Single Adapter Virtual Switch

A single adapter virtual switch is one that is supported or serviced by a single *physical* NIC. This NIC is what allows the virtual switch and the VMs access to the rest of the network. Figure 4.2 shows an example of how this can be implemented.

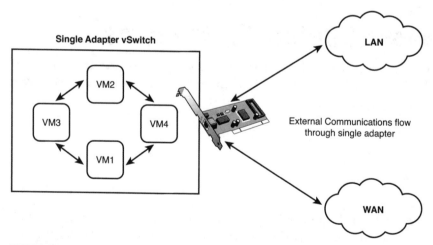

FIGURE 4.2
Single NIC vSwitch.

Multiple Adapter Virtual Switch

NIC teaming, or multiple adapter virtual switches, is a virtual switch that is supported by two or more NICs. This type of virtual switch allows for fault tolerance and High Availability. This is a typical scenario for mission-critical applications that you want to make sure have the maximum resources available to them and built-in failover and packet distribution. Figure 4.3 shows a sample configuration.

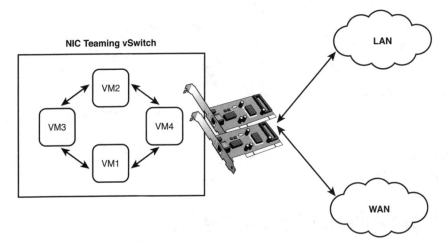

FIGURE 4.3
NIC Team vSwitch.

Types of Virtual Switch Ports

Now that we have covered the types of virtual switches, let's get down to the virtual switch ports. Ports on a virtual switch can be configured to handle different connection types as follows:

- ▶ Service Console
- ▶ VMkernel
- ▶ Virtual machine

This capability is helpful and allows the virtual switch to be a multifunction object rather than an object that does just one static task. To make things easier for you from a management standpoint, you have at your disposal what are known as *port groups*. A port group is a collection of ports on the vSwitch that all have the same connection type. So, instead of configuring each port individually on the vSwitch, you group them and give them a particular connection type.

In the following sections we explore the different port groups that can be configured and their usage scenarios.

EXAM ALERT

> The virtual switch port types touch on many aspects of virtualization with ESX, from networking to the different kinds of storage. For this reason, the exam will focus on the port types, so make sure you understand when each is used.

Service Console

The Service Console connection type allows for communication to and from the Service Console. During the installation of ESX 3.5, a Service Console port labeled vswif0 is automatically associated with vSwitch0, as illustrated in Figure 4.4. The Service Console requires that you configure the IP stack, including a dedicated IP address, a subnet mask, and a default gateway.

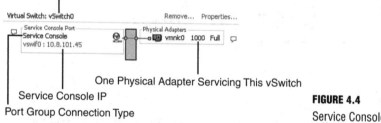

FIGURE 4.4

Service Console port group.

NOTE

> Additional Service Console ports enumerate as vswif1, vswif2, vswif3, and so on.

Because the Service Console is a critical component, you might want to think of providing some redundancy, and as such, two scenarios exist to help facilitate that, as follows:

> ▶ **Multiple Service Console ports:** Create a Service Console port group on two different virtual switches that are serviced by two different physical NICs and assign each service console a different IP address. This

creates a redundant second entry point into your ESX host should the primary fail. Figure 4.5 illustrates this scenario.

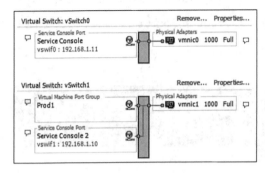

FIGURE 4.5
Multiple SC port groups.

▶ **Service Console NIC Team:** Add a second physical NIC to the same virtual switch where the original Service Console port groups reside, and therefore, you create redundancy at the physical level. If a NIC fails, the second one picks up seamlessly. In this scenario, you do not need a second IP address because it is being shared. Figure 4.6 illustrates this scenario clearly.

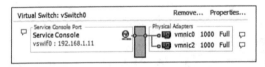

FIGURE 4.6
SC NIC Team.

VMkernel

A VMkernel port group connection type allows you to configure communication for technologies like VMotion, iSCSI, and NAS/NFS. This connection type requires you to configure the IP stack. The reason behind this is that these technologies will more than likely be connecting to different VLANs or different networks altogether. Figure 4.7 gives an example of how this works.

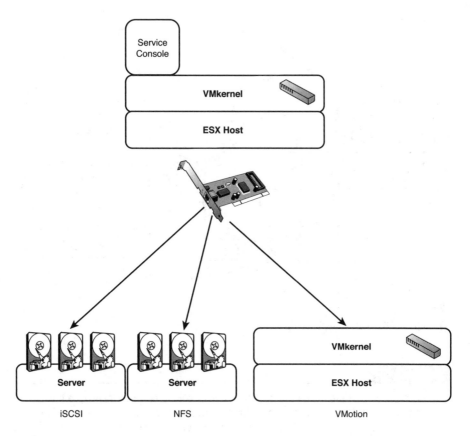

FIGURE 4.7
VLANs.

Virtual Machine

A virtual machine (VM) port group opens communication between the VMs configured on the virtual switch and the rest of the physical network by connecting the virtual switch to the physical switch by way of the NIC or NICs configured to support the virtual switch. Figure 4.8 shows this configuration scenario.

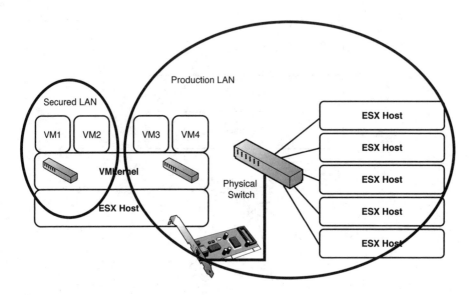

FIGURE 4.8
VM to physical network connectivity.

> **NOTE**
>
> Virtual machine port groups do not need the IP stack configured. Your network adminis-
> trator should configure the physical port that the physical NIC is plugged into to see the
> networks and VLANs that need to be accessed by the VMs on this virtual switch.

VLANs in Virtual Networking

A virtual local area network (VLAN) is a logical grouping of several different
LANs. Traditionally, a LAN spans a single segment, whereas a VLAN, being a
logical entity represented in software, is capable of breaking this barrier and
extending beyond the single segment limitation of a LAN by grouping different
LANs together.

Using VLANs allows you to dictate which ports on the switch are connected to
which IP segment, thereby reducing the need for additional hardware. You are
now capable of allocating different ports on the switch to different subnets.
Figure 4.9 further clears up this issue.

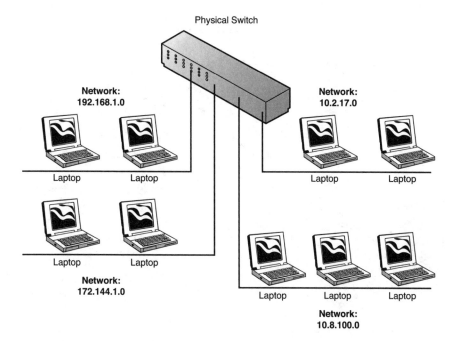

Physical Switch

Network:
192.168.1.0

Network:
10.2.17.0

Laptop

Laptop

Laptop

Laptop

Laptop

Laptop

Network:
172.144.1.0

Laptop

Laptop

Laptop

Network:
10.8.100.0

FIGURE 4.9
VLAN connectivity to different LANs.

Trunk Ports

A trunk port is a port on the physical switch that you configure to be aware of other VLANs that exist on other switches. Anything that plugs into this port is able to pass IP communications to all the visible VLANs. Traditionally, a switch could see and give access only to a single IP segment or subnet. With *port trunking*, you can now configure multiple ports on multiple switches to be part of the same VLAN. This characteristic helps overcome geographic limitations and eases management. Figure 4.10 illustrates trunk ports.

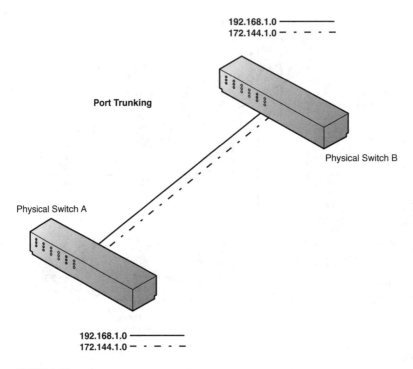

192.168.1.0 ——————
172.144.1.0 — · — — · —

Port Trunking

Physical Switch B

Physical Switch A

192.168.1.0 ——————
172.144.1.0 — · — — · —

FIGURE 4.10
Physical switch trunk port.

802.1Q VLAN Tagging

ESX has built-in support for *802.1Q VLAN tagging*. The first thing you do to get 802.1Q VLAN tagging to work is to connect a physical NIC to a port that is configured as a trunk port on the physical switch. You then assign this NIC to a vSwitch. What you have accomplished so far, then, is making all the VLANs that are configured on that trunked port visible to the vSwitch.

Now you create port groups on this virtual switch. Port groups, as the name implies, are groupings of several ports and are configured to see a particular VLAN by configuring a VLAN ID in the port group that matches the VLAN ID assigned on the physical switch. Now when you try to add virtual machines to these port groups, your VMs are part of the VLAN assigned to that port group. Figure 4.11 illustrates VLAN tagging.

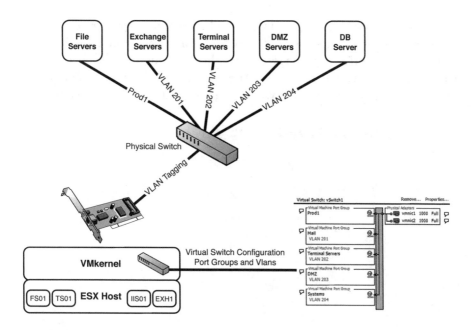

FIGURE 4.11
VLAN tagging.

Virtual Switch Policies

Virtual switches allow you some flexibility to configure them for optimal performance and maximized security. These settings can also be configured for each of the port groups configured on the virtual switch. When closely examining a virtual switch or port group properties, you find the following tabs:

▶ General

▶ Security

▶ Traffic Shaping

▶ NIC Teaming

You can get to these tabs by clicking Properties of a vSwitch in the Networking tab on the ESX host. You can then select the appropriate port group and edit its settings or select the vSwitch and edit its settings.

We examine security, traffic shaping, and NIC teaming in greater detail in the sections to follow, but first look at Figure 4.12, which shows the contents of the General tab. The General tab is the place where you limit the number of ports you want this virtual switch to have. After you modify the number of ports on the switch, you must restart the system before your changes will take effect.

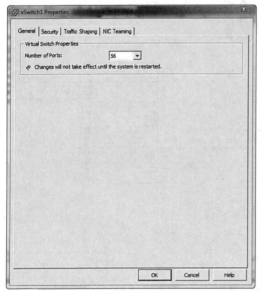

FIGURE 4.12
vSwitch policies.

Virtual Switch Security

Three types of Layer 2 security policies can be configured on virtual switches or port groups from the Security tab:

- ▶ **Promiscuous Mode:** If set to Accept, this setting would pass all the unicast frames that pass through the virtual switch to a virtual machine connected to that virtual switch. This setting is set to Reject by default to prevent frames destined for a particular VM from being read by other VMs. You should enable this mode only if you are running troubleshooting tests or running intrusion detection systems that require the system to investigate these frames.

- ▶ **MAC Address Changes:** If set to Reject, this setting would deny incoming IP traffic from reaching the VM if the MAC address defined in the guest operating system does not match the MAC address listed in the VM's configuration file or vmx, as illustrated in Figure 4.13. By default, this setting is set to Accept.

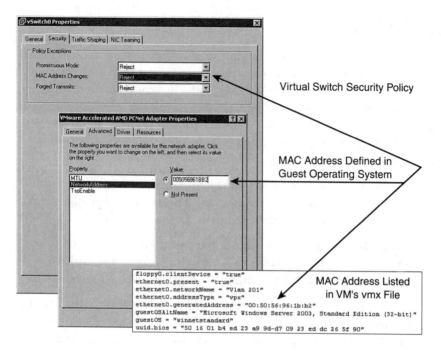

FIGURE 4.13
VM MAC match configuration file.

▶ **Forged Transmits:** This setting is the same as the MAC Address
Changes setting, except it controls the outgoing IP traffic rather than the
incoming. If set to Reject, this setting would deny outgoing IP traffic
from the VM if the MAC address specified in the guest OS does not
match the MAC address listed in the VM's configuration file or vmx. By
default, this setting is set to Accept.

TIP

For the highest level of security, set all the values to Reject.

When applying security to a virtual switch or to a port group, you need to
understand the policy processing and what takes precedence over what. You can
apply the policy as follows:

▶ **Virtual Switch:** When applying to the virtual switch, the policy propa-
gates to all the port groups configured on this virtual switch.

▶ **Port Group:** When applied to a port group, a policy overrides the policy
applied to the virtual switch and takes precedence over it.

Traffic Shaping

Traffic shaping gives you greater control over the amount of outgoing bandwidth available to virtual machines and enables you to tweak it and prioritize it. Traffic shaping is a great feature and can be useful in some cases in which adding more physical NICs is not permitted. However, given the relatively cheap cost of adding network interface cards, it would be much easier to add more NICs and increase network bandwidth using NIC teaming than it is to tweak bandwidth with traffic-shaping policies.

Traffic shaping is disabled by default; however, should the need arise for traffic shaping and should you need to enable it, you have three configurable settings that can help you tweak bandwidth:

▶ **Average Bandwidth:** Defines the average bandwidth this virtual switch should handle over time. It basically establishes the normal bandwidth load value for this vSwitch. It measures this in kilobits per second (kbps).

▶ **Peak Bandwidth:** Defines the maximum bandwidth that a virtual switch can handle. Packets received after the maximum has been reached are queued and processed as bandwidth is available. If the queue becomes full, any packets after that are bounced. This parameter is also set in kbps.

▶ **Burst Size:** Allows you to configure in kilobytes what you want the maximum burst size to be under normal conditions. The burst size also queues packets if the maximum is reached, and if the queue is full, any other packets are dropped.

NIC Teaming

NIC teaming provides for fault tolerance, redundancy, and load balancing of outgoing IP traffic from the virtual switch. You can adjust the settings on the NIC Teaming tab of the vSwitch Properties window, as shown in Figure 4.14.

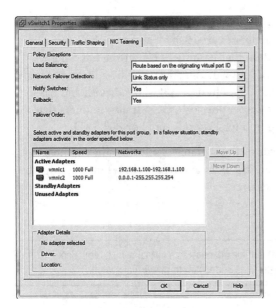

FIGURE 4.14
NIC teaming.

Load Balancing

You can select load-balancing policies in the Load Balancing drop-down list. There are four load-balancing policies that you can configure the virtual switch to take advantage of, as follows:

> ▶ **Route Based on the Originating Virtual Port ID:** This setting configures communications based on the virtual port where the VM is connected on the virtual switch. In essence, because every VM is configured on a virtual port ID and because this port ID rarely changes, communications are consistent.

EXAM ALERT

The exam might have a question about whether the port ID will change in the event of a VMotion. The answer is yes because the VM is moving from one vSwitch to another and a completely new host. Keep that in mind.

> ▶ **Route Based on Source MAC HASH:** This setting configures communications uplink based on the MAC address of the VM from which the traffic originated. This method has low overhead; however, in this setting, VMs cannot take advantage of multiple physical NICs' bandwidth, and they are limited to the bandwidth of the NIC to which they are connected.

▶ **Route Based on IP Hash:** When this setting is selected, each packet's source and destination IP addresses are hashed, and an uplink communication link is selected based on that hashing. This setting has a higher CPU utilization overhead but provides an advantage by allowing a single VM to take advantage of multiple physical NICs' bandwidth and has better load balancing of traffic across physical NICs. It also requires that the physical switches be configured for EtherChannel or 802.3AD.

▶ **Use Explicit Failover Order:** If this policy is selected, the topmost physical NIC in the list is always used, and if it becomes unavailable, the second NIC on the list takes over.

NOTE

When you use NIC teaming and add multiple adapters to a virtual switch, you also increase the bandwidth available to the VMs connected to the virtual switch.

Network Failover Detection

ESX 3.5 has built-in capabilities that would notify it when a network failover was detected from one physical NIC to the other, and you can configure this either based on virtual switch or port groups in one of two ways:

▶ **Link Status:** This method determines if there is a connection by whether a connection is detected on the port. If a cable is connected to the port, it reports the connection as a success; if not, it fails over.

▶ **Beacon Probing:** In addition to doing Link Status, this method is similar to a heartbeat in that it continuously sends packets between the adapters, and if a heartbeat is missed, it assumes there is an issue and fails over.

Notify Switches

The *Notify Switches* option is a great performance tweak. When set to Yes, it notifies physical switches of changes such as the following:

▶ Physical NIC failover occurs where a virtual NIC is now using a different physical NIC to pass its communication.

▶ A new physical NIC was added to a NIC team.

This feature is especially helpful because, without it, virtual machines would experience latency and slowness as the physical switches update their lookup tables. This is especially helpful after VMotions and, of course, in the event of failovers.

> **CAUTION**
>
> Do not set the Notify Switches option to Yes if you will be using Microsoft Network load balancing in Unicast mode. Check out the VMware knowledgebase article 1556 for more information. The knowledgebase is located at http://kb.vmware.com.

Failback

The Failback policy determines what happens when a failed physical NIC is functional again. There are two options:

▶ If this policy is set to Yes, when a failed adapter is restored to a functioning state, it immediately seizes the role of active physical NIC and retires the current active one to standby mode.

▶ If this policy is set to No, when a failed adapter is restored, it goes into standby mode and does not become active again until the next time a failover occurs.

Explicit Failover Order

When the Explicit Failover Order option is selected, you can manually control what happens in the event of a failover. For example, in the Active adapters, the topmost adapter is always the first one to be used; however, you can control which adapter is on top. The Standby adapters are the ones that are used in the event the active adapter fails; again, you can control which one is used first. The Unused adapters are simply out of commission and should not be used.

Networking Maximums

It is an inevitability that the VCP exam will include questions regarding networking maximums. Table 4.1 provides these figures to help make sure you are aware of them both for the exam and later for your day-to-day administration and design of ESX environments.

Table 4.1 Networking Maximums

Component	Maximum
Virtual Switches	127
Virtual Ports	1016
Port Groups	512
E100 NICs	26
E1000 NICs	32
Broadcom NICs	20
Ethernet Ports	32
NIC Teams	32

Exam Prep Questions

1. If you want to use iSCSI, what type of port group would you need to configure on a virtual switch?

   ○ **A.** Virtual Machine

   ○ **B.** Service Console

   ○ **C.** VMkernel

   ○ **D.** vSwitch

2. Select the three types of security policies that can be applied to either virtual switches or port groups.

   ○ **A.** IP Hash

   ○ **B.** MAC Address Changes

   ○ **C.** Forged Transmits

   ○ **D.** Promiscuous Mode

3. What is the default number of ports for a virtual switch?

   ○ **A.** 24

   ○ **B.** 56

   ○ **C.** 48

   ○ **D.** 54

4. Select the three load-balancing methods that can be used.

   ○ **A.** Route Based on IP Hash

   ○ **B.** Route Based on the Originating Port ID

   ○ **C.** NIC teaming

   ○ **D.** Route Based on Source MAC Hash

5. Which load-balancing method distributes load more efficiently and allows VMs to take advantage of more than a single NIC's available bandwidth?

   ○ **A.** IP Hash

   ○ **B.** MAC Hash

   ○ **C.** Port ID

   ○ **D.** NIC teaming

6. Which two methods are used to detect a network failure?

   ○ **A.** Notify Switches

   ○ **B.** Link Status

   ○ **C.** Alarm Notification

   ○ **D.** Beacon Probing

7. What is the maximum number of ports that can be configured on a virtual switch?

   ○ **A.** 1,014

   ○ **B.** 1,015

   ○ **C.** 1,016

   ○ **D.** 1,018

8. True or false: When you are using virtual switches, every virtual machine has its own MAC address.

   ○ **A.** True

   ○ **B.** False

9. True or false: If you edit the properties of a virtual switch and modify the virtual port count, you need to reboot the ESX host.

   ○ **A.** True

   ○ **B.** False

10. What are the two circumstances under which physical switches are notified of a change?

    ○ **A.** When a new physical NIC is added to a virtual switch

    ○ **B.** When a new physical NIC is removed from a virtual switch

    ○ **C.** When a physical NIC failover occurs

    ○ **D.** When a virtual NIC failover occurs

Answers to Exam Prep Questions

1. Answer **C** is correct. To configure iSCSI, you need to create a port group on your virtual switch that is of type VMkernel.

2. Answers **B**, **C**, and **D** are correct. MAC Address Changes, Promiscuous Mode, and Forged Transmits are the three security policies.

3. Answer **B** is correct. The default number of ports that are configured with a virtual switch is 56. In ESX Server 3.0, the default number of ports for the first vSwitch was 24 and subsequent switches would default at 56.

4. Answers **A**, **B**, and **D** are correct. The three types of load-balancing methods are Route Based on IP Hash, Route Based on Originating Port ID, and Route Based on Source MAC Hash.

5. Answer **A** is correct. Route Based on IP Hash is the ideal method if you want the most efficient bandwidth load balancing; it also allows VMs to take advantage of multiple physical NIC's bandwidth capabilities. It does, however, add a CPU load and requires the physical switches to be configured for EtherChannel.

6. Answers **B** and **D** are correct. Link Status and Beacon Probing are the two methods by which a network failure is detected.

7. Answer **C** is correct. The maximum number of virtual ports that can be assigned to a virtual switch is 1,016.

8. Answer **A**, True, is correct. Each virtual machine is assigned its unique MAC address.

9. Answer **A**, True, is correct. When you modify the virtual port count of an existing virtual switch, the changes do not take effect until after the ESX host is rebooted.

10. Answers **A** and **C** are correct. Notify Switches notifies physical switches when a physical NIC failover occurs or when a new physical NIC is added to a virtual switch.

CHAPTER FIVE

Storage Operations

Terms you'll need to understand:

- ✓ Fiber Channel
- ✓ Internet Small Computer System Interface (iSCSI)
- ✓ Network Attached Storage (NAS)
- ✓ Network File System (NFS)
- ✓ iSCSI Software Initiator
- ✓ Block-Level Transfer
- ✓ File-Level Transfer
- ✓ Hard Zoning
- ✓ Soft Zoning
- ✓ LUN Masking

Concepts and techniques you'll need to master:

- ✓ The components of the Fiber Channel SAN and how addressing works
- ✓ The difference between hard and soft zoning and how zoning works in a Fiber Channel SAN
- ✓ The difference between file-level and block-level transfers
- ✓ VMFS extents and multipathing

When you are planning a VMware Infrastructure deployment on an enterprise level or even on a small- or medium-size level, storage considerations occupy a large percentage of the discussion. The reason is that storage is an integral part of the deployment that unlocks features such as VMotion, High Availability, and Distributed Resource Scheduler. Storage also has a significant positive or negative impact on performance of the virtual machines that are loaded on the ESX hosts. For all those reasons and many more, being intimately familiar and comfortable with all the storage operations in a virtual infrastructure will be the deciding factor between a successful implementation and a mediocre one.

Storage in VI3

Storage as a general subject is so large and vast that it would probably take a book to cover all the options and technologies available. This chapter discusses the different storage technologies that VMware Infrastructure 3 supports and leaves the vendor selection to your planning phase when you decide to evaluate which solution fits your environment the best. The aim here is to pour a solid storage foundation upon which you can build sharp decision making when the time comes. VI3 presents four different storage architectures to choose from for your deployments:

- Local Storage
- Fiber Channel Storage
- iSCSI Storage
- Network Attached Storage (NAS)

These architectures, like anything else, have their pros and cons, and your selection depends on the deployment at hand, but that's not to say you cannot mix and match technologies. The importance of storage lies in the enterprise features that require the ESX hosts to see shared storage to allow for technologies like VMotion, Storage VMotion, HA, DRS, and others to work together. Without shared storage between ESX hosts, there would be no way of enabling these features because the hosts would not be able to see the VMs that reside on other storage Logical Unit Numbers (LUNs) to manipulate them in any way. That being said, these technologies also require a certain level of robustness to allow for these live migrations or recoveries to take place in a timely manner that is acceptable.

> **TIP**
>
> Prior to committing to buy any hardware in general for a Virtual Infrastructure, but before committing to any storage solutions in particular, make sure you check the VMware compatibility guide at http://www.vmware.com/pdf/vi35_san_guide.pdf.

While we are on the subject of performance, you should become intimately familiar with the two types of data transfer that are available:

- ▶ **Block-Level Transfer:** The storage area network (SAN) administrator carves up and presents a block of storage to a host. In this scenario, the host treats this storage as if it were local storage on the host. This is typically the case with Fiber Channel (FC) and iSCSI SANs. In this scenario, you can format the storage with the file system that is appropriate to the environment for which it is being deployed.

- ▶ **File-Level Transfer:** The host is presented with a logical pointer to a block of disk; a perfect example of this is a network drive letter in Windows. Windows sees the disk as a drive letter but does not have lock capabilities on the disk to format it. Windows sees only the storage and can use it but cannot claim ownership over it.

Based on the storage solution you choose, file level or block level, performance will vary. For example, block-level transfer in the forms of Fiber Channel and iSCSI render superior data transfer speeds than you would get using file-level transfer with NAS.

Fiber Channel

Fiber Channel storage area networks are the most efficient, most reliable, and best performing of all the other solutions. They are also the most expensive of them all. However, depending on your enterprise's needs and the types of applications that you plan to deploy, Fiber Channel may be the best solution, and thus, performance and reliability become the deciding factor over cost.

A Fiber Channel SAN is a high-speed transport protocol that moves SCSI commands between two nodes at speeds of up to 8GB.

Knowing how a Fiber Channel SAN works with ESX is critical if you plan on deploying ESX in that environment. FC SANs extend the following options to ESX:

▶ **SAN Boot ESX:** Allows you to configure the ESX Server's BIOS to point to the right LUN where ESX was installed and therefore boot from that LUN.

▶ **Create VMFS Datastores:** Allows you to create VMFS partitions and take advantage of a robust foundation where VMs run at an optimal level. This option also provides for a location where you can store VM templates and ISO images.

▶ **Enable Enterprise Features:** FC SANs allow for features like VMotion, Storage VMotion, DRS, and HA to have a shared disk or common playground that allows for these technologies to function properly.

▶ **Allow VMs Access to Raw LUNs:** Allows you to configure a VM to have access to a raw LUN; this is the same concept as attaching a LUN to a physical server and then allowing this physical server to use this LUN as if it were local disk. The same applies to a VM: You are presenting this LUN to it, and the VM treats this as a local disk and manages it according to the operating system installed on it.

ESX 3.5 supports 256 LUNs that range from 0–255, 0 being the first LUN. These LUNs are identified by the VMkernel during the boot process. However, many times you will find yourself adding a SAN LUN to ESX and wanting it to see it without having to reboot the server; this is where the rescan option, shown in Figure 5.1, can be a very handy tool. You can access the rescan tool by going to the Configuration tab of the ESX host and then choosing Storage Adapters.

FIGURE 5.1
Rescan LUNs.

> **NOTE**
>
> During the installation of ESX, the wizard sees only the first 128 LUNs.

FC SAN Architecture

Familiarizing yourself with the different components that make up the Fiber Channel architecture is imperative in your virtual infrastructure deployment. The following sections cover the different components that make up the FC network:

- ▶ Host bus adapters
- ▶ Fiber Channel switches
- ▶ Logical Unit Numbers
- ▶ Storage systems
- ▶ Storage processor

Host Bus Adapters

A host bus adapter (HBA) is a physical device that is typically installed in a server and is similar to the network interface card (NIC) except it uses a different protocol and different type of cable. It is used to connect the host to a Fiber Channel network.

Every HBA is assigned a unique 64-bit address known as the World Wide Name (WWN), which identifies this device on the Fiber Channel network. The WWN is similar in functionality to a MAC address that is found on NICs. Figure 5.2 shows a typical WWN as noted from an ESX 3.5 host.

FC HBA WWN

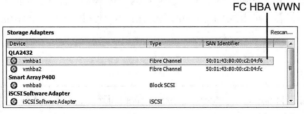

FIGURE 5.2

World Wide Name.

Fiber Channel Switches

A Fiber Channel switch, also known as the "fabric," is similar in functionality to an Ethernet switch except it supports FC ports, FC cables, and a different protocol. FC switches create the framework by which Fiber Channel devices can communicate with one another in a secure, optimal way.

Logical Unit Numbers

A Logical Unit Number (LUN) is a logical grouping of physical disks, sometimes referred to as Just a Bunch Of Disks (JBOD), or storage containers that are JBOD with the added advantage of RAID for fault tolerance. A Logical Unit (LU) can be a JBOD, a storage container, or part of a JBOD or storage container.

Storage Systems

A storage system is the collection of actual physical hard drives that are available in their rawest format and ready to be carved up into LUNs.

Storage Processor

A storage processor, also referred to as a controller, is the actual maestro or brain that creates the LUNs, implements security, and controls and regulates route access to the LUNs from the hosts.

Masking

LUN masking is the process of obscuring or hiding specific LUNs from being visible to hosts. LUN masking is implemented at the HBA or SCSI controller level. LUN masking should not be viewed as a secure way of preventing access to LUNs but rather an administrative measure to prevent operating systems from corrupting each other's LUNs. An example would be a Windows operating system: If you don't hide LUNs from a Windows operating system, it attempts to write a signature on all the visible disks, thereby corrupting some LUNs that were not its own to begin with. LUN masking prevents such nuisances by hiding these LUNs and limiting visibility only to the host's operating system.

> **NOTE**
>
> The reason LUN masking should not be considered a strong security measure is that an HBA WWN can be spoofed or forged.

Zoning

Zoning in a Fiber Channel SAN is the logical grouping of physical devices that are allowed to communicate together. Zoning is the compartmentalization of the fabric to break it down into smaller, more secure, and optimally managed subsets with controlled interference. The devices that are connected to the Fiber Channel fabric should not be allowed to freely interact with one another. Zoning regulates which devices should be communicating. There are two primary types of zoning in a Fiber Channel SAN:

▶ **Hard Zoning:** Implemented at the Fiber Channel switch level. It prevents physical access to any device that is not a member of the zone, thus making this type of zoning a more secure one.

▶ **Soft Zoning:** Also implemented at the Fiber Channel switch level. It is the method of obscuring ports so that they are not visible to devices outside their native zone. Therefore, what you can't see, you can't access. That being said, the security risk in this scenario lies in the fact that if you can discover the physical address of the device, you can still contact it and communicate with it.

NOTE

In most Fiber Channel deployments, seasoned SAN administrators always use a combination of hard and soft zoning to better manage the SAN.

FC Addressing

Addressing, as its name implies, is a method of providing a unique identifier that allows an ESX host to reach a LUN or partition. Just like your home address allows others to reach you, the VMkernel also has an address scheme that connects an ESX host's HBA to the drives. Figure 5.3 breaks down the addressing scheme.

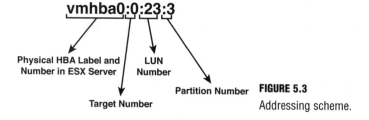

vmhba0:0:23:3

Physical HBA Label and
Number in ESX Server

LUN
Number

Target Number

Partition Number   **FIGURE 5.3**

Addressing scheme.

The addressing scheme components are as follows:

▸ **Physical HBA label and number in ESX Server:** A default label that identifies the device as an HBA. The label is "vmhba." A number is appended to this label that distinguishes the HBAs that are installed in the host. So if you have two or three HBAs, you can identify them by the appended number.

▸ **Target number:** The path or route that the storage processor presents to reach the SCSI disks. If you have two storage processors, depending on which SP will be used to route your request, the SP's number is appended to the target.

▸ **LUN number:** The number identifying the LUN. So if the traffic is destined for LUN 11, 11 would be appended.

▸ **Partition number:** The number of the target partition where traffic is destined. If you are trying to reach partition 3, 3 is appended.

Figure 5.4 illustrates a sample address that is destined to a LUN and also a sample address that is destined to a partition. The figure also shows how the traffic flows from the ESX host to its destination. Taking a closer look at what is going on in Figure 5.4, you can see that the top scenario is that of an ESX host that has two HBAs that are single ports. vmhba0 is trying to get to partition 3 on LUN 23 via storage processor 0, and thus, the address would be vmhba0:0:23:3; while vmhba1 is trying to get to LUN 24 via storage processor 1, and its address translates into vmhba1:1:24.

In the bottom scenario in Figure 5.4, an ESX host has two dual-port HBAs connecting to two dual-port storage processors. vmhba0 is again trying to access partition 3 on LUN 23; however, this time it is configured to have two paths to this partition:

▸ **vmhba0:0:23:3**

This path uses storage processor 0 to get to partition 3.

▸ **vmhba0:1:23:3**

This path uses storage processor 1 to get to partition 3.

Similarly, vmhba1 is trying to get to LUN 24 in two different paths:

▸ **vmhba1:0:24**

This path uses storage processor 0 to get to LUN 24.

▸ **vmhba1:1:24**

This path uses storage processor 1 to get to LUN 24.

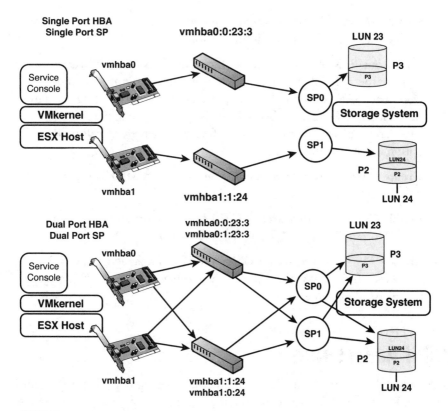

FIGURE 5.4
FC addressing.

iSCSI

Internet Small Computer System Interface (iSCSI) is an IP-based storage networking architecture that is capable of transmitting SCSI commands over your existing Ethernet infrastructure. This option is attractive to some organizations because the cost of deploying an iSCSI-based SAN is much cheaper than that of deploying a Fiber Channel SAN, and the performance benchmarks of iSCSI are impressive and yield excellent results. Fiber Channel remains a more robust solution, but with advancement and the availability of 10GB Ethernet, iSCSI will continue to yield impressive performance benchmarks.

Another reason iSCSI is attractive is that you can use your existing Ethernet architecture and you do not need to deploy special switches or cabling to support it. iSCSI can be deployed over your LAN, WAN, or even over the Internet.

ESX Server supports iSCSI and extends the same support and feature capabilities as it does the Fiber Channel solution, as follows:

▸ **SAN Boot ESX:** Allows you to configure the ESX Server's BIOS to point to the right LUN where ESX was installed and therefore boot from that LUN. This option is supported only if you are using the hardware initiator. The reason behind that is the software initiator is software based and the driver does not load before ESX Server; therefore, the option is not available.

▸ **Create VMFS Datastores:** Allows you to create VMFS datastores on iSCSI LUNs.

▸ **Enable Enterprise Features:** iSCSI LUNs support enterprise features like VMotion, Storage VMotion, HA, and DRS.

▸ **Allow VMs Access to Raw LUNs:** Allows you to assign a raw iSCSI LUN directly to a VM the same way you can assign a raw LUN directly to a physical machine.

iSCSI Addressing

iSCSI, like Fiber Channel, also has a unique way of assigning addresses to initiators and targets for them to quickly, easily, and accurately route packets to one another. The iSCSI addressing scheme consists of the following:

▸ **iqn:** iqn, which stands for iSCSI Qualified Name, is a standard label that is affixed at the beginning of the naming convention.

▸ **Date:** This string specifies the year and the month in which the organization registered a valid domain or subdomain.

▸ **Reversed Domain:** The organizational naming authority basically consists of the domain name of the organization presented backward—for example, .com.vmware.

▸ **Alias:** This optional string is represented by a colon (:) and is appended at the end of the name string followed by the friendly name or alias given.

When you break it down, the iSCSI naming convention looks something like this:

iqn.2007-02.com.eliaskhnaser:ipstor

Software Initiator

The software initiator driver that is used in ESX is a modified version of the Cisco iSCSI Initiator Command Reference and renders the NIC in the ESX server a multifunction NIC. When the software initiator is enabled, the vmkiscsid driver is loaded in the Service Console. For this reason, when you're configuring the software initiator, both the Service Console and the VMkernel need access to the iSCSI storage. Because the software initiator driver is loaded in the Service Console, it is now the SC's responsibility to initiate the session and to handle security and authentication, and it is then the VMkernel's responsibility to handle the input/output (I/O) traffic.

When configuring the software initiator's networking parameters, you have two options to choose from (see Figure 5.5):

> ▶ **One vSwitch with Two Port Groups:** In this scenario, you create one vSwitch and add two port groups, one for the SC and one for the VMkernel. You want to make sure that both the SC and the iSCSI storage are on the same subnet. Remember we mentioned earlier that both the SC and the VMkernel need to have access to the iSCSI storage before it will work properly; this scenario addresses this situation.

> ▶ **Two vSwitches:** In this scenario, you create two vSwitches for each port group and each can be on a different subnet; as long as routing is enabled between them, it is a viable solution. Many administrators prefer to keep things separated and less prone to errors and thereby would find this approach much more appealing.

EXAM ALERT

Make sure you always have an SC port group that has access to the iSCSI storage to ensure that your iSCSI implementation works.

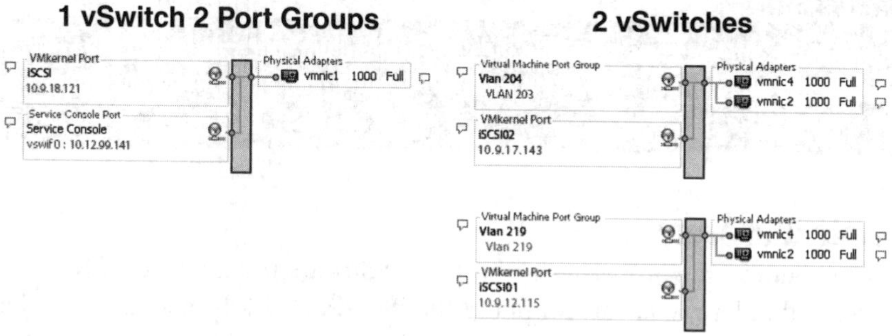

---

1 vSwitch 2 Port Groups

VMkernel Port
iSCSI
10.9.18.121

Physical Adapters
vmnic1 1000 Full

Service Console Port
Service Console
vswif0 : 10.12.09.141

2 vSwitches

Virtual Machine Port Group
Vlan 204
VLAN 203

Physical Adapters
vmnic4 1000 Full
vmnic2 1000 Full

VMkernel Port
iSCSI02
10.9.17.143

Virtual Machine Port Group
Vlan 219
Vlan 219

Physical Adapters
vmnic4 1000 Full
vmnic2 1000 Full

VMkernel Port
iSCSI01
10.9.12.115

FIGURE 5.5

Software initiator vSwitch configurations.

Enabling the Software Initiator

The *iSCSI software initiator*, being software based, needs to be enabled before the existing NICs can be set in multifunction mode. Enabling the software initiator is a two-step process:

1. Enable it in the Service Console by opening TCP port 3260 on the SC firewall. To do this, you need to edit the Security Profile, which is located under the Configuration tab. Check the box next to Software iSCSI Client. See Figure 5.6 for an example.

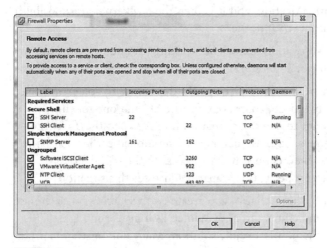

FIGURE 5.6
Enable iSCSI Daemon in the SC.

2. Edit the properties of the iSCSI software initiator in the Storage Adapters link under the Configuration tab. Select Configure and then Enable.

EXAM ALERT

Although there are two steps to enable the software initiator, the process does not work properly without your configuring a VMkernel port group and configuring the IP stack.

Dynamic Discovery

The second tab on the properties of the iSCSI Software Initiator is the Dynamic Discovery tab. Here, you can configure the iSCSI server's IP address with the associated port that can be queried for available targets. This method is also known as the SendTargets method because it establishes a discovery session with the SendTargets Server, also known as the iSCSI Server, and the server responds back with a list of all the available targets that you can connect to.

CHAP Authentication

Using the CHAP Authentication tab, you can enable or disable CHAP authentication. If it is enabled, you are prompted to enter a CHAP name. To make your name selection easy, you can use the software initiator name, if you choose, by selecting that option, as shown in Figure 5.7. You are then prompted to enter the CHAP secret. The CHAP secret that you enter must match the secret on the destination device that you are establishing communications with.

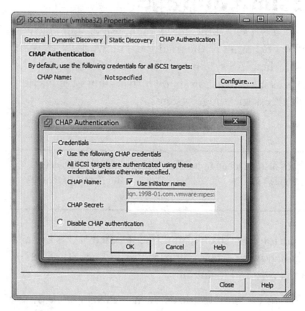

FIGURE 5.7
CHAP authentication.

Hardware Initiator

The hardware initiator has all the benefits of the software initiator described previously but also has better performance metrics. You can see when using a software initiator that you put a strain on the ESX host's CPU because it is used to process all the TCP packets. By using a hardware initiator, you offload the CPU processing burden from the host's CPU to the hardware initiator, thereby increasing performance. The hardware initiator also has two main advantages over the software initiator:

► The hardware initiator allows ESX to boot from a SAN LUN.

► The hardware initiator uses Static Discovery.

Static Discovery is a tab on the iSCSI initiator properties that allows you to manually specify the IP address of targets that you know ESX can access.

Network Attached Storage

Network Attached Storage (NAS) is a self-sufficient storage system—an entity on its own that can be attached via Ethernet to the traditional network. NAS is different from SAN in that, with the NAS system, a complete entity is attached to the network, whereas a SAN is a network on its own that allows connections from storage devices to gain access to storage systems.

> **NOTE**
>
> It is possible to have NAS devices also attached to the Fiber Channel network; however, one of the main reasons for using NAS is the capability to attach to the existing Ethernet network.

NAS is less expensive than both Fiber Channel and iSCSI-based SANs but also yields lower performance benchmarks when compared to FC or iSCSI SANs. NAS, however, is easier to manage and maintain.

Whereas NAS supports different types of protocols, such as *Network File System (NFS)* and *Common Internet File System (CIFS)*, which is also known as Server Message Block (SMB), ESX 3.5 supports only NFS and more specifically NFS 3.

> **NOTE**
>
> NAS disk drives have traditionally been SCSI, but you can build NAS on almost any type of disk, including ATA.

ESX Features on NFS Datastores

ESX supports NFS datastores; therefore, you are able to store VM files, templates, and iso images on NFS datastores just as you would on FC or iSCSI datastores. ESX trusts NFS datastores to perform the following tasks:

- VMotion
- DRS
- HA
- VCB

Table 5.1 puts forth the features that are supported by ESX on the different storage types to make it easier for you to identify what is supported where.

Table 5.1 Storage Systems Feature Support on ESX

Feature	Local	NFS	iSCSI	Fiber Channel
VMFS	✓	X	✓	✓
RDM (Raw Disk Mapping)	✓	X	✓	✓
VMotion	X	✓	✓	✓
HA	X	✓	✓	✓
VCB	✓	✓	✓	✓
DRS	X	✓	✓	✓
MSCS (Microsoft Cluster Server)	X	X	X	✓

Configuring NFS Datastores

When configuring an NFS datastore for use with ESX, you need to know a few points that will make it easier for you to complete the configuration in a successful manner. Aside from the GUI portion of creating an NFS datastore, you should familiarize yourself with some of the syntax in /etc/exports because this file defines which system can access the shares on the NAS device. The syntax is as follows:

- **Share name:** This is the name of the directory that will be shared on the NAS device.
- **Subnet:** This defines which subnet is allowed to access this share.

- ▶ **sync:** This ensures the completion of a write request before accepting additional requests.

- ▶ **rw:** This enables read and write requests on the NAS device.

- ▶ **no_root_squash:** This enables the root user or UID0 to access NFS with extended privileges.

NFS addressing is in the form of an IP address followed by the share name. When configuring it in ESX, you need to create a dedicated VMkernel port group on a vSwitch that is separate from that of the Service Console because it requires an IP address differentiation between it and the Service Console.

Virtual Machine File System

So far in this chapter we have looked at the different hardware storage solutions. Now let's focus our attention on what file system (software) leverages the hardware solutions we discussed previously. This brings us to the topic of the Virtual Machine File System (VMFS).

VMFS is a VMware proprietary file system that was designed and optimized to host virtual machine files, templates, and iso images. VMFS is a lightweight file system with little overhead. Unlike other file systems such as Windows NTFS, which allows only a single host access to the file system at one time, VMware's VMFS allows multiple hosts access at the same time without stepping on each other. This process is handled by the metadata file, a file that keeps track of the different changes that each attached host makes to the file system.

EXAM ALERT

The metadata files present on every VMFS volume are represented by files with the .fs extension.

Another reason VMware chose to build its own file system rather than use an existing file system like NTFS or ext is that it wanted a file system with the least overhead. For example, VMFS does not have any of the overhead of NTFS that it requires for security. Therefore, VMFS has one purpose only, and that is to provide VMs with a superior, well-optimized space to operate and accelerate.

But how, you might ask, does VMFS allow multiple hosts to lock the volume to write to it? VMFS uses file-level locks rather than entire volume-level locks, so by locking only the file being used, it allows other hosts to access other files on the partition and write to them at the same time. The only time a lock is placed on the entire partition is when the metadata file is being accessed; this is why, during the planning of your storage solution, LUN sizing is critical, because you don't want to put so much disk I/O on your LUNs that it slows down performance.

Performance is affected when hosts are queued to write to the metadata file. You therefore should be very cautious to design LUNs that can perform without having to wait for locks on the metadata to be released so that they can lock the metadata and write to it.

Extending a Datastore

ESX allows you the flexibility of extending a VMFS volume to address space limitations on existing volumes. Extending a VMFS volume is a dynamic process, which means you can add more space without interrupting productivity. The maximum size that you can allocate to a VMFS is 2TB. To get around this limitation, you can add extents to an existing VMFS volume. The maximum size of an extent is also 2TB, but you can add up to 32 extents to a single VMFS.

> **EXAM ALERT**
>
> A VMFS volume with extents can be as large as 64TB. The maximum number of extents that can be added to a single VMFS is 32, and the maximum size of each extent is 2TB (32 * 2 = 64TB).

So if you want an 8TB VMFS datastore, you create the VMFS datastore at 2TB in size and then add three extents, each 2TB in size, which totals 8TB. We strongly recommend that you carefully scale out your VMFS to avoid taking a performance hit. Even though you can get an 8TB VMFS, it does not necessarily mean you should. As we discussed before, every VMFS volume has a metadata file that gets locked by a different host when it is making updates to the volume. The larger the volume, the longer hosts have to wait to lock and write to the metadata file and the more performance suffers.

> **CAUTION**
>
> When using multiple extents, you should be aware that the first extent in the set is the one that hosts the metadata. Loss or corruption of the first extent leads to data loss on the other extents.

When an extent has been assigned to a datastore, you cannot remove that extent without destroying the entire datastore and the contents on it. So, although adding an extent is a relatively easy process, the capability to remove an extent and preserve the datastore is not supported at this time. Figure 5.8 illustrates a VMFS with several extents that form the extent set or extent group.

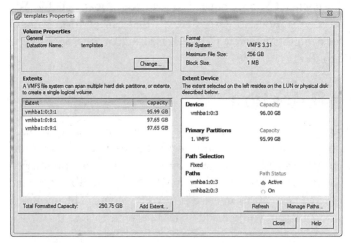

FIGURE 5.8
VMFS extents.

Multipathing

Multipathing is a concept that allows the ESX host to have more than one path to the storage systems configured for this host. This method is used to ensure continuous uninterrupted access to this storage by configuring the different ports on the HBAs in the ESX host to be aware of more than one way to reach the storage systems. So, in essence, it is designed to provide High Availability in the event of a hardware failure. The two types of multipathing available are as follows:

▶ **Fixed:** The default method of access used with active/active storage. It dictates that the ESX Server will use the preferred path to the storage systems. In the event that this path is not available for any reason, it automatically reverts to the alternate paths.

▶ **Most Recently Used (MRU):** The default method of access used with active/passive storage devices. It dictates that the ESX server will continue to use the most recent path to the storage systems until this path becomes unavailable, at which point it will revert to using the other path.

Multipathing in an ESX Server environment should not be confused with automatic load balancing, as this is not the case. Multipathing in this implementation is used as a failover method, and this is why only one path to the storage systems is active at any given time. Managing your paths in ESX Server is a relatively easy and straightforward task. Navigate to the Configuration tab. Choose Storage and then Properties (storage system of your choice). Click Manage Paths. Then select the device for which you want to configure pathing and click Change, as shown in Figure 5.9. You can then either enable or disable the state of this path. In some cases, you may want to disable a certain path to the storage devices for maintenance purposes or if you are reconfiguring your SAN. If you choose Enabled, this path actively participates in load balancing and failover. Disabled, of course, completely disables the path so that it cannot be used as an access route to the storage devices.

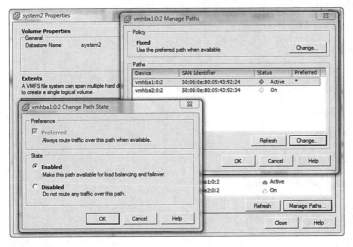

FIGURE 5.9
Multipathing management interface.

NOTE

You can use preferred paths only with the fixed policy.

Although multipathing in a SAN environment requires some configuration and has some configuration options to consider, with iSCSI, it is built in and utilizes the underlying IP network to achieve this. In a routed network, if a specific path to a device is not available, another route is provided to ensure the packet reaches the destination. To achieve multipathing with iSCSI, you really just have to do NIC teaming. By adding a second physical NIC to the vSwitch where iSCSI is configured, you achieve multipathing.

Exam Prep Questions

1. How many bits make up the unique address assigned to every HBA?

   ○ **A.** 32

   ○ **B.** 34

   ○ **C.** 62

   ○ **D.** 64

2. What is the name of the unique address that identifies every HBA on the Fiber Channel network?

   ○ **A.** World Wide Identifier

   ○ **B.** World Wide Name

   ○ **C.** World Wide Source

   ○ **D.** World Wide NetID

3. What is the method of hiding or obscuring LUNs on a per host basis known as?

   ○ **A.** Hard zoning

   ○ **B.** Soft zoning

   ○ **C.** LUN masking

   ○ **D.** Storage processor zoning

4. Identify the LUN number from vmhba0:2:3:4.

   ○ **A.** 0

   ○ **B.** 2

   ○ **C.** 3

   ○ **D.** 4

5. How many LUNs does ESX Server see during the installation process?

   ○ **A.** 32

   ○ **B.** 64

   ○ **C.** 128

   ○ **D.** 256

6. Choose the two iSCSI discovery methods that ESX 3.5 supports.

   ○ **A.** Dynamic Configuration

   ○ **B.** Static Configuration

   ○ **C.** SendTargets

   ○ **D.** Fixed Targets

7. What is the default authentication method for iSCSI?

   ○ **A.** Kerberos

   ○ **B.** CHAP

   ○ **C.** NTLM

   ○ **D.** Radius

8. True or false: VMotion is supported when you are using an NFS datastore.

   ○ **A.** True

   ○ **B.** False

9. True or false: VMware best practice calls for separating iSCSI traffic on its own network.

   ○ **A.** True

   ○ **B.** False

10. What is the iSCSI daemon or service name that runs in the Service Console?

   ○ **A.** vmiscsib

   ○ **B.** vmiscsi

   ○ **C.** vmkiscsi

   ○ **D.** vmkiscsid

Answers to Exam Prep Questions

1. Answer **D** is correct. The unique address that is assigned to every HBA is made up of 64 bits.

2. Answer **B** is correct. The unique 64-bit address that is assigned to every HBA is known as the World Wide Name or WWN.

3. Answer **C** is correct. LUN masking is the method of obscuring LUNs on a per host basis.

4. Answer **C** is correct. vmhba0 identifies the HBA adapter number in the ESX host. The second number, which is 2 in this example, identifies the target. The third number, which is 3, identifies the LUN number. The fourth number, which is 4, identifies the partition number.

5. Answer **C** is correct. During the installation of ESX Server, the installer sees only the first 128 LUNs. After ESX Server is installed and up and running, it can see a maximum of 256 LUNs.

6. Answers **B** and **C** are correct. The two iSCSI methods supported by ESX are Static Configuration and SendTargets.

7. Answer **B** is correct. iSCSI uses CHAP as the default method of authentication.

8. Answer **A**, True, is correct. VMotion is supported on NFS datastores.

9. Answer **A**, True, is correct. VMware best practices recommend that iSCSI be separated on its own network.

10. Answer **D** is correct. The iSCSI daemon that runs in the Service Console is vmkiscsid.

CHAPTER SIX

Administration with VirtualCenter 2.5

Terms you'll need to understand:

✓ Datacenter

✓ Inventory

✓ Root Folder

✓ Guided Consolidation

✓ Maps

✓ Lockdown Mode

✓ Clusters

✓ Folders

✓ Core Services

✓ Distributed Services

Concepts and techniques you'll need to master:

✓ VC database requirements and sizing

✓ VC hierarchal inventory design

✓ The management capabilities of VC

✓ The software and hardware requirements for a VC Server

The importance of VirtualCenter (VC) is that it is the one fundamental piece of the VMware Infrastructure suite that enhances the value for the enterprise. VirtualCenter unlocks all the enterprise features that make the VMware Infrastructure so valuable; features like VMotion, High Availability, and others all rely on VirtualCenter. It is the backbone of the infrastructure that can make ESX hosts aware of each other and make them work together in resource pools, for example. This chapter covers installation of VirtualCenter, design of a functional VC inventory, and administration with VC.

Planning and Installing VC

VirtualCenter 2.5 is a Windows-based application that allows you to control both ESX hosts and their virtual machines. It is also the application that allows you to use enterprise technologies such as VMotion, High Availability, and Distributed Resource Scheduler. VirtualCenter 2.5 also introduces the following new technologies to complement and enhance its other features:

- ▸ **VMware Update Manager:** An automated tool used for patch management of ESX hosts and virtual machines.

- ▸ **VMware Converter Enterprise for VirtualCenter:** A conversion tool that allows you to perform physical to virtual machine migration in addition to virtual machine to virtual machine migrations into the VI3 infrastructure.

- ▸ **Guided Consolidation:** Toned-down version of VMware Capacity Planner, a tool used to analyze a physical server infrastructure and recommend physical machines that are good candidates for conversion to virtual machines.

VirtualCenter is a framework that requires several elements to be functioning to make the entire suite work properly. Depending on the deployment scenario of your VirtualCenter Server and its different elements, sometimes ports need to be open to allow the flow of communications to take its proper course. Table 6.1 shows ports and their use in the VC deployment.

Table 6.1   VC Port Matrix

Flow (From -> To)	Port
VC to License Server	27000 and 27010
VC to Oracle DB	1521
VC to SQL DB	1433
Web Access and SDK Clients to VC	80 and 443
VC to ESX Hosts	902
VI Client to VC Server and ESX Hosts	443
ESX Server to ESX Server	902
VM Remote Console Traffic	903
NFS Transactions	2049
iSCSI Transactions	3260
VMotion Incoming Requests	8000

VC Blueprint

Understanding the architecture behind VirtualCenter greatly impacts the level of understanding you possess of the technology. VirtualCenter is not complicated software; on the contrary, it is very cleanly built and well defined. Figure 6.1 illustrates how the VirtualCenter blueprint is laid out.

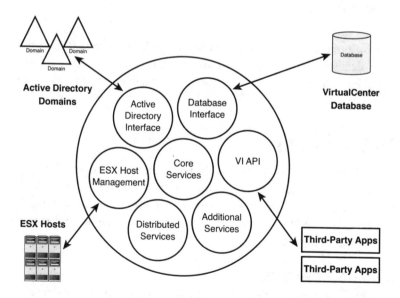

FIGURE 6.1
VirtualCenter blueprint.

The following different architectural pieces make up the blueprint:

- **Core Services:** The main module of VirtualCenter, the basic heart of the application that gives way to VM provisioning, Task Scheduler, events logging, and so on.

- **Distributed Services:** The module that gives way to features like VMotion, HA, and DRS. This is the place where the features that require a separate license stem from.

- **Additional Services:** The place where independent modules stem from, technologies such as VMware Converter Enterprise and Update Manager.

- **Database Interface:** The link that is established with a database server that provides VC with a centralized repository for all its data.

- **ESX host management:** The interface that allows VC to plug into ESX hosts and manage them.

- **Active Directory Interface:** The link that is established with an Active Directory domain to extend user and group support to VirtualCenter.

- **Virtual Infrastructure Application Programming Interface (VI API) and Virtual Infrastructure Software Development Kit (VI SDK):** The programming codethat provide a framework for developers of custom applications.

VirtualCenter communicates and issues commands to ESX Servers it manages using the vpxa daemon. However, if you are using the VI client to connect directly to the ESX host and issue commands to manage it that way, the vmware-hostd daemon, also known simply as hostd, is used.

VC Preinstallation

As with any application with a critical role in the enterprise, proper planning, sizing, and preinstallation steps and tasks exist that you should be familiar with to successfully complete VirtualCenter installation. Before you can size hardware and software, you need to know the minimum requirements, and that is what we cover in the following sections.

VC Hardware Requirements

The minimum hardware requirements for a VirtualCenter Server vary depending on the roles this server will play. The more roles you add to a server, the more hardware you will most likely throw at for it to perform its functions in an optimal manner. Therefore, if you decide that the server hardware will run the VirtualCenter Server and also the VirtualCenter database, the hardware requirements are one thing, and if the server hardware will support only the VirtualCenter Server, the hardware is in a different configuration. The following minimum requirements are for a server that runs VirtualCenter Server only:

- ▶ **CPU:** 2GHz or better processor.

- ▶ **Memory:** 2GB or more.

- ▶ **Storage:** A minimum of 560MB is needed, of which 245MB are for program installation and 315MB for the temporary directory. Best practice calls for a minimum of 2GB disk space for the installation.

- ▶ **Networking:** A network interface card (NIC) that supports 10/100MB, with 1GB being the best practice recommendation.

VC Software Requirements

Now that we have covered the minimum hardware requirements, let's shift our attention to the software requirements needed to host VirtualCenter Server. Keep in mind that VirtualCenter is a 32-bit application and therefore is supported on 32-bit operating systems. This is not to say it will not work on a 64-bit operating system; it is just not supported. The following operating systems are supported, however:

- ▶ Windows XP Professional SP2

- ▶ Windows 2000 Server SP4 with Update Rollup 1

- ▶ Windows Server 2003 SP1

- ▶ Windows Server 2003 R2

VC Database Design

The server is only as good as the data repository that supports it, so no matter how great VirtualCenter is, it is only as good as the database that supports it. For this reason, designing a good database back end is imperative for performance, scalability, and stability.

When you are planning for a VirtualCenter database, best practice calls for hosting the database on a separate dedicated server. In other words, it is not recommended to have the database and VirtualCenter on the same server. That being said, the following databases are supported by VirtualCenter Server:

- ▶ Microsoft SQL Server 2005 Express.

- ▶ Microsoft SQL Server 2000 Standard SP4 and Enterprise. If this option is selected, DAC 2.8 is a required installation on the client.

- ▶ Microsoft SQL Server 2005 Enterprise SP1, SP2, and Express. If this option is chosen, MDAC 2.8 is a required installation on the client.

- ▶ Oracle 9iR2, 10gR1 (10.1.0.3 and higher), 10gR2.

CAUTION

When you use Microsoft SQL Server 2005 Express, the database size limit is 4GB. If the VC database reaches this size limit, performance degradation occurs. Best practice calls for using this type of database only for test or demonstration purposes, but not for production.

EXAM ALERT

VMware supports the Microsoft SQL Express database for up to 5 ESX hosts with a maximum of 15 virtual machines on each.

Prior to installing VirtualCenter Server, you need to complete the following preparatory steps if you choose to use Microsoft SQL Server as your database software of choice:

- ▶ You need to create a database on the database server and a database user with either the sysadmin server role or the db_owner fixed database role assigned to it.

- ▶ You should create a system DSN, otherwise known as an ODBC connection, on the VirtualCenter Server that points to the database server. This process ensures that when the installation wizard needs to connect to the database, it knows how to communicate with it.

- ▶ You need to configure your DSN connection to use SQL server authentication.

NOTE

The only time you should use Windows authentication is when your VirtualCenter Server and your SQL Server are on the same server host.

EXAM ALERT

SQL authentication is supported on both local and remote instances of a SQL database server.

Database Sizing

After installing VirtualCenter Server, you are provided with a small bunch of useful tools; among them is a calculator that allows you to design your database size based on a number of different parameters. For instance, you tell the calculator how many ESX hosts you have and how many virtual machines you have, and it estimates the database size you need. Figure 6.2 illustrates what this calculator looks like.

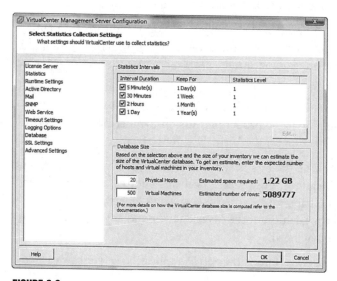

FIGURE 6.2

VC database sizing.

To access this sizing tool, follow these steps:

   1. Log in to VirtualCenter using the Virtual Infrastructure client.

   2. From the menu bar, select Administration.

   3. Choose VirtualCenter Management Server Configuration.

   4. Choose Statistics.

On the right pane of the statistics window, you enter your values and the calculator crunches your numbers for you.

VC Installation

VirtualCenter Server can be installed on a physical server or on a VM. The advantages of hosting it on a VM are endless, including its capability to participate in HA and DRS, making the server even more reliable and stable. Some administrators might hesitate to put VirtualCenter on a VM and allow it to participate in HA or DRS because they fear that they don't want to put the server that published these technologies in a position where it is also taking advantage of its technologies due to fear of complications. VMware does recommend and support this type of configuration for VirtualCenter. With the many deployments that we have made, we think this solution is a good one.

When you are ready to perform the installation, you should become familiar with the components of VirtualCenter and the order in which they should be installed so as to avoid any complications. For that matter, this order is recommended:

1. **Database Server:** This step includes creating the database on the database server, assigning it the proper permissions, and creating the associated ODBC connection on the VirtualCenter Server.

2. **License Server:** The use of a license server is imperative to enable some enterprise-level features. We covered licensing and the license server in greater detail in Chapter 4, "Virtual Networking Operations." Refer to that chapter for installation of the license server and any other licensing explanation you may need.

3. **VirtualCenter Server:** This is the actual application server software to be installed.

4. **VI Client:** This is the application that you use to log in to VirtualCenter from a GUI and manipulate it.

During the installation of VirtualCenter, you have the opportunity to modify the communications ports that VirtualCenter will use. You have a chance to modify the following. In most cases, the default values work just fine.

▶ **HTTP Web Service** is configured by default on port 80 and is used for client connections to VC via a web browser.

▶ **HTTPS Web Service** is configured by default on port 443 and is used for client connections to VC via a secure web browser.

▶ **Heartbeat (UDP)** is configured by default on UDP 902 and is used by VC to maintain ESX host connectivity. In other words, as long as VC is receiving packets from the ESX hosts on these ports, the ESX host is online and communicating, and if VC stops receiving a heartbeat, it assumes the ESX host is down.

▶ **Web Server Port** is configured by default on port 8086 and is used by the Apache web server.

VC Services

If you installed VirtualCenter on a server that is part of an Active Directory domain, you can add users and groups from that domain and any trusted domain directly into VC. Furthermore, once part of a domain, the Domain Admins group is automatically added and granted full control over hosts and VMs. So, if this is not something you desire, you should plan accordingly. After the installation of VC, a number of Windows services are added, as follows:

▶ **VMware Capacity Planner Service:** This service controls the Guided Consolidation feature of VC.

▶ **VMware Converter Enterprise Service:** This service controls VMware Converter, which allows you to migrate physical machines to virtual machines or virtual machines to virtual machines.

▶ **VMware Infrastructure Web Access:** This service controls your ability to log in and manage VMs from a web browser.

▶ **VMware License Server:** This service controls whether the license server is online or offline.

▶ **VMware Mount Service for VirtualCenter Service:** This service is used during the creation or cloning of VMs.

▶ **VMware Update Manager Service:** As the name implies, this service controls the Update Manager.

▶ **VMware VirtualCenter Server Service:** The most important service and heart of VC, this service is what makes VirtualCenter Server run. If this service is not running, VC will not run, and as a result, all its service offerings will not run either.

NOTE

Some of the services listed assume that the license server and VirtualCenter Server are installed on the same server per best practices. Some of these services may not be present in your deployment based on the method by which you installed the different components in your environment.

Designing a Functional VC Inventory

Depending on the size of your environment and how much you expect it to grow in the future, designing a functional VirtualCenter inventory is critical because doing so will make it much easier for you to apply security and enact role-based access to the different hosts and VMs within this inventory. An organizational hierarchy is important also because it gives you quick access to the systems you are trying to reach, whereas putting all the hosts and all the VMs in one folder will make finding what you are looking for more time consuming and frustrating if you are dealing with several dozen virtual machines. In the following sections, we discuss the different ways you can group and organize resources to gain the maximum flexibility and the easiest management and controlled access possible.

Folders

At the top of the inventory's hierarchy sits the *root folder*, which is, as the name implies, the topmost structure. The *Alpha* folder presents itself sometimes as Hosts and Clusters and other times as Virtual Machines and Templates, depending on the Inventory view you are in. You can use *folders* and *subfolders* to organize VMs and hosts in a way that is functional to your enterprise. A word of caution here: Make sure you do not overuse or overorganize your hierarchy because that, too, can make finding objects difficult for you and very difficult for others browsing the inventory.

If you want to break the VMs into folders, you can divide them based on the overall function they serve. Some people might want to break them down based on the function of the server. So, for example, file servers go in one folder, whereas database servers go in another and so on. We have found that dividing the VMs based on what they do in the enterprise may be easier. For example, if you have a Citrix or Terminal Server implementation in your environment and you group all your Citrix or Terminal Server-related VMs in one folder, users can more easily find the server they are looking for. You would use the same approach to Microsoft Exchange, where you group all servers in the same folder. Figure 6.3 illustrates how folders could be used.

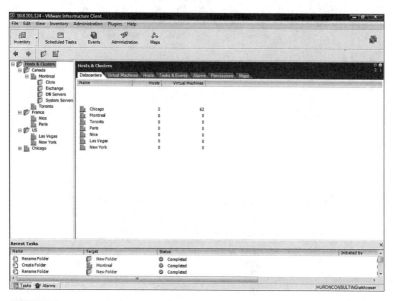

FIGURE 6.3
Folder structure based on application.

Datacenters

Before you can add any hosts or VMs to the inventory, you need to create at least one *datacenter*. A datacenter is the logical repository of hosts and VMs. You can create a folder under the root and then add a datacenter, but you cannot create a folder and add hosts and VMs before first adding a datacenter. The best approach to a datacenter setup is to follow what you currently have in your organization. Therefore, if you have two datacenters, create two datacenter objects and group them in folders accordingly and based on geographical location. Figure 6.4 illustrates how a datacenter could be laid out.

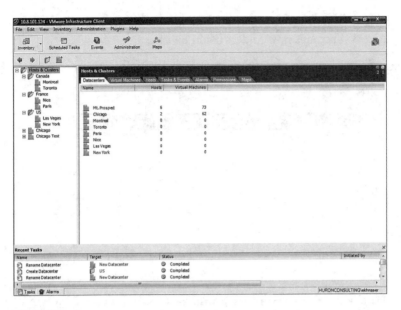

FIGURE 6.4
Datacenter layout.

Virtual machines in one datacenter cannot be VMotioned to another datacenter. Objects are manipulated in their parent datacenter. However, you can clone a virtual machine from one datacenter to another.

Clusters

Clusters are created by grouping multiple ESX hosts under the same resource pool. By doing that, you allow these ESX hosts to pool resources and distribute load among them in the most efficient way. You also allow these hosts to calculate and take into consideration one or more host failures and the ability to restart VMs on different hosts. When you create a resource pool, you can enable it to be a High Availability resource pool only, a Distributed Resource Scheduler resource pool only, or both at the same time, which is what best practice calls for. Keep in mind that when you are creating a resource pool, the maximum number of hosts that it can support is 32. Figure 6.5 illustrates a cluster that is both VMware HA and VMware DRS enabled.

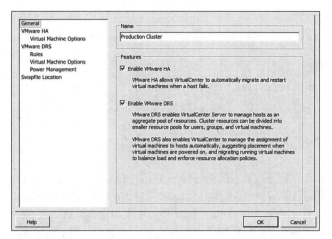

FIGURE 6.5
HA and DRS cluster.

Administration with VirtualCenter

When you access VirtualCenter via the VI client, you are presented with numerous tabs from which you can administer, manage, and support your infrastructure. The following sections focus on these tabs and tools in VirtualCenter and how you can use them in an efficient way.

VMware Infrastructure Client Tabs

The following subsections cover the following VI client tabs:

- ▶ Inventory
- ▶ Scheduled Tasks
- ▶ Events
- ▶ Administration
- ▶ Maps
- ▶ Consolidation

Inventory Tab

The Inventory tab allows you to switch the view of the hierarchy between

- ▶ Hosts and Clusters
- ▶ Virtual Machines and Templates
- ▶ Networks
- ▶ Datastores

As their names imply, a view of Hosts and Clusters primarily focuses on displaying the hosts and the different cluster configurations. You can, however, still drill down on every host or in every cluster and find the VM or template you are looking for. On the other hand, a view of Virtual Machines and Templates displays all the VMs and templates available. Similarly, a view of Networks or Datastores primarily displays the different network configurations and the available datastores. Figure 6.6 shows where you can change the views.

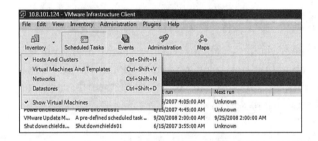

FIGURE 6.6
Inventory views.

Scheduled Tasks Tab

Scheduled tasks are an extremely helpful method of automating certain tasks to be performed at a given time. Without scheduled tasks, get ready to be up and bright at 3:00 a.m. to power down a host or run an update or any other task that would be required after hours or when load is at a minimum. Scheduled tasks allow you to perform these tasks in an automated manner. Figure 6.7 shows the Scheduled Tasks tab and some available scheduled tasks.

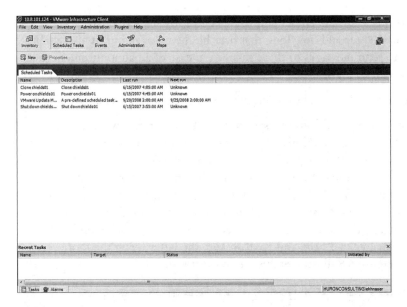

FIGURE 6.7
Scheduled tasks.

Events Tab

The Events tab is an imperative first step in any troubleshooting undertaking that you will engage in. This panel displays the different events that have occurred. This may include errors that have been registered, alarms that have been triggered, or tasks that have been completed. From this panel, you also have access to search with query keywords and display relevant results. If looking at all the events in one panel is too cumbersome and you want a more focused list, you can select any object in the inventory and browse its Tasks & Events window, which displays information on this object only.

Administration Tab

The Administration tab offers several tabs that allow you to manipulate different functions in the infrastructure. These tabs are

- ▶ **Roles:** This tab is discussed in greater detail with security and access control topics in Chapter 8, "VMware Infrastructure Security and Web Access." On this tab, you can define or view a defined role based on access to VirtualCenter.

- ▶ **Sessions:** This tab shows you who is currently logged in to VirtualCenter and how long that user has been logged in. It also enables you to send messages to these sessions in case of an announcement that you want to make.

- ▶ **Licenses:** This tab allows you to view licenses within the environment.

- ▶ **System Logs:** Like events, system logs are imperative when you are troubleshooting, and this tab gives you a list of system-related logs that you can browse through. You may also search system logs by keyword. Because there may be more than one version of the vpxd-index file, which is the file that holds the system logs, make sure you are using the latest one. The most recent one is usually incremented by a number, and the higher the number, the more recent the file. So, for example, you may have `vpxd-2.log` and `vpxd-3.log`, the latter being the more recent one. Figure 6.8 illustrates this tab in greater detail.

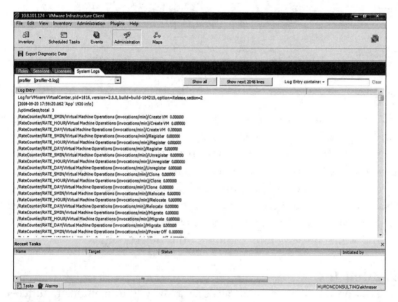

FIGURE 6.8
System logs.

Maps Tab

Maps are a fantastic way of graphically understanding the topology and what is connected to what. They can be used in many different ways. Say you want to find out which hosts are connected to which datastores or which VMs are on which hosts. Maps can be useful in making sure the VMotion requirements are met by inspecting the ESX hosts in question and making sure they see the correct networking and storage. The more seasoned you become with ESX, the more you will appreciate the power that maps offer you, especially in larger, more complicated environments. Figure 6.9 shows the Maps tab; it shows, on the right, the different criteria that can be selected that would update maps to reflect your selection.

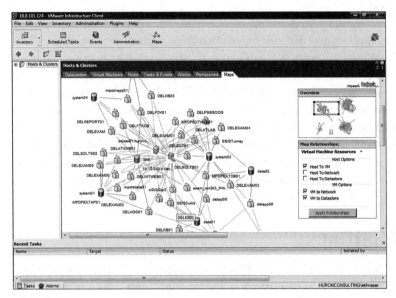

FIGURE 6.9
Maps tab.

Consolidation Tab

Guided Consolidation is covered in greater detail in Chapter 7, "Virtual Machine Operations." On this tab, you plan and execute a Guided Consolidation. The tools under this tab allow you to discover, analyze, and consolidate physical servers into virtual machines on ESX hosts.

Lockdown Mode

Lockdown mode allows you to control direct VI client access to an ESXi host. In other words, you shouldn't directly log in to hosts that are being managed by VirtualCenter because this may cause issues. To prevent administrators from logging in to a host directly, you can modify the Security Profile by selecting an ESXi host, choosing Configuration > Security Profile > Edit, and checking the box next to Enable Lockdown Mode. This prevents any direct access to this ESXi host.

EXAM ALERT

As of this writing, the Lockdown mode is available and shows up only on ESXi hosts.

Plug-ins

Plug-ins are applications that can be enabled from within VirtualCenter. Plug-ins extend the capabilities of VirtualCenter by giving it more features. Plug-ins are written to connect through the framework that VirtualCenter provides. As of this release, there are two plug-ins for VirtualCenter: VMware Update Manager and VMware Converter Enterprise. This is not to say that VMware could not release a plug-in tomorrow that would take advantage of the VC framework; that's the beauty and power of VC. Plug-ins are also installed and upgraded separately, which makes installing them independent from the VC installation. When a plug-in is enabled, the VI client GUI is modified, and new features appear accordingly to help manage the new plug-ins.

Client Settings

Because the VI client is the arm by which you manipulate VirtualCenter, knowing how to tweak some of its settings is an important step. You can modify the Timeout settings of the VI client so it is more tolerant to slow WAN connections or even limit the number of VI clients that can concurrently connect to VC. You can access these settings from the File menu: Select Edit and then Client Settings.

VirtualCenter Maximums

When you are planning, designing, and building any environment, it is critical that you know your limits so that you can plan accordingly and be able to scale properly. Table 6.2 provides some configuration maximums for VirtualCenter.

Table 6.2 VirtualCenter Limits

Description	Limit
VMs per VC Server	2000
ESX hosts per VC Server	200
ESX hosts per cluster (HA and DRS)	32

VirtualCenter Server Backup and High Availability

The first thing you should know before we get into the discussion of how to back up and recover VirtualCenter is that if the VC Server goes offline, your environment will not stop working. As a matter of fact, everything will continue to function normally. You will be limited only to what new tasks you can perform, and when the VirtualCenter Server is back online, it will resume its responsibilities.

Now let's talk about what you can do to back up VC Server or to provide some redundancy and High Availability. First, you can put your VirtualCenter Server on a VM and make it part of a cluster. That way, it is taking advantage of both HA and DRS. This takes care of ensuring the server stays up but does not protect you in case of operating system corruption or crashes. To protect against that, you can always have a copy of the VC virtual machine stored somewhere safe that you can recover from in case of emergency.

If the idea of having VirtualCenter on a VM does not appeal to you, you can have a cold standby server that is the exact replica of the VC Server in production. In the event that the production server goes offline, you can recover in a relatively short period. You can also mix and match. Therefore, instead of having a physical server in standby, doing nothing and collecting dust, you can P2V your VC to a VM and turn it off. Then you can use it in the event your physical server should go offline. Being able to do this would hold you up until you recover your server.

Another approach would also be to use clustering of the VC Server, either between two physical servers or two virtual servers, or a mix of physical and virtual. Clustering can also be extended to the database because both Microsoft SQL and Oracle offer clustering.

The options and configurations you can use to protect against a VC failure are numerous. The choice you make depends on what you see as the most efficient solution for your environment. Remember to keep it simple. As long as you have a good backup of your database and a good strategy on how to handle outages in VC, you should be good to go.

Exam Prep Questions

1. Which VirtualCenter interface allows developers to write third-party applications for use with VC?

   ○ **A.** VC API

   ○ **B.** VI API

   ○ **C.** VC SDK

   ○ **D.** VM API

2. How many ESX hosts can you have per cluster?

   ○ **A.** 16

   ○ **B.** 24

   ○ **C.** 32

   ○ **D.** 36

3. Which file is responsible for holding the system logs?

   ○ **A.** vpxd-logs

   ○ **B.** vpxd-events

   ○ **C.** vpxd-alerts

   ○ **D.** vpxd-index

4. What is the maximum number of virtual machines that can be managed by a single VirtualCenter Server?

   ○ **A.** 1000

   ○ **B.** 1500

   ○ **C.** 2000

   ○ **D.** 2500

5. Which option is not a VirtualCenter inventory hierarchy?

   ○ **A.** Hosts and Clusters

   ○ **B.** Datacenters

   ○ **C.** Networks

   ○ **D.** Datastores

6. Which two technologies are considered VirtualCenter plug-ins?

- ○ **A.** Guided Consolidation
- ○ **B.** VMware Consolidated Backup
- ○ **C.** Update Manager
- ○ **D.** VMware Converter Enterprise

7. Consider a scenario in which ESX Servers are separated from a VirtualCenter Server by a firewall. What port would you need to open to allow authentication communications?

- ○ **A.** 902
- ○ **B.** 903
- ○ **C.** 904
- ○ **D.** 906

8. True or false: You can create a database for VirtualCenter using the setup wizard during the installation of VirtualCenter.

- ○ **A.** True
- ○ **B.** False

9. True or false: It is recommended that VirtualCenter Server and the license server be installed on the same server.

- ○ **A.** True
- ○ **B.** False

10. What is the maximum number of ESX hosts that can be managed by a single VirtualCenter Server?

- ○ **A.** 100
- ○ **B.** 200
- ○ **C.** 500
- ○ **D.** 1000

Answers to Exam Prep Questions

1. Answer **B** is correct. The interface that allows developers to create third-party applications for use with VirtualCenter is the VI API.

2. Answer **C** is correct. The maximum number of ESX hosts that is supported per cluster is 32.

3. Answer **D** is correct. The file responsible for indexing the system logs is vpxd-index.

4. Answer **C** is correct. The VMware Configuration Maximum states that the maximum number of virtual machines to be managed by a single VC Server is 2000.

5. Answer **B** is correct. Datacenters is not a correct VirtualCenter hierarchy; the other hierarchy that is missing from the list is Virtual Machines and Templates.

6. Answers **C** and **D** are correct. The two technologies that are VirtualCenter plug-ins are VMware Update Manager and VMware Converter Enterprise.

7. Answer **A** is correct. Port 902 needs to be open when ESX hosts and VirtualCenter Server are separated by a firewall for authentication communications to flow back and forth.

8. Answer **B**, False, is correct. The VirtualCenter database cannot be created by the setup wizard during the installation of VC and must be created prior to the installation of VirtualCenter.

9. Answer **A**, True, is correct. VMware best practice calls for the VC Server and the license server to be installed on the same server because this setup avoids any possible communication issues, and given that VC features rely heavily on a license server being present, the recommendation is that they share the same server.

10. Answer **B** is correct. The VMware Configuration Maximums state that the maximum number of ESX hosts that can be managed by a single VC Server is 200.

CHAPTER SEVEN

Virtual Machine Operations

Terms you'll need to understand:

✓ Cold Cloning
✓ Hot Cloning
✓ Cold Migrations
✓ Snapshots
✓ Guided Consolidation
✓ Templates
✓ VMware Tools
✓ Converter Enterprise
✓ Virtual Hardware
✓ Remote Cloning

Concepts and techniques you'll need to master:

✓ What templates are and how to best leverage them and use them in the VI3 environment

✓ How to use guest operating system customization for Windows and Linux

✓ How to use VMware Converter Enterprise to convert physical and virtual machines to ESX virtual machines

✓ How to use Guided Consolidation to discover, analyze, and implement server consolidation

In this chapter, we start tackling some of the daily operations that an administrator faces when working with a VMware Infrastructure environment, such as the creation and administration of virtual machines—one of the fundamental reasons we use a virtual infrastructure in the first place. As far as the VCP exam goes, you can rest assured that the topic of virtual machine operations dominates because it is one of the most basic functions a VI administrator is expected to perform and understand thoroughly.

Virtual Machine Defined

A virtual machine (VM) serves the same purpose and behaves in the same manner as a physical machine except, instead of being a collection of hardware devices, it is a collection of software or virtual devices. A virtual machine is made up of the same components found in a physical machine, and similar to the way a physical machine's components establish a baseline upon which you can install a guest operating system, a virtual machine's virtual components establish a similar framework upon which you can install a guest operating system. In this sense, a virtual machine is made up of a bunch of files that carry its configuration and specify its name, how many CPUs are assigned to it, how much memory is allocated, and so on.

> **TIP**
>
> When you are naming a virtual machine, best practices call for not using special characters in its display name because the Service Console might have issues with that.

Virtual Hardware

The power of a virtual machine is that it provides a uniform platform upon which an operating system can be installed. It does this by allocating a standardized motherboard for all supported guest operating systems to use. This motherboard is based on an Intel 440BX with an NS338 SIO chipset. This standardization is what makes the VM so portable and so compatible with a wide collection of supported operating systems.

When you are installing an operating system, it does not matter whether you are installing it on *physical* or *virtual hardware*. As a matter of fact, the guest OS does not even know the difference between physical and virtual; the only thing that matters is that it sees the necessary components it needs to complete the installation.

A virtual machine can have several different virtual hardware components added to it:

▶ **6 Virtual PCI Devices:** Although six virtual PCI devices are supported, one is automatically allocated to the virtual video adapter, thereby leaving you with five available PCI devices that you can allocate to Ethernet and SCSI adapters as follows:

　　▶ **4 NICs:** You can have a maximum of four network interface cards in every VM. Considering that NICs are PCI devices and that the maximum number of *available* PCI devices is five, you have to equally allocate NICs and SCSI adapters.

　　▶ **4 SCSI Adapters with 15 Devices Otherwise Known as Hard Drives:** You can allocate a maximum of four SCSI adapters. Given that these are PCI devices and that you have only five *available* PCI slots in every VM, you have to plan accordingly to distribute SCSI and Ethernet adapters in your VM configuration.

▶ **4 IDE Devices per VM:** You can have up to four CD-ROM/DVD-ROM drives.

▶ **2 Floppy Drives:** You can have up to a maximum of two floppy drives.

▶ **1, 2, or 4 vCPUs:** To take advantage of the ability to add multiple processors to a VM, you need a separate virtual SMP license.

▶ **64GB RAM:** Up to 64GB of RAM can be physically allocated to a VM's use.

▶ **2 Serial Ports:** Up to 2 serial ports can be allocated to a VM's use.

▶ **2 Parallel Ports:** Up to 2 parallel ports can be allocated to a VM's use.

EXAM ALERT

At this time, ESX Server VMs do not support USB or audio adapters.

Figure 7.1 illustrates these different virtual hardware components.

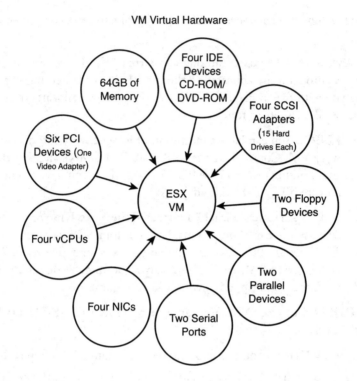

VM Virtual Hardware

FIGURE 7.1
VM virtual hardware.

The bare minimum components that are required for every virtual machine are

- vCPU

- Memory

- Boot mechanism (CD-ROM, floppy, or virtual disk)

All other components are considered optional.

Virtual Machine Files

Every virtual machine is made up of files that together make up its environment. You should become intimately familiar with these files because they are at the core of your proper understanding of how a virtual machine is constructed. These files are as follows:

▶ *name_of_VM*.vmx: This file contains the configuration of the VM—the way it is built and constructed. This file is literally the blueprint of the VM that defines how many vCPUs are assigned, how much memory is allocated, and so on.

▶ *name_of_VM*.vmdk: This file contains all the relevant information about the VM's virtual hard disk.

▶ *name_of_VM* -flat.vmdk: This file makes up the hard drive and contains all the data.

▶ vmware.log: This file contains the VM's log files.

▶ .nvram: This file contains the BIOS of the VM.

▶ vmware-#.log: This file contains old VM logs, and the # enumerates starting with 1.

▶ *name_of_VM*.vswp: This is the VM's swap file.

▶ *name_of_VM*.vmsd: This file contains information about any available snapshots for this VM.

The VM may have additional files if snapshots exist or if raw disk mappings are in place. Raw disk mappings can be in the form of a SAN LUN that is directly attached to the VM. Another point to note here is that when you have only one hard drive configured for a VM, the files that make up the hard drive appear as VM.vmdk and vm-flat.vmdk, but when you add a second hard drive, the second hard drive's files appear as vm_1.vmdk and vm_1-flat.vmdk. Adding a third hard drive enumerates accordingly, but it is important to note that the enumeration process starts at 1.

Creating a Virtual Machine

The process of creating a virtual machine is one that you should be comfortable with as you are preparing to take the VCP exam. Therefore, we do not go into detailed steps as to how to go about creating the VM because this straightforward wizard-driven process allows you to configure all the components we have discussed up to this point in the chapter. These components include vCPU, memory, virtual disk, and so on. We do, however, want to highlight the importance of the configuration of the virtual disk during the creation of the virtual machine. We do that in the next section, but first let's quickly tackle a few issues pertaining to how to launch console access to the VM to manipulate it.

The VI client is the tool used to initially launch the VM's console to install a guest operating system on it. After a guest operating system is installed, though, the VM console is not typically used, but rather tools like RDP, SSH, or VNC are used. That being said, the console can be used to access the VM's BIOS or to control power cycling the VM or editing some of its settings.

> **TIP**
>
> When you are using the VI client to launch the console, if a Windows operating system is installed, you can use the key combination Ctrl+Alt+Ins to initiate a Ctrl+Alt+Del command to access the Graphical Identification and Authentication (GINA) and log in. You can also do this by clicking VM on the File menu of the console and selecting Send Ctrl+Alt+Del.

Installing a Guest Operating System

The easiest way to install a guest operating system inside a VM is to mount an ISO file as a CD-ROM and install it that way. The other options that you have are to mount either the ESX CD-ROM or the client from where you are connecting, meaning the machine you are using to access the VM Console, which can be your local desktop or laptop. You can use the CD-ROM devices to install the guest operating system. Figure 7.2 illustrates these options.

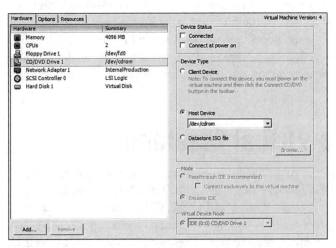

FIGURE 7.2
Virtual machine settings.

However, the most efficient way is to store the ISO image files in a shared location, whether on a VMFS datastore or an NFS datastore that is accessible by all ESX servers. This makes deployment easier and more reliable. ESX 3.5 currently supports the following guest operating systems:

- Windows NT 4.0 all the way to Windows Server 2008

- Red Hat Enterprise Linux 2.1, 3, 4, and 5

- Red Hat Linux 7 to 9

- Ubuntu 5.04, 5.10, 6.06, 6.1, and 7.04

- NetWare 4.2, 5.1, 6.0, and 6.5

- Solaris 10 x86

- SLES 7 to 10

Virtual Disk

A few clicks into the VM creation wizard, and you are presented with a screen that prompts you to select the storage adapter type, as shown in Figure 7.3. Your options are either Bus Logic or LSI Logic. The setup wizard selects the ideal adapter based on the operating system you are about to install; however, this step allows you to customize this selection if the need arises. Keep in mind that if you choose Typical at the beginning of the virtual machine creation wizard, you are not shown this step. To be prompted with this step, you must select Custom at the beginning of the virtual machine creation wizard..

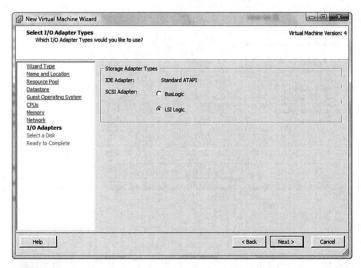

FIGURE 7.3
SCSI adapter type.

Up next, you are prompted to select a disk and, as you can see in Figure 7.4, your options are as follows:

- ▶ **Create a New Virtual Disk:** As the name implies, this option creates a new virtual disk.

- ▶ **Use an Existing Virtual Disk:** With this option selected, you can browse for an existing virtual disk and associate it with the virtual machine you are creating.

- ▶ **Raw Device Mappings:** This option is the one you would use if you were attaching a SAN LUN directly to this virtual machine.

- ▶ **Do Not Create a Disk:** This option does not create a virtual disk and therefore renders this VM as a shell only. The VM cannot be powered on unless you specify some kind of a booting mechanism, such as booting from a CD-ROM, an ISO image, or even a floppy.

EXAM ALERT

You can create a VM without a virtual disk, but it needs some kind of a booting mechanism before you can power it on.

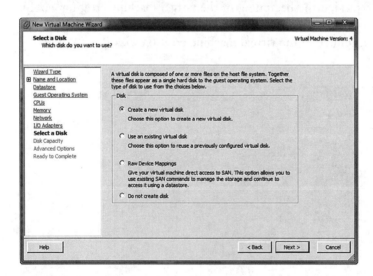

FIGURE 7.4

Provision virtual disk.

If you choose to create a new virtual disk, your next screen in the setup wizard looks like Figure 7.5. Here, you can enter the desired size of the virtual hard disk. Keep in mind while you're doing this that the maximum size of disk you can use is 2TB. But more important in this screen is the method of storing the virtual disk. Your options are Store with the Virtual Machine and Specify a Datastore. This choice is important because it allows you to separate multiple hard disks associated with a single VM to different locations. The importance of this lies in performance, so you should separate the operating system files from the data files. Typically, operating system files are stored with the VM, whereas data files are stored on a separate datastore service by different SAN LUNs.

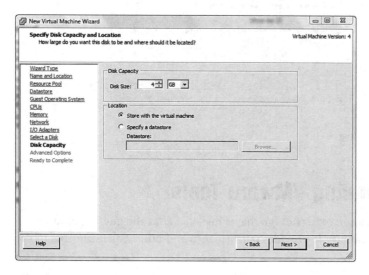

FIGURE 7.5
Disk capacity and storage location.

The final step in the virtual disk configuration is illustrated in Figure 7.6. Here, you can configure the virtual disk on a specific SCSI node. This step also gives you the option to tweak the disk mode. By default, the disk mode allows you to use snapshots. If you opt to use independent disks, by checking Independent, you sacrifice the use of snapshots because they are not supported. Independent Disk has two modes, as follows:

▶ **Persistent:** Thisoption means that the changes made to the disk are immediately committed to the disk and are final; you cannot undo them.

▶ **Nonpersistent:** This mode means that when the VM is powered off or recycled, all the changes since the last power on are discarded and you revert to the original state of the disk.

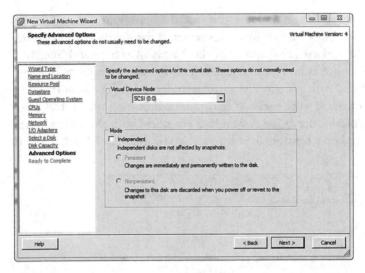

FIGURE 7.6
Independent disk modes.

Understanding VMware Tools

VMware Tools is a software package that is installed after the guest operating system is up and running. It provides performance and other enhancements to the VM's operability:

- A better virtual NIC adapter driver

- An enhanced SCSI adapter driver

- Better memory management

- OS quiescing for snapshots and VCB

- Time synchronization

- A better mouse driver

- The capability to gracefully shut down a VM

- An enhanced video driver for the virtual video card

When the VMware Tools package is installed, you can configure the tools further by double-clicking the VMware Tools icon in the taskbar. One of the more important tasks to consider is time synchronization. By default, when the VMware Tools are installed, time synchronization is disabled between the VMs and the Service Console or the ESX host. This feature is disabled by default because Windows-based VMs sync time with the domain controller that has the FSMO role of PDC emulator. Enabling time synchronization between the VMs and the SC may cause potential issues because the VMs don't know where to turn for time synchronization. Should they use VMware Tools and the time synchronization with the SC, or should they use the domain controller? To get around this problem, you can configure your ESX host to either sync its time with the PDC emulator or configure both your ESX host and your PDC emulator to sync time from the same external source.

> **EXAM ALERT**
>
> Time synchronization is an important design consideration. For more information on this topic, refer to the VMware white paper "TimeKeeping in Virtual Machines" at http://www.vmware.com/pdf/vmware_timekeeping.pdf .

Understanding and Working with Templates

Everything in a virtual infrastructure is derived one way or another from your day-to-day functions. Consider the concept of *templates*, for example. Templates in a virtual infrastructure are the equivalent of images in a physical environment. So, before the concept of virtualization became popular, what administrators and engineers did—and still do—is provision servers from images. Images are created by configuring a system either by creating just an operating system image or by creating an operating system and application's image. When the time comes for a new server to be deployed, you do so from these images, thus saving time and effort.

Templates are the same: They are a quick and easy way to provision VMs on the fly. The advantage of templates over traditional images is not just in the significant speed by which you can provision VMs, but also in your ability to update the template.

Templates in a VI3 environment allow for the quick provisioning of similarly configured virtual machines. Templates are objects that cannot be powered on.

Creating Templates

There are a couple of different ways of creating a template, depending on the situation you are in and what you are trying to accomplish. To create a template, you first have to create a virtual machine, configure this virtual machine to your liking in terms of operating system tweaks, install the necessary drivers and applications, and when you are ready to create a template, simply right-click this VM and you are presented with the following two options:

▶ **Clone to Template:** With this option, you are cloning the current VM to a template. You use this option if you want to continue to use the existing VM because by turning it into a template, you cannot power it on anymore.

▶ **Convert to Template:** With this option, you convert the VM into a template that is powered off. You typically use this option if the sole purpose of creating the VM is to make it into a template.

> **EXAM ALERT**
>
> When you are cloning to template, you must turn off the source VM that you are about to clone.

Now that you have created a template, you should also be familiar with how to update this template. As you are likely aware, master images constantly need updating, whether that is for security patches, new application versions, or anything else. To accomplish this, you simply find the template you want to update, right-click it, and select Convert to Virtual Machine. At this point, that template is converted back to a VM. You can power it on, update accordingly, and then when you are ready, convert it back to a template.

Templates Storage

Storage seems to dominate almost every aspect of a VI, and the reason is simple: You are doing everything in files, and files need to be stored somewhere. Understanding the different options available makes finding things and sharing things easier, but can also help save on space if you tweak certain settings at your disposal. During the process of creating a template, you are offered two methods by which to store it. As shown in Figure 7.7, the choices are as follows:

▶ **Normal:** The default method, this option does not conserve space and has the advantage of rapid virtual machine provisioning.

▶ **Compact:** This option attempts to compress the template files and conserve space but sacrifices deployment speed when the time comes for VM provisioning.

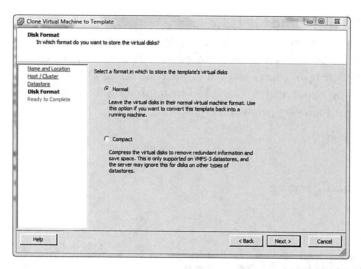

FIGURE 7.7
Template storage format.

Guest OS Customization

When you are deploying from a template or master image, one of the challenges is making sure the newly deployed VM has its own unique identity and is not an exact replica of the template or any other VM on the network because that would cause numerous issues. Two completely identical VMs cannot and should not exist. For that matter, many tools exist from OS vendors to address these issues. VMware ESX leverages these tools and streamlines the customization process.

Windows-Based OS Guest Customization

Windows-based operating systems use what is known as the Sysprep files, which are a bunch of small applications and tools that Microsoft makes available to customize its operating systems. For VirtualCenter to take advantage of this feature, these files need to be copied to the VirtualCenter server in the following location:

```
C:\Documents and Settings\All Users\Application Data\VMware\VMware
VirtualCenter\Sysprep\<OS>
```

Linux-Based OS Guest Customization

Linux-based operating systems do not need any special attention. All the files and tools needed for configuration are installed as part of the VirtualCenter install because they are open source and can be included in the VC distribution without any licensing requirements. Guest OS customization for Linux allows you to customize the following parameters:

- ▶ Computer name

- ▶ Domain name

- ▶ DHCP or static IP settings

- ▶ DNS

Deploying Virtual Machines

Deploying a virtual machine is a straightforward task; you can deploy it in two ways:

- ▶ **Deploy from Template:** Simply identify the template you want to use, right-click it, and choose Deploy from Template. This option preserves the template in its existing state and creates a duplicate as a virtual machine. It's as simple as that.

- ▶ **Clone:** Simply identify a virtual machine, right-click it, and select Clone. This option creates an exact replica of the virtual machine that is currently running. We strongly recommend you use guest operating system customization to avoid issues on your network and in your domain, such as SID conflicts, same IP conflict, and so on. You can also use Clone to clone an existing template. Say you want to keep a certain template but create an additional one with extra features. You can clone the template by creating a baseline image you can work from and then modify the new template.

It is important to know that you can clone or deploy virtual machines across datacenters.

Managing Virtual Machines

At the heart of the VI environment is the management of virtual machines because they enable you to perform your daily tasks. The following sections are dedicated to some important techniques you need to be familiar with to make it easier for you to manage your environment.

Cold Migration

A *cold migration* is used to move a virtual machine from one ESX host to another while the machine is powered off. Cold migrations are useful because they allow you to move VMs between ESX hosts that may have different CPU families that would otherwise prevent VMotion from working properly. Cold migrations are also useful to move VMs to local disks that may or may not be visible to all ESX hosts.

When you are using cold migrations, the wizard offers to relocate the VM's files in addition to moving it to a different host. Cold migrations are also useful when you simply want to relocate the VM's files from one datastore to another rather than move the actual VM to a different host.

What Are Snapshots?

Snapshots are a moment-in-time capture of a virtual machine's state; this includes its settings, memory, and disk states. This feature is useful especially in development or testing when you need to repeatedly go back to a point in time and try different fixes to a potential problem. This feature is also useful in educational areas where you are trying to demonstrate something but need to repeatedly revert to a VM's state after the demonstration is over.

A virtual machine can have multiple snapshots that are all managed by the Snapshot Manager, which you can access by right-clicking a VM and selecting Snapshots and then Snapshot Manager.

Virtual machine snapshots consist of the following files:

- ▶ *name_of_VM*-00000#-delta.vmdk: This is the differences file that basically registers the changes that have happened on this VM. The # is a sequential number that is enumerated starting at 1.

- ▶ *name_of_VM*-00000#.vmdk: This file contains the snapshot description.

- ▶ *name_of_VM*-Snapshot#.vmsn: This file holds the state of the memory and is typically the size of the maximum memory allocated for this VM.

Using VMware Converter Enterprise

VMware *Converter Enterprise* is an add-on product that is used to extend VirtualCenter capabilities. Its primary function is to convert physical or virtual machines into ESX-compatible virtual machines. Converter Enterprise can be used to accomplish the following tasks:

- **P2V and V2V:** Converter Enterprise can convert a physical machine to a virtual machine (P2V) and also can convert other VMware VMs, such as Workstation, Fusion, ACE, and Player to ESX VMs (V2V).

- **Convert Third-Party VMs to ESX VMs:** Converter Enterprise can convert Microsoft Virtual PC or Virtual Server VMs to ESX VMs.

- **Restore VCB Images to ESX VMs.**

- **Export ESX VMs to Other Formats.**

- **Customize VirtualCenter VMs.**

When using Converter Enterprise against a Windows operating system, you are able to customize and resize the volume being restored and also change its identity, whereas if you are using a non-Windows operating system, you are bound by the original settings and cannot modify them.

Converter Enterprise Components

As with any other product, Converter Enterprise has a prerequisite set of components that need to interact together to make the process work. These components are as follows:

- **Server:** This component initiates import and export of VMs through the VI client or via CLI.

- **CLI:** The command-line interfave component actually carries out the commands issued by the server component. Whether the server commands were issued from the VI client or CLI, the CLI component is the one responsible for carrying them out.

- **Agent:** This component is tasked with preparing a physical machine for conversion.

- **Client Plug-in:** This component modifies the VI GUI and enables the Converter Enterprise features.

Converter Enterprise Installation

VMware Converter Enterprise is a Windows-based application that is typically installed on the same server as VirtualCenter because it requires intimate connection with this server in any case. However, you can install Converter Enterprise on a standalone physical or virtual server, provided that a connection exists to VirtualCenter 2.5. Converter Enterprise has the following requirements:

- ▶ Windows 2000 Server, Windows XP
- ▶ Windows Server 2003 (32- and 64-bit)
- ▶ Windows Vista (32- and 64-bit)
- ▶ Windows Server 2008 (32- and 64-bit)

After it is installed, VMware Converter Enterprise needs to be enabled from within the VI Client. To do so, do the following:

1. Click on Plugins from the File menu.
2. Click on Manage Plugins.
3. Select Available Plugins.
4. Select Install.

EXAM ALERT

After installing any plug-ins, you should always make sure you enable them from the Plugins > Manage Plugins > Installed menu.

Cloning

Cloning is the process of copying or converting a physical or virtual disk to a new virtual disk. Cloning makes an exact replica of the source disk. VMware Converter Enterprise is capable of the following cloning methods:

- ▶ **Hot Cloning:** The process of cloning a machine while it is online without taking it offline or affecting its productivity.
- ▶ **Cold Cloning:** The process of cloning a machine while it is not online.
- ▶ **System Reconfiguration:** The process of rehabilitating an imported virtual machine so that it functions properly in an ESX environment.

▶ **Remote Cloning:** The process of cloning a machine using the agent over the network. This means you do not need to physically be there or manipulate it in any way; everything is done remotely.

▶ **Local Cloning:** The process of cloning with the Converter Enterprise software being present on the local machine, such as on a CD-ROM.

Cloning Modes

When cloning, you are offered two methods by which you can clone:

▶ **Volume-based cloning:** You clone only the volumes available on the source machine. This method is useful because it allows you to resize the volumes being cloned. For example, if you want to resize a volume to a smaller size, you can do that, at which point the conversion takes place at a file level rather than at a block level, had you not modified the size downward. It is done at a file level to ensure no data loss occurs. Block level does not understand what exists and simply clones block by block whether or not data exists on these blocks. This mode is supported by hot and cold cloning.

▶ **Disk-based cloning:** This method takes the exact copy of the entire disk and creates a replica. It replicates everything, even free space. If you are cloning a 6GB hard drive, you end up with a 6GB hard drive. This mode is supported only with cold cloning.

Using Guided Consolidation

Guided Consolidation is a new feature of VirtualCenter 2.5 aimed particularly at new users who are just starting out in virtualization and server consolidation as a whole. This intelligent concept is a scaled-down version of a more robust product offering from VMware known as Capacity Planner. Guided Consolidation is ideally used in small- to medium-sized organizations with about 100 physical servers. Guided Consolidation can discover and analyze only Windows-based operating systems. As mentioned earlier, the aim of this product is to quickly introduce new users to the benefits and power of virtualization.

Guided Consolidation analyzes systems based on their performance metrics and determines whether they are good candidates for virtualization. The machines that Guided Consolidation can discover and analyze in the enterprise are not limited to physical machines; they can be virtual machines as well, running a different platform than ESX. As long as they are Windows boxes, they can be discovered and analyzed. The final step in the Guided Consolidation process is to recommend and implement a plan that will convert physical or non-ESX virtual machines to ESX virtual machines and place them on the most suited ESX host. This process is done while these machines are live and therefore not jeopardizing any uptime for these systems.

Guided Consolidation depends on the following two services to function properly:

- **VMware Capacity Planner Service:** Also known as the Data Collector service, this service is installed on the VirtualCenter Server and is responsible for discovering the systems by using either LAN Manager or Active Directory. When the systems are discovered, this service is responsible for querying them for performance metrics to make recommendations on whether they are virtualization candidates.

- **VMware Converter Service:** This service is responsible for converting physical and virtual machines to ESX virtual machines. We covered the Converter in great detail earlier in this chapter. Think of it as the implementation arm of Guided Consolidation: It is the Converter that does the actual dirty work and implements the Guided Consolidation recommendations on potential virtualization systems.

Discovery and Analysis

The Discovery and Analysis task is the first step in the Guided Consolidation process. To start this process, log in to VirtualCenter using the VI client and then click on the Consolidation tab. This brings you to a window that prompts you to start the analysis. After you click Start Analysis, a wizard starts and guides you through the Discovery and Analysis process.

For this process to work properly, you need a user account with the following privileges:

- Member of local administrators group on VC server.

- User must have the Log on as Service user right.

- User must have Read access to Active Directory to be able to query it.

- User with Administrator rights on target machines to be queried. You can enter different credentials for this step of the process.

> **TIP**
>
> Typically, you would create a single user account for the purpose of doing all these tasks. We have described the simplest approach to doing this.

Performing the Consolidation

When the Discovery and Analysis is complete, you are shown a list of servers that can be consolidated; you can then select these servers and click on Plan Consolidation. This starts the process and walks you through the consolidation process, which uses Converter Enterprise to convert the servers to ESX VMs and gives you the option of placing them on specific ESX Servers if you choose to do so.

Virtual Machine Maximums

The VCP exam will surely quiz you on configuration maximums for virtual machines. For this reason, we provide you with Table 7.1, which supplies the configuration maximums for virtual machines with ESX 3.5.

Table 7.1   Virtual Machine Configuration Maximums

Component	Maximum
vCPUs	4
Memory	64GB
SCSI disk size	2TB
Devices per VM (Windows and Linux)	60
NICs	4
IDE devices	4
Floppy devices	2
CD-ROM/DVD-ROM devices	4
SCSI controllers	4
Devices per SCSI controller	15
Parallel ports	2
Serial ports	2
VM swap size	65,532MB
PCI devices	6
Remote console connections	10

Exam Prep Questions

1. Which two services from the following list are required for proper Guided Consolidation operation?

   ○ **A.** VMware Capacity Planner Service

   ○ **B.** VMware Guided Consolidation Service

   ○ **C.** VMware VirtualCenter Server Service

   ○ **D.** VMware Converter Service

2. Which cloning modes are valid cloning modes? (Choose two.)

   ○ **A.** LUN-based

   ○ **B.** Volume-based

   ○ **C.** Disk-based

   ○ **D.** Partition-based

3. How many available PCI devices can you add to a virtual machine?

   ○ **A.** 4

   ○ **B.** 5

   ○ **C.** 6

   ○ **D.** 8

4. What is the maximum amount of physical memory that you can allocate to a virtual machine?

   ○ **A.** 16GB

   ○ **B.** 32GB

   ○ **C.** 64GB

   ○ **D.** 128GB

5. Which two SCSI adapters are available?

   ○ **A.** NetxLogic

   ○ **B.** Bus Logic

   ○ **C.** LSI Logic

   ○ **D.** VMI Logic

6. Which two methods can be used to create a template?

  ○ **A.** Clone to Template

  ○ **B.** Convert to Template

  ○ **C.** Make Template

  ○ **D.** Snapshot to Template

7. What is the maximum disk size you can allocate to a virtual machine?

  ○ **A.** 1TB

  ○ **B.** 2TB

  ○ **C.** 4TB

  ○ **D.** 8TB

8. True or false: VMware Converter Enterprise requires that you install a client on every machine that needs to be converted into a VM.

  ○ **A.** True

  ○ **B.** False

9. True or false: VMware Guided Consolidation queries only Windows-based machines.

  ○ **A.** True

  ○ **B.** False

10. What must be installed on VirtualCenter for Guest OS customization to work for Windows-based systems?

  ○ **A.** Sysprep files

  ○ **B.** RIPREP

  ○ **C.** SID Changer

  ○ **D.** Nothing; all files are copied during VC install

Answers to Exam Prep Questions

1. Answers **A** and **D** are correct. VMware Guided Consolidation requires the VMware Capacity Planner Service and the VMware Converter Service to be running for the entire process to work. The Capacity Planner Service discovers analysis and recommends systems for virtualization, while the Converter turns them into virtual machines.

2. Answers **B** and **C** are correct. The two valid cloning modes are Volume-based and Disk-based. Partition-based and LUN-based do not exist.

3. Answer **B** is correct. You can add a maximum of six PCI devices to a virtual machine; however, because one PCI device is always allocated for the video adapter, you have only five available PCI devices you can add.

4. Answer **C** is correct. ESX 3.5 introduced increased memory support for VMs, raising it to 64GB of memory per VM.

5. Answers **B** and **C** are correct. The two SCSI adapters that are available are Bus Logic and LSI Logic. NetxLogic and VMI Logic do not exist.

6. Answers **A** and **B** are correct. The two methods to create a template are Clone to Template and Convert to Template.

7. Answer **B** is correct. The maximum disk size you can allocate to a virtual machine is 2TB.

8. Answer **B**, False, is correct. VMware Converter Enterprise does not require you to manually install a client on machines you want to convert to VMs.

9. Answer **A**, True, is correct. VMware Guided Consolidation queries and analyzes only Windows-based machines. This product is intended for new users as a way to introduce them to virtualization. For a more robust analysis, you should use VMware Capacity Planner.

10. Answer **A** is correct. The Sysprep files need to be copied to the VirtualCenter for every Windows operating system that will use Guest OS customization.

CHAPTER EIGHT

VMware Infrastructure Security and Web Access

Terms you'll need to understand:

✓ Roles

✓ Privileges

✓ vpxuser

✓ Web Access

✓ Generate Remote Console URL

Concepts and techniques you'll need to master:

✓ What a role is and how to create it and assign users and groups to it

✓ How to assign permissions to objects in the inventory

✓ The difference between VirtualCenter security and ESX Server security

✓ The limitations of Web Access

With great power comes great responsibility. Your responsibility is to make sure that the virtual infrastructure you have deployed is secure and that role-based access has been implemented so that the right users have the necessary security permissions to perform their daily tasks. This chapter is dedicated to security in VMware Infrastructure.

VI Security Model

The VMware Infrastructure security model consists of both VirtualCenter security and ESX Server security. The security model revolves around users and groups that are assigned *roles*. These roles constitute a collection of rights or *privileges* to perform certain tasks.

Users, Roles, Privileges, and Permissions

The cornerstones of the VMware Infrastructure (VI) security model are the users, groups, roles, privileges, and permissions that you can assign at different levels and to different objects within your infrastructure. Properly configuring and assigning these rights and permissions enables you to enforce accountability. Taking a closer look at each of these cornerstones helps you better design your security solution:

▶ **User and group:** An account that is allowed to log in to the VMware infrastructure. A group is a collection of accounts with rights to log in and perform other tasks within the VMware Infrastructure.

▶ **Role:** A collection of privileges that a user or group is allowed to perform.

▶ **Privilege:** An allowed action or function within a role. In other words, a privilege allows a user or group to perform a certain task.

▶ **Permission:** A right assigned to an object in the inventory and grants a user or group the right to interact with that object according to selected roles and privileges.

NOTE

You can choose from about 100 preconfigured privileges.

Working with Roles

Familiarizing yourself with roles is an imperative task of building your access control into the Virtual Infrastructure. To help you get started, Table 8.1 shows a set of default roles available to you.

Table 8.1   Default Roles

Default ESX Roles	Default VirtualCenter Roles	Custom Roles
No Access	No Access	User-created roles
Read-Only	Read-Only	
Administrator	Administrator	
	Virtual Machine Administrator	
	Datacenter Administrator	
	Virtual Machine Power User	
	Virtual Machine User	
	Resource Pool Administrator	
	VCB User	

The easiest way to get to the Roles panel is to log in to ESX Server or VirtualCenter using your VI client. Click the Administration tab and then the Roles tab, as shown in Figure 8.1.

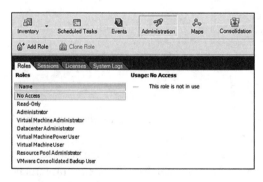

FIGURE 8.1
Roles panel.

On the Roles panel, you can right-click any role and edit it. However, we recommend that you maintain the integrity of the existing roles and create your own custom roles if the need arises. To do so, you can right-click anywhere in the Roles pane and click Add to start the new role creation, as shown in Figure 8.2.

> **NOTE**
>
> Custom roles cannot be shared between ESX Server and VirtualCenter.

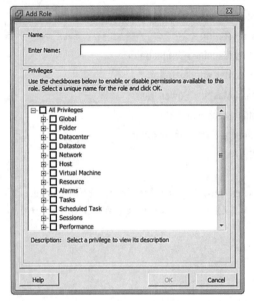

FIGURE 8.2
Add new role.

Assigning Permissions

After you have crafted the appropriate roles for your environment, it is time to apply them to the right inventory object to allow your users and groups access only to the part of the inventory tree that you want them to have access to. To apply permissions, find the object in the tree on which you want to implement security, right-click it, and select Add Permission. This brings you to a screen similar to the one shown in Figure 8.3 that allows you to choose a user or group and assign the corresponding role that you want the user or group to have for this inventory object.

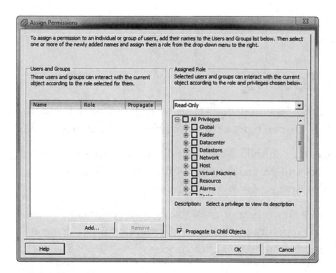

FIGURE 8.3
Assign permissions.

When assigning permissions, you may choose to have these permissions propagate from the object where the permission originated and downward to all the child objects. To do this, simply place a check mark in the check box next to Propagate to Child Objects, as shown in Figure 8.3.

If a conflict arises when assigning permissions, the most restrictive of the permissions takes precedence. For instance, if a user is part of a group in the Administrator role but the user is explicitly assigned a Read-Only role on a particular object, the most restrictive of the permissions takes precedence, thereby allowing the user only Read-Only permissions to the object. Keep in mind though that if permissions do not propagate down to any child objects, the user has Read-Only permission over the object but has full permissions over the child objects. The reason behind this is Propagate permissions is not enabled, which means you are slapping explicit permissions on this object only, but not its child object. The child objects in this case inherit the permissions given to the user's group.

EXAM ALERT

Knowing how permissions are applied and the precedence of permissions are topics that are sure to come up on the exam.

When explicitly assigned, permissions take precedence and the most restrictive permissions are enforced.

VirtualCenter Security

VirtualCenter is a Windows-based application to be installed on a Windows-based operating system. It has two types of directory repositories to select from:

▶ **Local:** If VirtualCenter is installed on a Windows server that is part of a workgroup, the users and groups that are local members of this server can be configured to have access in VirtualCenter.

▶ **Domain:** If VirtualCenter is part of an Active Directory domain, in addition to the ability to configure local users and groups, you can also configure users and groups from Active Directory.

By default, the local Administrators group is assigned the Administrator role at the top of the inventory list in VirtualCenter. If the VC server is member of a domain, the Domain Admins group is also added by default.

ESX Server Security

The ESX Server security revolves around the Service Console, and because the Service Console operating system is based on Red Hat Linux, the users and groups that you find in the ESX Server are Linux users and groups. These users and groups can be configured to grant direct access to an ESX host.

NOTE

ESX Server users and groups do not sync and cannot be used to assign roles and privileges in VirtualCenter.

TIP

Do not configure permissions using ESX users and groups. The reason behind this is the permissions you assign on a per ESX Server level do not propagate to other ESX hosts; therefore, using a common users and groups directory makes it easier to manage permissions.

By default, the following users are assigned the Administrator role in ESX Server:

▶ *root* is the equivalent of the administrator in the Windows world and is the highest user account that is created by default.

▶ *vpxuser* is added to the Administrators group in ESX after the ESX Server is joined to VirtualCenter. VirtualCenter uses this user to authenticate itself to the ESX host to send preapproved commands.

While the vpxuser is used to authenticate VirtualCenter to ESX Server and pass preapproved commands, the root account actually executes these commands. So in this case, the vpxuser acts merely as a secure bridge between VirtualCenter and the ESX host, while the root user account is tasked with executing VirtualCenter tasks.

Web Access

Web Access is designed to allow you to manage virtual machines from anywhere without requiring special software to be installed on the host from which you are trying to connect. Web Access is not as robust or feature friendly as the VI client, and it allows for limited functionality but can be useful when you need to perform certain tasks from a machine that does not have the VI client installed or if you need to pass an administrative tool with limited features to a group like the helpdesk, for example.

To access Web Access, you need to point your Internet browser to either the IP address or fully qualified domain name (FQDN) of your ESX host or your VirtualCenter Server. If you point to your ESX host, you are able to manage virtual machines that are on this host only. If you log in to VirtualCenter Web Access, you are able to manage all your VMs.

After logging in to Web Access, you can select any VM in the list and you are able to perform the following tasks, shown in Figure 8.4:

▶ Enumerate VMs

▶ Launch console access to a VM

▶ Manipulate all power functions against a VM

▶ View a VM's status

▶ Edit VM configuration

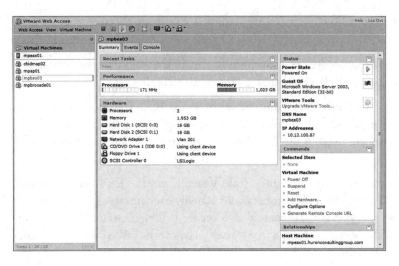

FIGURE 8.4

Virtual machine Web Access view.

EXAM ALERT

The exam will surely challenge your knowledge of the difference between Web Access and the full VI client. Know the limitations of the Web Access compared to the full VI client.

CAUTION

You cannot create VMs from Web Access; this function requires the VI in order to be completed.

NOTE

To launch a VM's console from Web Access, you need to have installed the VMware Virtual Infrastructure plug-in in your browser.

Web Access Minimum Requirements

The minimum system requirements to successfully connect and log in to Web Access are as follows:

On a Windows machine:

- Internet Explorer 6.0 or higher
- Firefox 1.0.7 or higher
- Netscape Navigator 7.0 or higher
- Mozilla 1.x

On a Linux machine:

- Firefox 1.0.7 or higher
- Mozilla 1.x
- Netscape Navigator 7.0 or higher

Remote Console URL

One of the very cool things you can do with Web Access is to generate a regular web URL to a particular virtual machine. This URL gives you or any user you send it to direct access to this virtual machine. This capability is useful when you want to provide someone access to a virtual machine directly; you can just as easily paste the URL link into an email and send it to that person.

To generate a URL for a VM, you can simply click the Generate Remote Console URL link shown in Figure 8.4. This brings you to a screen similar to the one shown in Figure 8.5 that allows you to configure different settings to control which user interface features the user has access to.

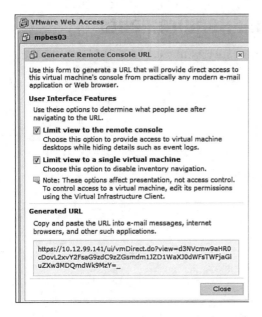

FIGURE 8.5
Generate Remote Console URL window.

Exam Prep Questions

1. What is a collection of privileges called in the security model of a VMware Infrastructure?

    ○ **A.** Role

    ○ **B.** Right

    ○ **C.** Access

    ○ **D.** Permission

2. Choose two roles that are default VirtualCenter roles.

    ○ **A.** Night-shift Operator

    ○ **B.** VCB User

    ○ **C.** Backup Administrator

    ○ **D.** Virtual Machine User

3. Which version of Internet Explorer is the minimum that can be used with Web Access?

- ○ **A.** 4.0
- ○ **B.** 5.0
- ○ **C.** 6.0
- ○ **D.** 7.0

4. Choose the roles that are not default ESX Server roles.

- ○ **A.** Read-Only
- ○ **B.** No Access
- ○ **C.** Datacenter Administrator
- ○ **D.** Resource Pool Administrator

5. Which version of Mozilla Firefox is the minimum that can be used with Web Access?

- ○ **A.** 1.0.4
- ○ **B.** 1.0.5
- ○ **C.** 1.0.6
- ○ **D.** 1.0.7

6. True or false: When using Web Access, you can access VMs only by accessing the VirtualCenter Server.

- ○ **A.** True
- ○ **B.** False

7. Approximately how many privileges are there by default in VMware Infrastructure?

- ○ **A.** 50
- ○ **B.** 75
- ○ **C.** 100
- ○ **D.** 150

8. True or false: Web Access can be used to create virtual machines.

- ○ **A.** True
- ○ **B.** False

9. True or false: ESX Server and VirtualCenter Server users and groups can be synchronized.

   ○ **A.** True

   ○ **B.** False

10. Which two user accounts are assigned to the ESX Server Administrator role by default?

    ○ **A.** adm

    ○ **B.** vpxuser

    ○ **C.** vpx

    ○ **D.** root

Answers to Exam Prep Questions

1. Answer **A** is correct. A collection of privileges is known as a role in a VMware Infrastructure.

2. Answers **B** and **D** are correct. From the list provided, the two roles that are available by default on a VirtualCenter server are VMware Consolidated Backup (VCB) User and Virtual Machine User.

3. Answer **C** is correct. Internet Explorer version 6.0 is the minimum that can be used to access Web Access.

4. Answers **C** and **D** are correct. The two roles that are not default ESX Server roles are Datacenter Administrator and Resource Pool Administrator.

5. Answer **D** correct. The minimum version of Mozilla Firefox that is supported with Web Access is 1.0.7.

6. Answer **B**, False, is correct. You can access the Web Access console by either pointing to the ESX Server or VirtualCenter Server IP address or FQDN. When pointing to the ESX host, you see only the VMs on that host, whereas when pointing the web access to the VC server, you see all the VMs.

7. Answer **C** is correct. There are approximately 100 privileges by default.

8. Answer **B**, False, is correct. Web Access cannot be used to create virtual machines. Web Access can be used only to manage VMs. To create virtual machines, you need to use the VI client.

9. Answer **B**, False, is correct. ESX Server and VirtualCenter Server users and groups cannot be synchronized.

10. Answers **B** and **D** are correct. The two user accounts that are assigned the administrator role by default on the ESX Server are root and vpxuser.

CHAPTER NINE

Managing VMware Infrastructure Resources

Terms you'll need to understand:

✓ Resource Pools

✓ Clusters

✓ Shares

✓ Limit

✓ Reservation

✓ Expandable Reservation

✓ VMotion

✓ Distributed Resource Scheduler (DRS)

✓ Affinity

✓ Anti-Affinity

Concepts and techniques you'll need to master:

✓ How does VMotion work?

✓ What is a resource pool?

✓ How does VMware Distributed Resource Scheduler work?

✓ How do the Affinity and Anti-Affinity rules work?

Understanding resource management is the single most important component of designing and maintaining your virtual infrastructure. To properly identify how many virtual machines (VMs) you can load on your ESX hosts, you must understand how resource management works. Furthermore, to plan for scalability and high availability, you must thoroughly understand resource management. This chapter covers resource management in a VMware Infrastructure 3 environment.

VM CPU and Memory Management

Understanding how virtual machines address their resources, particularly their CPU and memory resources, is extremely important. As Figure 9.1 illustrates, the three settings that control the VM's CPU and Memory resource management are as follows:

▶ *Limit* defines the maximum that a VM can consume in CPU (measured in megahertz, or MHz) and memory (measured in megabytes, or MB).

▶ *Reservation* is the minimum that a VM needs in terms of CPU and memory resources to be able to function properly.

▶ *Shares* identify the frequency and priority a VM will have in terms of accessing time slices on the physical CPU and memory. All VMs are assigned shares. The more shares a VM is assigned, the more priority it has over physical resources.

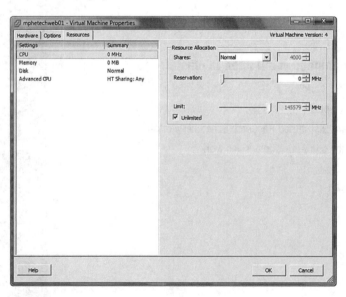

FIGURE 9.1

Virtual machine resource management.

A virtual machine's vCPUs are always scheduled at the same time. When you're assigning shares, keep in mind the number of vCPUs configured for any given VM. A reservation of 1,000 shares might be adequate for a VM that has only one vCPU, but a VM of two vCPUs will have to divide these 1,000 shares into 500 shares per vCPU, and that might or might not be adequate depending on what this VM's function will be. Similarly, reservation of 1,000 shares for a VM that has four vCPUs renders each vCPU with 250 shares, which further diminishes the functionality of the VM.

EXAM ALERT

Don't forget, each vCPU will get 1,000 shares. However, if, for example, you set a reservation of 1000 MHz on a VM that has more than one vCPU, it is at that point when the 1,000 shares are divided among the vCPUs.

The Available Memory setting, which is a fourth setting option enabled only for the memory configuration of a VM, is the initial memory that you configure for a VM during its creation. You can always modify this option, after the VM is created. With this in mind, if the Available Memory and Reservation values differ, the VMkernel compensates for this discrepancy by creating a swap file for the difference between the two values. An example of this would be if the Available Memory setting is configured for 2GB and the reservation is set to 1GB; then the VMkernel creates a swap file to compensate for the difference.

NOTE

A virtual machine does not power on if its CPU and memory reservation is not met.

When assigning shares to a virtual machine, you have four options: High, Normal, Low, and Custom. Table 9.1 outlines how these settings translate in number of shares for CPU and memory. Depending on the version of VirtualCenter that you are using, these values will change. When the book was written, VMware had just released Update 1. The values in Table 9.1 are currently valid for Resource Pools, as for VMs, the values should read: High=2000, Normal=1000, and Low=500.

Table 9.1   CPU/Memory Share Value Calculations

Share Setting	Number of CPU Shares	Number of Memory Shares
High	8000 * # of vCPUs	80 * Available memory
Normal	4000 * # of vCPUs	40 * Available memory
Low	2000 * # of vCPUs	20 * Available memory
Custom	Manually specified	Manually specified

Using Resource Pools to Govern CPU/Memory Resources

A *resource pool* allows you to group virtual machines and apply the same resource policy on them. Resource pools can be created for a single ESX host or to a *Distributed Resource Scheduler (DRS)* cluster to govern the CPU and memory resources. Grouping virtual machines also makes it easier to implement security and delegate administration to other users and groups. You should also know that you can create child resource pools and further compartmentalize VMs.

> **NOTE**
>
> Every ESX host, by default, is a resource pool known as the Root Resource Pool. The Root Resource Pool exists prior to your creating any resource pools under this host.

Resource pools have the same settings as virtual machines; therefore, you can control a resource pool's CPU and memory shares, limits, and reservations. As Figure 9.2 illustrates, a resource pool has an additional *expandable reservation* option, which allows child resource pools to tap into the parent resource pool and harness whatever resources are available to satisfy its own shortage. An expandable resource is used only when the resource pool cannot secure enough resources to satisfy its policy.

> **TIP**
>
> Use expandable reservation wisely because it can consume all the parent's resources.

You can view a resource pool's data using either of the following methods:

► Highlight the resource pool in the inventory and then select the Summary tab.

► Choose the Resource Allocation tab while the resource pool is selected in the inventory.

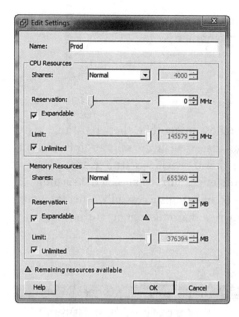

FIGURE 9.2
Resource pool properties.

VMotion

VMotion is probably the most popular and most sought after feature in the VMware infrastructure suite. The VMotion feature allows a running virtual machine to be migrated without interruption from one host to another, provided that some prerequisites are met on the originating and destination hosts.

VMotion is an enterprise-level feature and thereby requires VirtualCenter before it can be enabled. VMotion, as you see later in the section "Distributed Resource Scheduler," is used in conjunction with DRS to make sure VMs are always spread out on the most appropriate host, thereby balancing the resource availability of these hosts.

VMotion Host Prerequisites

With VMotion, for the VM to successfully port from one host to another, the following requirements must be satisfied on the source and destination hosts:

- ▶ Access to all datastores on which the VM is configured

- ▶ Virtual switches that are labeled the same, so that when the VM is ported from one host to another, its configuration is the same and finds the same resources

- ▶ Access to the same physical networks for the VM to continue to function after being ported from one host to another

- ▶ Compatible CPUs

- ▶ Gigabit network connection

When you initiate a VMotion from one host to another, the wizard that starts the process warns you if there are errors that prevent the migration from completing successfully. The VMotion wizard also provides warnings that you take into account and possibly address after the migration is completed. Warnings do not prevent the VMotion process from completing successfully, whereas errors do. Table 9.2 outlines the different scenarios that might generate an error or a warning.

Table 9.2   VMotion Errors and Warnings

VMotion Errors	VMotion Warnings
A VM is connected to an internal vSwitch on the source host.	A VM is configured for an internal vSwitch but is not connected to it.
A VM has a removable disk such as a CD/DVD-ROM or floppy connected to it.	A VM is configured for a removable CD/DVD-ROM or floppy but is not connected to it.
A VM has CPU affinity assigned.	A VM has a snapshot.
	A heartbeat cannot be detected from the VM to be migrated.

TIP

If your ISO or FLP image files are mounted in a shared network location where all the ESX hosts involved have access, you receive a warning only during VMotion. That's whether the virtual CD or floppy drive is connected.

Enabling VMotion

To enable VMotion, you need to create a VMkernel port group with VMotion enabled on all ESX hosts that will participate in the VMotion process, as shown in Figure 9.3. The virtual switch where this port group is created should bear the same label on all ESX hosts. Typically, VMotion is configured on a dedicated virtual switch on all ESX hosts.

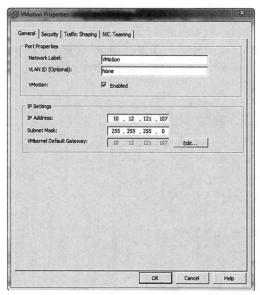

FIGURE 9.3
Port group with VMotion enabled.

VMotion also requires that the physical NIC that you choose to service the virtual switch where VMotion is enabled should be a Gigabit or higher.

VMotion CPU Requirements

One of the main obstacles to a successful VMotion migration is the CPU; VMotion requires a strict CPU approach, so keep the following guidelines in mind:

- ▶ VMotion does not work across CPU vendors, so if you have an ESX host that is running an AMD processor and one that is running an Intel processor, VMotion errors out and does not work.

- ▶ VMotion does not work across CPU families, so you are not able to migrate between a Pentium III and a Pentium 4, for example.

- ▶ Hyperthreading, the number of CPU cores, and the CPU cache sizes are not relevant to VMotion.

- ▶ VMotion does not work across CPUs with different multimedia instructions—for example, a CPU with *Streaming SIMD Extensions 2* (SSE2) and a CPU with *Streaming SIMD Extensions 3* (SSE3).

- ▶ Nx/xD hides or exposes advanced features in the CPU of an ESX Server. In most cases, this hidden feature is controlled by VMware for stability reasons (see Figure 9.4). In the event that the guest operating system requires it, however, the VI client exposes this feature in the properties of a VM. If it is enabled, the CPU characteristics of the host and destination must match; if disabled, an occurring mismatch is ignored and VMotion proceeds.

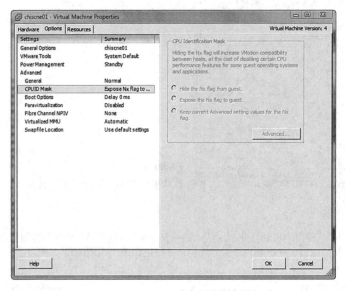

FIGURE 9.4
Nx/xD feature exposed in VI client.

CPU vendors Intel and AMD now offer a technology known as *virtualization assist* that aids virtualization. Intel has its VT technology, and AMD has its AMD-V technology, both of which are enabled in the BIOS of a computer.

NOTE

Virtualization assist needs to be enabled before you can migrate 64-bit VMs from one host to another.

In the presence of these technologies, you can enable the VMs whose operating system supports the virtualization assist technology to improve their performance. To do this, you can right-click the VM in question and click Edit Settings. Click the Options tab, find the Paravirtualization section, and enable it. Figure 9.5 illustrates this process clearly.

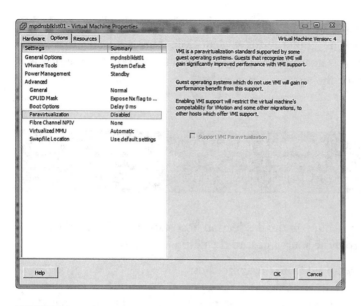

FIGURE 9.5
Enabling Paravirtualization.

The VMotion Stages

Because the virtual machine to be VMotioned resides on a datastore that is visible and accessible to both the source and the destination ESX host, the only thing that VMotion needs to do is to copy the VM's memory from one host to another. Because the VM's memory resides on the physical memory of the source host, that memory is what needs to be copied. That being said, the two ways to initiate a VMotion are as follows:

- ▶ Select one or more VMs and then right-click and choose Migrate.

- ▶ Simply drag and drop a VM from one host to another.

When the VMotion process begins, the four stages that it goes through are as follows:

1. Once VMotion is initiated, a memory bitmap is created to track the changes, and the process of copying the physical RAM from one host to another begins.

2. Quiesce the VM and copy the contents of the memory bitmap. Quiesce can be defined in simpler terms as a cut-over. This is the only time at which the VM is unavailable. This is a very short period of time that is transparent for the most part to the user.

> **EXAM ALERT**
>
> The Quiesce period is the only time during which the VM is not available, but the outage time is short, typically between 1/2 to 1 1/2 seconds. This time period is so transparent that you may lose a single ping in some cases.

3. The virtual machine on the destination host starts and moves all connectivity to it from the source host to the destination host.

4. The VM is removed from the source host.

During your monitoring of the VMotion process, you might notice that it will pause at 10% completion as part of the identification process.

> **NOTE**
>
> The speed at which VMotion completes its process depends on bandwidth availability and congestion on the VMotion network, as well as the size of the RAM dedicated to the VM being moved.

Distributed Resource Scheduler

VMware DRS is an enterprise-level feature that uses VMotion to load balance the CPU and memory resources of all ESX hosts within a given DRS cluster. DRS is also used to enforce resource policies and respect placement constraints.

DRS functions efficiently using *clusters*. A cluster is the implicit collection of CPU and memory resources across ESX hosts that are members of this cluster to allow for the creation of VMware DRS clusters and VMware High Availability (HA) clusters. A cluster, which can have a maximum of 32 nodes, is an object that appears in the VirtualCenter inventory and, like all other objects, can be assigned permissions.

After you add ESX hosts as nodes in a DRS cluster, DRS then monitors these ESX hosts. If DRS detects high CPU utilization or high memory utilization on a particular host, it uses VMotion to migrate some VMs off the host with resource constraints to a host that is not experiencing resource constraints. DRS constantly plays this role to ensure that all ESX hosts never have resource constraints.

DRS Automation Process

The DRS automation process involves *initial placement* of the virtual machines when they are first powered on and later on dynamically load balancing VMs on the best-suited host that will render the best performance. As shown in Figure 9.6, the automation process options are as follows:

▸ **Manual:** If you select this option, VirtualCenter suggests which VM needs to be initially placed on which host at power on and will later suggest which VM should be migrated to a different host; however, VirtualCenter does not perform either task automatically.

▸ **Partially Automated:** If you select this option, VMs are automatically placed at power on; however, for future load balancing, VirtualCenter will only suggest the migration but will not perform it.

NOTE

The advantage of using Manual or Partially Automated is that you get greater control of which VMs are moved where and when. The disadvantage, of course, is you have to manually intervene for this task to be completed. Typically, Manual or Partially Automated is used on sensitive VMs that you want to constantly monitor.

▸ **Fully Automated:** If you select this option, VirtualCenter suggests and performs the initial placement of VMs at power on and automatically migrates them to maintain the most adequate load balancing.

When set to Manual or Partially Automated, DRS recommends VMs that need to be migrated to improve performance and maintain proper load balancing in the cluster. To view these recommendations, you can select the DRS cluster in the VirtualCenter inventory and click on the DRS Recommendations tab, as shown in Figure 9.7.

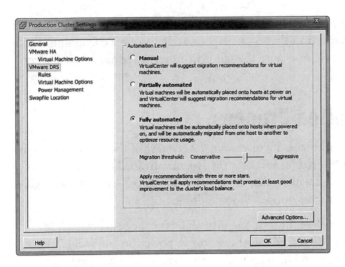

FIGURE 9.6

DRS cluster automation.

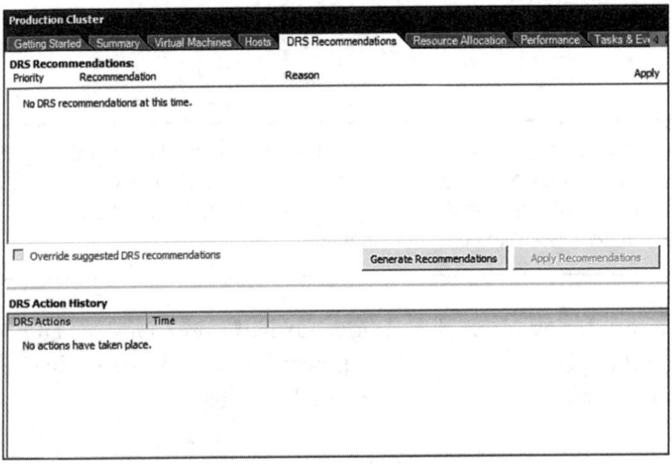

FIGURE 9.7

DRS recommendations.

EXAM ALERT

The DRS recommendations are available as long as they are valid. If anything should change that would render them inaccurate, these recommendations are changed or updated.

EXAM ALERT

Automation levels set at the virtual machine level override those set at the DRS cluster level.

If you choose a fully automated load-balancing schedule, you can also control the frequency at which migrations occur. DRS analyzes the VMs and rates them on a five-star basis, with five stars meaning the VM must move from one host to another and one star meaning the VM does not necessarily need to move or, if moved, the change is not significant. Your options are as follows:

▶ **Most Conservative:** This option means DRS migrates VMs very infrequently and only when it must (that is, when VMs have five stars).

▶ **Moderately Conservative:** This option means that DRS migrates VMs with four stars or more. This option promises significant improvement.

▶ **Default:** This option moves VMs with three stars or more and promises good improvement.

▶ **Moderately Aggressive:** This option moves VMs with two stars or more and promises moderate improvement.

▶ **Aggressive:** This option migrates VMs with one star or more and promises slight improvement.

DRS automation levels can also be managed on the virtual machine level, where you manually assign the automation level for each VM in the cluster. To configure the automation level based on the VM, right-click the cluster where the VM is a member and go to Edit Settings. On the left pane, select Virtual Machine Options. You then are presented with a list of VMs that are members of this cluster on the right. You can change the automation level manually. Figure 9.8 shows an example.

FIGURE 9.8
VM level automation.

DRS Cluster Validity

Monitoring a DRS cluster to ensure that there are no errors is critical. A resource pool can be in one of three states: valid, overcommitted, or invalid. A DRS cluster is considered to be valid, functioning, and healthy when the resource availability satisfies all the reservations and supports all running VMs. In the event that a DRS cluster is not considered valid, resource pools notify you that there is a problem by changing the color of the resource pool in the VI client as follows:

► *Yellow* means that the resource pool is *overcommitted* in terms of resources.

► *Red* means that the resource pool has violated the DRS cluster rules or high-availability rules and is thereby considered *invalid*.

DRS Rules

DRS allows you to set rules that govern whether VMs can exist on the same ESX host at the same time or if they should always be separated and never exist on the same host at the same time. This capability can be extremely useful if you are trying to avoid a single point of failure for a particular VM and want to make sure that the DRS algorithm never places VMs assigned in the rules on the same host. That being said, you can choose to have the VMs on the same host at all times, so if one VM is migrated, the other follows as well. These rules are known as

▶ **Affinity:** This rule implies that VMs should be on the same ESX host at all times.

▶ **Anti-Affinity:** This rule implies that VMs cannot exist on the same ESX host at the same time.

You can access these rules by right-clicking your cluster and pointing to Edit Settings. You then see the Rules section on the left. Select it and click on Add. Figure 9.9 shows an example of how you can set a rule to never allow two VMs to be on the same host at the same time.

FIGURE 9.9
DRS rules.

Exam Prep Questions

1. Which items are not settings that would affect a virtual machine's resource allocation? (Select all that apply.)

   ○ **A.** Cycles

   ○ **B.** Expandable

   ○ **C.** Reservations

   ○ **D.** Shares

2. Which setting controls the maximum CPU time measured in MHz that a virtual machine is allowed to use?

   ○ **A.** Limit

   ○ **B.** Reservation

   ○ **C.** Shares

   ○ **D.** Affinity

3. What color is assigned to a DRS cluster that is overcommitted?

   ○ **A.** Red

   ○ **B.** Orange

   ○ **C.** Blue

   ○ **D.** Yellow

4. Which setting is an invalid level when Fully Automated DRS cluster load balancing is selected?

   ○ **A.** Conservative

   ○ **B.** Aggressive

   ○ **C.** Default

   ○ **D.** Low

5. Which of the following is not a DRS cluster automation level? (Select all that apply.)

   ○ **A.** Manual

   ○ **B.** Semi Manual

   ○ **C.** Fully Automated

   ○ **D.** Semi Automated

6. What is the name given to the topmost resource pool?

   ○ **A.** Resource Pool

   ○ **B.** Default Resource Pool

   ○ **C.** Root Resource Pool

   ○ **D.** Master Resource Pool

7. How many cluster nodes are supported for each DRS cluster?

   ○ **A.** 16

   ○ **B.** 24

   ○ **C.** 32

   ○ **D.** 36

8. True or false: If a virtual machine's available memory and its reservation memory setting differ, the VMkernel generates a VM-specific swap file for the difference between the two settings.

   ○ **A.** True

   ○ **B.** False

9. True or false: Resource pools can be used with a standalone ESX host or a DRS cluster.

   ○ **A.** True

   ○ **B.** False

10. Which of the following is not a requirement of the source and destination host for VMotion to work properly?

   ○ **A.** Gigabit Ethernet

   ○ **B.** Virtual switches that are configured and labeled identically

   ○ **C.** Access to the same shared storage

   ○ **D.** Access to each host's Service Console

Answers to Exam Prep Questions

1. Answers **A** and **B** are correct. Cycles and Expandable are not settings that you can use to control a virtual machine's resource allocation. Cycles is not valid, and Expandable is available only on Resource Pools. The three settings that affect a VM's resource allocation in terms of CPU and Memory are Shares, Reservations, and Limits; therefore, answers C and D are incorrect.

2. Answer **A** is correct. Limit is the setting that controls the maximum a CPU can use measured in MHz; therefore, answers B, C, and D are incorrect.

3. Answer **D** is correct. A DRS cluster that is overcommitted is assigned the color yellow; therefore, answers A, B, and C are incorrect.

4. Answer **D** is correct. Low is not a valid frequency level when Fully Automated is selected; therefore, answers A, B, and C are incorrect.

5. Answers **B** and **D** are correct. Semi Manual and Semi Automated are invalid and do not exist. The three levels of automation are Manual, Partially Automated, and Fully Automated; therefore, answers A and C are incorrect.

6. Answer **C** is correct. The Root Resource Pool is the name given to the topmost resource pool; therefore, answers A, B, and D are incorrect.

7. Answer **C** is correct. VMware DRS clusters support up to 32 ESX hosts or nodes per cluster; therefore, answers A, B, and D are incorrect.

8. Answer **A**, True, is correct. When the Available Memory and the Memory Reservation settings differ, the VMkernel generates a swap file for the difference.

9. Answer **A**, True, is correct. Resource Pools can be created for a single ESX host or for a DRS cluster.

10. Answer **D** is correct. Access to each host's service console is not a requirement for the successful VMotion process; therefore, answers A, B, and C are incorrect.

CHAPTER TEN

Monitoring VMware Infrastructure Resources

Terms you'll need to understand:

✓ Hyper-Threading

✓ Hardware Execution Context (HEC)

✓ Transparent Memory Page Sharing

✓ Balloon-driver

✓ Alarms

Concepts and techniques you'll need to master:

✓ How the balloon-driver works

✓ How transparent memory page sharing works

✓ How to use host-based and VM-based alarms

✓ Virtual memory and virtual CPU optimization

This chapter focuses primarily on how to monitor your VMware Infrastructure. You learn about optimizing and monitoring resources used by virtual machines (VMs) and hosts, including virtual CPUs and virtual memory. The chapter concludes with a discussion of alarms.

Resource Optimization Concepts

The two most important resources for virtual machines are virtual CPU and virtual memory. Knowing and understanding the different concepts and techniques used to manipulate these two resources are absolutely critical and are fundamental in your understanding of how the VMware Infrastructure works. This section focuses on the different mechanisms used by ESX for virtual CPU and virtual memory optimization.

Virtual CPU

You can configure a virtual machine with one, two, or four virtual CPUs (vCPUs). For a vCPU to get physical CPU time, the vCPU needs to be scheduled on a *Hardware Execution Context (HEC)*. An HEC is a thread that is scheduled on a physical processor. The number of HECs available for scheduling depends on the number of physical cores available in the system. vCPUs must be scheduled at the same time or not at all, so, for example, a two-vCPU virtual machine must be scheduled on two HECs at the same time or not all. The same applies to a four-vCPU virtual machine; it either gets scheduled on four HECs at the same time or not at all.

> **NOTE**
>
> To configure a VM with two or four vCPUs, you need the underlying host to have two or four physical processors or cores.

> **EXAM ALERT**
>
> If any physical CPU in an ESX host fails, the entire host will crash, and there will be no redundancy capabilities.

To determine the number of HECs available, you have to look at the physical processor configuration of your system. Today, processors with multiple sockets are available; a socket is also a complete processor that is either packaged with other sockets in the same core or available alone in the core. If you have a single core, dual socket system without hyper-threading, for example, you then have two HECs. If you have a single core, quad socket, you then have four HECs and so on. The following sections describe hyper-threading and vCPU load balancing.

Hyper-threading

Hyper-threading is an Intel Corporation technology that allows you to schedule multiple threads on the same processor at the same time. Hyper-threading does not increase CPU capacity, however. Hyper-threading is enabled in the BIOS of the system, and when enabled, it increases the number of available HECs on which vCPUs can be scheduled. Even with the capability to schedule multiple threads on the same physical CPU at the same time, if contention occurs, one thread would have to wait while the other finishes execution. For this reason, when VMs have high vCPU utilization, the VMkernel ignores the second thread if it exists. That is, hyper-threading does not increase a VM's vCPU capabilities if the VM is CPU intensive.

vCPU Load Balancing

The VMkernel is responsible for dynamically scheduling vCPUs and the Service Console (SC). VMkernel schedules and reschedules vCPUs on different HECs every 20 milliseconds, with the exception of the Service Console, which is always scheduled on the first HEC or physical CPU 0 and is never changed.

The VMkernel's sole purpose in this constant migration of the vCPUs from one HEC to another is to maintain the most adequate load. The VMkernel determines where it schedules the different vCPUs and on which HECs.

> **EXAM ALERT**
>
> It is very likely that the VCP exam will challenge your knowledge as far as which physical CPU where the SC is always scheduled.

Virtual Memory

The VMkernel uses the following techniques to control and allocate virtual memory when memory is scarce:

► Transparent memory page sharing

► Balloon-driver or vmmemctl

► VMkernel swap

EXAM ALERT

The VCP exam may use the term *balloon-driver* at times and at other times may use the official name of the technology, which is *vmmemctl*, so be prepared.

The following sections dig into each one of these concepts. You find out how they work and how they yield and release memory to satisfy an ESX host in times of memory need.

Transparent Memory Page Sharing

Transparent memory page sharing detects when VMs are accessing the same memory pages, and instead of allocating different copies of the same memory space for each VM, it maps all the VMs that are accessing the same memory space to a single copy. The technique of transparent memory page sharing holds true as long as the VMs are just reading the same memory space—so in other words, as long as they are in Read-Only mode.

As soon as a VM needs to write to memory, the VMkernel creates a copy of this memory space specifically for this VM, which can then write to it. Transparent memory page sharing is enabled by default unless specifically disabled.

Consider an example of how this mechanism works. Say you have 10 VMs that are all running Windows Server 2003. Because they all run the same operating system, they are all accessing the same file and thus require the same memory pages. So these 10 VMs can access the same memory pages in Read-Only mode. As soon as any one of these VMs needs to write to memory, a private copy is then created for it.

Balloon-driver (vmmemctl)

A *balloon-driver* (also referred to as *vmmemctl*) is a guest operating system device driver that is installed as part of the VMware Tools installation. Its function is simple: When an ESX system comes under physical memory strain, the VMkernel randomly selects a VM, inflates the device driver inside the guest operating system, and consumes all the available memory that is not being used by the operating system. It then releases this acquired memory to the ESX system to ease its memory requirements. When the need for this memory ceases to exist, the device driver is deflated or stopped, and the memory is returned to the guest operating system.

This mechanism comes into play only when an ESX system is hungry for memory resources. It is also worth noting that VMs are completely unaware of this concept. To a VM, a device driver simply started inside the guest operating system and consumes all this memory.

You can configure the balloon driver to consume up to 75% of the memory of the virtual machine. This is an advanced VMkernel setting named Mem.CtlMaxPercent and can be set between 0% and 75%. It is set to 65% by default. As you can see in Figure 10.1, to modify this setting, you need to go to the Configuration tab on your ESX host, select Advanced Settings on the left pane, and click on Mem.

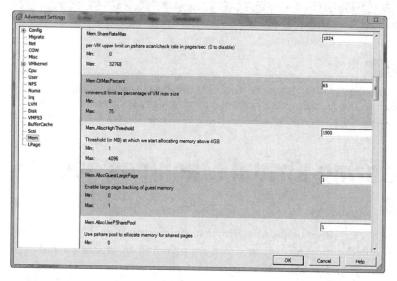

FIGURE 10.1
Mem.CtlMaxPercent setting.

VMkernel Swap

Every virtual machine needs a swap file that is created when the VM is powered on and is deleted when the VM powers off. The swap file size is the difference between the VM's memory limit and its reservation. Unless otherwise specified, the swap file is located with the VM's boot disk.

When the VMkernel requires memory, the VM's memory pages are copied into the swap file to allow the VM to continue to function and then relinquish this memory to the VMkernel. This measure is a last resort in case the balloon-driver cannot allocate enough memory to satisfy the VMkernel's needs. As with any other system, when heavy paging occurs, the VM's performance suffers.

Because ballooning can consume only up to 75% of a VM's memory and because ballooning is set to 65% by default, the 10% difference would have to be allocated by the VMkernel swap. For example, in the event that an ESX host becomes starved for memory resources and a VM's balloon-driver is inflated for 65% of its memory but the VMkernel has requested 75%, the remaining 10%

is allocated by swap. You should note that swapping is less desirable than ballooning and causes a VM's performance to suffer, whereas ballooning has less of a performance strain on the VM.

EXAM ALERT

When the VMkernel swaps memory to disk, a significant performance penalty is noticeable.

NOTE

If the VMkernel requests it, a VM's entire memory is written to the page file and released to the VMkernel. This happens only in times of extreme memory strain on the ESX host.

Monitoring Virtual Machines and Hosts

Monitoring the resource usage of a virtual machine or a host is a critical first step in a troubleshooting process or if you are planning an expansion and need to know where your performance metrics stand as far as resources. The Virtual Infrastructure (VI) client offers you the Performance tab for both virtual machines and hosts; this tab allows you to view real-time or historical graphs for the following resources:

- ▶ CPU
- ▶ Memory
- ▶ Disk
- ▶ Network

TIP

To compare multiple VMs side by side, you can tear off the performance charts of those VMs and arrange them side by side to make comparing them easier.

In the sections to follow, we cover those resources in greater detail and examine how you can gather the necessary performance metrics needed. Performance metrics are great to have for troubleshooting purposes, of course, but they are also very useful in justifying additional hardware purchases or hardware upgrades.

CPU

The most important indicator that a VM is not getting enough time on the physical CPU is the CPU ready metric, which indicates that a vCPU is requesting a time slice on the physical CPU but cannot get scheduled fast enough. The vCPU is thereby queued, which results in poor performance. Figure 10.2 shows a vCPU's ready graph that is available only in real-time. You cannot view this metric in the historical database.

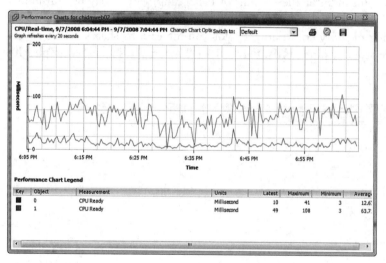

FIGURE 10.2
CPU ready graph.

The following conditions can affect the CPU ready time:

- ▶ **Overall CPU Utilization:** This can affect CPU ready time because when the overall CPU utilization is high, other VMs are also competing for this resource, which drives up this counter.

- ▶ **Number of Resource Consumers:** When an ESX host is running several VMs, it is more than likely that the VMkernel will start to queue the VMs' access times to the physical CPU as a result of the numerous simultaneous requests.

- ▶ **Load Correlation:** This means that if a task being executed on the physical CPU initiates multiple other tasks or threads when it is completed, ready time is affected.

▶ **Number of vCPUs in a VM:** When multiple vCPUs are present in the VMs, they are scheduled at the same time on the physical CPUs or not at all. A four-vCPU VM requires four physical CPUs to be available for the schedule to be successful. In high ready times, this is challenging because all the CPUs must be free of contention to be scheduled.

Memory

You can monitor memory usage in the same manner as you would CPU usage. However, when a virtual machine is running out of memory, check the performance graph and monitor the amount of ballooning, which may be consuming memory. In this event, you can VMotion the VM to another host that is not experiencing memory constraints, or you can increase its shares, which would give it priority over other VMs. Figure 10.3 shows a VM's memory graph with ballooning.

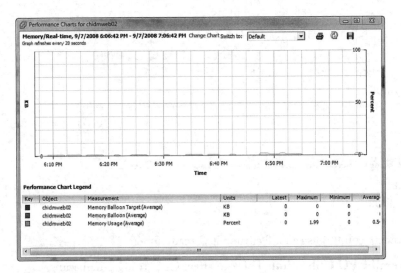

FIGURE 10.3
VM's memory graph.

> **NOTE**
>
> As with CPU ready time, ballooning shows up only in the real-time view of the graphs, and not the historical view.

Disk

Disk contention is a performance metric that many people often dismiss as a nonissue. Disk contention, however, can significantly degrade virtual machine performance. You can monitor disk saturation using the performance graph inside the VI client or using third-party tools. In the event that disk saturation is detected, you should move the VM's files to another storage device that is not having disk contention, change the path that leads to the storage device if that path is saturated, and then ensure that you are using a RAID level that is adequate for the application you have deployed.

> **NOTE**
>
> Keep in mind that the installation of the VMware Tools improves disk access, so make sure they are installed.

Network

Network bandwidth-intensive applications often require you to migrate the VMs to other physical NICs that are less utilized to maximize performance. You may also consider traffic shaping as another technique by which you can control network bandwidth. The use of the performance graphs or other third-party tools can help you detect high utilization of network bandwidth.

Monitoring with Alarms

Alarms are thresholds that you configure on either a host or a virtual machine. The alarm sends you a notification when a certain threshold has been reached. Alarms allow you to quickly respond to a potential problem and address it before it causes major problems.

When an alarm threshold is reached, the VI client displays a message. Because you typically are not monitoring or logged in all the time, you can configure options to notify you of this alarm. Figure 10.4 shows the Actions tab in Alarm Settings and the different methods by which you can configure the alarm to notify you. You can also configure it to perform a certain task when an alarm threshold is reached, such as run a script, send an email, or even use the Short Message Service (SMS).

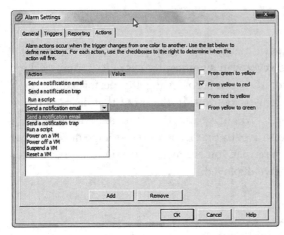

FIGURE 10.4
Alarms Action tab.

After you have configured your alarms with the proper actions to perform, you should make sure that VirtualCenter (VC) knows how to deliver these messages to you. If you chose to be notified by email when a certain threshold is reached, for example, you need to configure VC with the proper SMTP settings to route this email to you successfully. The same goes for SNMP traps. From within VC, click on Administration > VirtualCenter Management Server Configuration. As you can see in Figure 10.5, you can then click on the Mail to configure email delivery or SNMP to configure its settings

CAUTION

If the CMTP server is reporting the alarm, you may never be notified because the server that is charged with delivering the notification is suffering from a warning. Situations like these are what necessitates that you have alternate means of notification delivery, such as a monitoring server, for example.

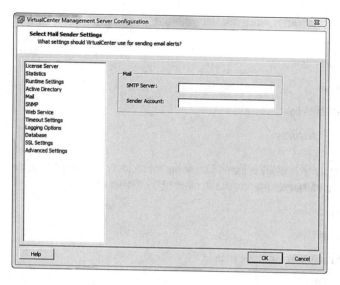

FIGURE 10.5

VirtualCenter Management server configuration.

Exam Prep Questions

1. True or false: Transparent memory page sharing is enabled by default and cannot be turned off.

   ○ **A.** True

   ○ **B.** False

2. True or false: A virtual machine's swap file is deleted once the VM is powered off.

   ○ **A.** True

   ○ **B.** False

3. Which technology allows for the scheduling of multiple threads on the same CPU?

   ○ **A.** CPU affinity

   ○ **B.** CPU threading

   ○ **C.** Memmaker

   ○ **D.** None of the above

4. What is the key indicator that a virtual machine's vCPU is losing competition time for physical CPU scheduling?

- ○ **A.** CPU ready time
- ○ **B.** CPU time
- ○ **C.** Context switches
- ○ **D.** % CPU Scheduler

5. Which virtual memory technology is used to consume the memory of a virtual machine and release it to the VMkernel for allocation to other VMs? (Select all that apply.)

- ○ **A.** Balloon-driver
- ○ **B.** VMkernel swap
- ○ **C.** Transparent memory page sharing
- ○ **D.** Vmmemctl

6. On which physical processor does the Service Console always run?

- ○ **A.** CPU0
- ○ **B.** CPU1
- ○ **C.** CPU2
- ○ **D.** Distributes the load on multiple CPUs for redundancy

7. What is the interval at which the VMkernel dynamically and constantly changes the vCPU's HECs?

- ○ **A.** 20 seconds
- ○ **B.** 20 milliseconds
- ○ **C.** 25 seconds
- ○ **D.** 25 milliseconds

8. True or false: The Service Console is constantly scheduled on different HECs.

- ○ **A.** True
- ○ **B.** False

9. True or false: The balloon-driver, if inflated, is configured by default at 75% of the VM's memory.

   ○ **A.** True

   ○ **B.** False

10. How many physical CPUs are needed to support a virtual machine that is configured with four vCPUs? (Select all that apply.)

    ○ **A.** Single socket, quad core

    ○ **B.** Quad socket processor

    ○ **C.** Dual socket, single core

    ○ **D.** Single socket, dual core

Answers to Exam Prep Questions

1. Answer **B**, False, is correct. Transparent memory page sharing is turned on by default, but you can turn it off if you choose to do so.

2. Answer **A**, True, is correct. A virtual machine's swap file is deleted when the VM is powered off and is re-created when the VM is powered on.

3. Answer **D** is correct. The technology that allows for the scheduling of multiple threads on the same CPU is known as hyper-threading; therefore, answers A, B, and C are incorrect.

4. Answer **A** is correct. The key indicator that a virtual machine is losing compete time for a physical CPU time slice is the CPU ready time; therefore, answers B, C, and D are incorrect.

5. Answers **A** and **D** are correct. Vmmemctl, which is also known as the balloon-driver, is the virtual memory technology that is used to grab memory from one VM and release to the VMkernel, which will then allocate it to another VM; therefore, answers B and C are incorrect.

6. Answer **A** is correct. The Service Console is always scheduled on physical CPU0 and never changes; therefore, answers B, C, and D are incorrect.

7. Answer **B** is correct. The VMkernel dynamically and constantly changes the vCPU's HECs every 20 milliseconds; therefore, answers A, C, and D are incorrect.

8. Answer **B**, False, is correct. The Service Console does not participate in the VMkernel's constant scheduling and rescheduling of HECs and remains on the same CPU at all times.

9. Answer **B**, False, is correct. The balloon-driver is configured by default at 65% of the VM's memory.

10. Answers **A** and **B** are correct. A virtual machine with four vCPUs requires four physical CPUs to be scheduled on; therefore, answers C and D are incorrect.

CHAPTER ELEVEN

Backup and High Availability

Terms you'll need to understand:

✓ VMware Consolidated Backup (VCB)

✓ High Availability (HA)

✓ Admission Control

✓ Host Isolation

✓ Cluster-in-a-box

✓ Cluster-across-boxes

✓ Physical-to-virtual cluster

Concepts and techniques you'll need to master:

✓ The different techniques by which you can back up a virtual machine

✓ The different techniques by which you can back up the Service Console

✓ How VCB works

✓ How an ESX host can become isolated

What good is an environment without a good backup strategy? This chapter explores the different options by which you can back up your VMware Infrastructure. The chapter also explores VMware High Availability (HA) and the ability to sustain host failures and ensure that your critical virtual machines (VMs) can be restarted on other hosts that are online.

Backup Scenarios

You should think of and treat backup strategies for VMs and their ESX host the same way you would approach physical machines. The same best practices and methodologies apply. The only different scenario covered is VMware Consolidated Backup (VCB).

Virtual Machine Backup Options

As far as virtual machines are concerned, you can back them up using any of the following methods:

▶ Installing a backup agent inside the guest operating system. This is the same as when you install a backup agent inside a physical machine's guest operating system. You can then do file-level backups as frequently as your data changes or as frequently as your environment requires.

▶ Backing up the virtual machine files. Because a virtual machine is encapsulated inside regular files, you can back up or archive these files by installing a backup agent inside the Service Console and then back up those files. When using this method, you can power off the VM and back up the files. Alternatively, if you need the VM to continue to be online, you can take a snapshot of it and back up the snapshot files.

When considering backup of virtual machine data, make sure that you have your application files stored on separate drives. This makes the process of backing up the data easier. This also concentrates the backup process on the data rather than the operating system files, which should be backed up infrequently because they do not change and you don't want to have to back them up repeatedly. The system drive should be backed up in the event that you want to restore the entire virtual machine to the state it was in when you made the backup. The point to keep in mind here is that you are backing up the system drive for the Registry and the application-specific files that are installed with the virtual machine.

Host Backup Options

The ESX host is primarily the Service Console. Because the Service Console is used for command-line advanced options, its files rarely change and most of the configurations you make in your VMware Infrastructure are stored in the VirtualCenter database. That being said, backing up the Service Console is not really worth the time and effort involved. You can easily reinstall ESX and make the changes rather than deal with executing a backup and restore operation of the Service Console.

However, if you want to back up your Service Console, you can do so using one of the following two methods:

▶ Installing a backup agent inside the Service Console and backing up the files accordingly. This would be the same traditional agent backup approach that you would take with any physical machine running any guest operating system.

▶ Using third-party software to create a complete image of the ESX server and then using this same third-party software to restore the entire image and return the state of the ESX host to the point when you took the image originally.

EXAM ALERT

Pay attention to the Host backup section because you are sure to get a question on this topic on the VCP exam.

VMware Consolidated Backup

VMware Consolidated Backup (VCB) is an alternative method of backing up and restoring virtual machines at the file level or image level. VCB is based on snapshots. It works by taking a snapshot of the virtual machine that needs to be backed up; this snapshot is then copied to a location where the backup proxy server can back it up.

The advantage of VCB is that you can take the network completely out of the equation. If you take a snapshot of a running VM and then you copy the snapshot files to another SAN LUN that is visible to the backup server, this server can then back up those files directly. Consequently, you have taken the network out of the equation all the way to the backup server. Now, obviously, depending on what type of backup system you are using and how the backup server is connected to your backup robot, the network can remain out of the equation or can be used to move the files from the backup server to the backup tape library.

By using VCB, you have the following advantages:

▶ Because you are dealing with snapshot-level backups, there is no need for a backup window because no downtime is required to back up the VM. The VM is backed up while it is powered on.

▶ Backup load is moved away from the ESX host because you are taking a snapshot and moving this snapshot to another location to be backed up directly by the backup proxy server. By doing so, you offload all the processing requirements needed from the ESX host to the backup server.

▶ The backup agent is optional. When using VCB, you take advantage of the VMware Tools that are installed inside the VM that allow for VCB to take place, thereby giving you the option to use the backup agent only if you want to restore directly to this virtual machine. Instead of restoring directly to a VM, you may opt to install a backup agent on a select few VMs and then restore any files to these VMs. At that point, you can copy the restored files to their final destination. This would save money and management of backup agents on multiple virtual machines.

When running VCB, you have full support for file-level backup of Microsoft Windows guest operating systems and image-level backups of any guest operating system.

EXAM ALERT

Knowing the capabilities and limitations of VCB is critical because you will surely be quizzed on this subject on the exam. VCB is a most critical component of the VI suite.

High Availability

VMware *High Availability (HA)* deals primarily with ESX host failure and what happens to the virtual machines that are running on this host. When an ESX host fails for any reason, all the running VMs also fail. VMware HA ensures that the VMs from the failed host are capable of being restarted on other ESX hosts.

Many people mistakenly confuse VMware HA with fault tolerance. VMware HA is not fault tolerant in that if a host fails, the VMs on it also fail. HA deals only with restarting those VMs on other ESX hosts with enough resources. Fault tolerance, on the other hand, provides uninterruptible access to resources in the event of a host failure.

EXAM ALERT

The VCP exam is sure to challenge your knowledge on the difference between HA and fault tolerance. Make sure you have a clear understanding of the difference.

VMware HA maintains a communication channel with all the other ESX hosts that are members of the same cluster by using a heartbeat that it sends out every 15 seconds or 15,000 milliseconds. When an ESX server misses a heartbeat, the cluster initiates the restart of the VMs on the failing ESX host on the remaining ESX hosts in the cluster. VMware HA also constantly monitors the ESX hosts that are members of the cluster and ensures that resources are always available to satisfy requirements in the event of a host failure.

TIP

VMware HA is a reactive system, which means it kicks in to react to a problem; in this case, the problem is a failed host. A reactive system would be perfect if combined with a proactive system, and this is exactly what you get if you enabled VMware HA and VMware DRS on the same cluster. DRS is a proactive system that is constantly busy trying to load-balance resources on ESX hosts.

Virtual Machine Failure Monitoring

Virtual Machine Failure Monitoring is technology that is disabled by default. Its function is to monitor virtual machines, which it queries every 20 seconds via a heartbeat. It does this by using the VMware Tools that are installed inside the VM. When a VM misses a heartbeat, VMware HA deems this VM as failed and attempts to restart it. Think of Virtual Machine Failure Monitoring as sort of High Availability for VMs. Because VMware HA is for ESX hosts, this new feature will potentially (when it's out of the experimental phase) use VMware HA to provide VMs with a better failure monitoring and response method.

NOTE

Virtual Machine Failure Monitoring can detect if a virtual machine was manually powered off, suspended, or migrated, and thereby does not attempt to restart it.

EXAM ALERT

Before the release of ESX 3.5 Update 2, Virtual Machine Failure Monitoring was an experimental technology.

HA Configuration Prerequisites

HA requires the following configuration prerequisites before it can function properly:

- ▶ **VirtualCenter:** Because VMware HA is an enterprise-class feature, it requires VirtualCenter before it can be enabled.

- ▶ **DNS Resolution:** All ESX hosts that are members of the HA cluster must be able to resolve one another using DNS.

- ▶ **Access to shared storage:** All hosts in the HA cluster must have access and visibility to the same shared storage; otherwise, they would have no mechanism to know to restart the VMs.

- ▶ **Access to same network:** All ESX hosts must have the same networks configured on all hosts so that when a VM is restarted on any host, its connection is preserved.

Service Console Redundancy

Recommended practice dictates that the Service Console have redundancy. VMware HA complains and issues a warning if it detects that the Service Console is configured on only one vSwitch. As Figure 11.1 shows, you can configure Service Console redundancy in one of two ways:

- ▶ Create two Service Console port groups, each on a different vSwitch.

- ▶ Assign two physical network interface cards (NICs) in the form of a NIC team to the Service Console vSwitch.

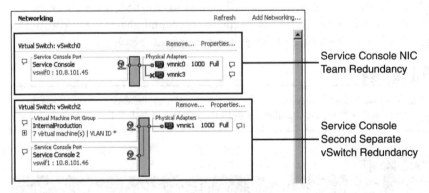

FIGURE 11.1
Service Console redundancy.

In both cases you need to configure the entire IP stack with IP address, subnet, and gateway. The Service Console vSwitches are used for heartbeats and state synchronization and use the following ports:

- ▶ Incoming TCP port 8042

- ▶ Incoming UDP port 8045

- ▶ Outgoing TCP port 2050

- ▶ Outgoing UDP port 2250

- ▶ Incoming TCP port 8042–8045

- ▶ Incoming UDP port 8042–8045

- ▶ Outgoing TCP port 2050–2250

- ▶ Outgoing UDP port 2050–2250

Failure to configure SC redundancy will result in a warning message when you enable HA. So, to avoid seeing this error message and to adhere to best practice, configure the SC to be redundant.

EXAM ALERT

Service Console redundancy is an important topic and will more than likely be one of the questions on the exam.

Host Failover Capacity Planning

When configuring HA, you have to manually configure the maximum host failure tolerance. This is a task that you should thoughtfully consider during the hardware sizing and planning phase of your deployment. This would assume that you have built your ESX hosts with enough resources to run more VMs than planned to be able to accommodate HA. For example, in Figure 11.2, notice that the HA cluster has four ESX hosts and that all four of these hosts have enough capacity to run at least three more VMs. Because they are all already running three VMs, that means that this cluster can afford the loss of two ESX hosts because the remaining two ESX hosts can power on the six failed VMs with no problem if failure occurs.

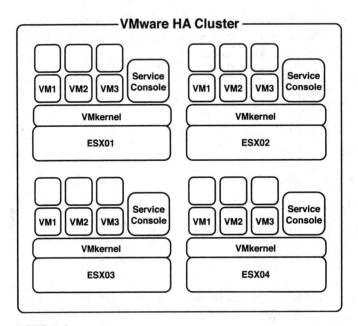

FIGURE 11.2
HA capacity planning.

During the configuration phase of the HA cluster, you are presented with a screen similar to that shown in Figure 11.3 that prompts you to define two cluster-wide configurations as follows:

▶ **Host Failures:**

  ▶ **Number of Host Failures Allowed:** This setting allows you to configure how many host failures you want to tolerate. The allowed settings are 1 through 4.

  ▶ **Restart Priority:** This setting allows you to specify a cluster-wide restart priority for VMs. The available settings are High, Medium, Low, Use Cluster Setting, and Disabled. The section "Virtual Machine Recovery Priority" later in this chapter explores how you can override this setting by specifying VM-specific restart policy.

  ▶ **Isolation Response:** This setting defines what happens when an ESX host becomes isolated. The available settings are Leave Powered On, Power Off, and Use Cluster Setting. The next section, "Host Isolation," covers this setting in greater detail.

- ▶ **Admission Control:**

  - ▶ **Do Not Power On Virtual Machines If They Violate Availability Constraints:** Selecting this option indicates that if no resources are available to satisfy a VM, it should not be powered on.

  - ▶ **Allow Virtual Machines to Be Powered On Even If They Violate Availability Constraints:** Selecting this option indicates that you should power on a VM even if you have to overcommit resources.

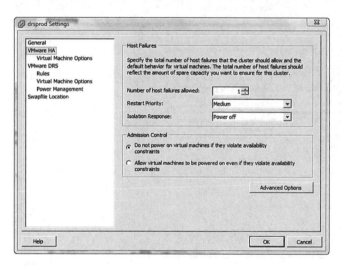

FIGURE 11.3
HA cluster-wide policies.

Host Isolation

A network phenomenon known as a *split-brain* occurs when the ESX host has stopped receiving a heartbeat from the rest of the cluster. The heartbeat is communicated via the Service Console gateway and is queried for every 15 seconds. If a response is not received, the cluster thinks the ESX host has failed. This re-emphasizes the need for redundancy at the Service Console level because it is the mechanism by which an ESX host announces to the rest of the cluster that it is still alive. Having multiple Service Console port groups greatly reduces the probability of *host isolation*.

You can control what happens to VMs in the event of a host isolation. To get to the VM Isolation Response screen, right-click the cluster in question and click on Edit Settings. You can then click on Virtual Machine Options under the VMware HA banner in the left pane. As shown in Figure 11.4, your Isolation Response options are as follows:

▶ **Leave Powered On:** As the label implies, this setting means that in the event of host isolation, the VM remains powered on.

▶ **Power Off:** This setting defines that in the event of an isolation, the VM is powered off.

▶ **Use Cluster Setting:** This setting forwards the task to the cluster-wide setting defined in the window shown previously in Figure 11.3.

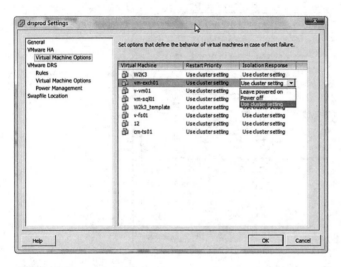

FIGURE 11.4
VM-specific isolation policy.

In the event of an isolation, this does not necessarily mean that the host is down. Because the VMs might be configured with different physical NICs and connected to different networks, they might continue to function properly; you therefore have to consider this when setting the priority for isolation. When a host is isolated, this simply means that its Service Console cannot communicate with the rest of the ESX hosts in the cluster.

Virtual Machine Recovery Priority

Should your HA cluster not be able to accommodate all the VMs in the event of a failure, you have the ability to prioritize on VMs. The priorities dictate which VMs are restarted first and which VMs are not that important in the event of an emergency. These options are configured on the same screen as the Isolation Response covered in the preceding section. As you can see in Figure 11.5, you can set a VM's restart priority to one of the following:

▶ **High:** VMs with a high priority are restarted first.

▶ **Medium:** This is the default setting.

▶ **Low:** VMs with a low priority are restarted last.

▶ **Use Cluster Setting:** VMs are restarted based on the setting defined at the cluster level defined in the window shown previously in Figure 11.3.

▶ **Disabled:** The VM does not power on.

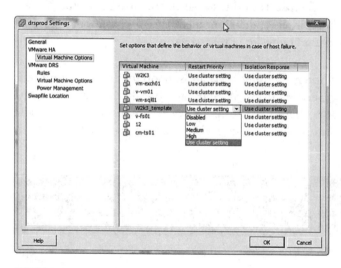

FIGURE 11.5
VM restart priority.

The priority should be set based on the importance of the VMs. In other words, you might want to restart domain controllers and not restart print servers. The higher priority virtual machines are restarted first. VMs that can tolerate remaining powered off in the event of an emergency should be configured to remain powered off to conserve resources.

Clustering

The main purpose of a cluster is to ensure that critical systems remain online at any cost and at all times. Similar to physical machines that can be clustered, virtual machines can also be clustered with ESX using three different scenarios:

▶ **Cluster-in-a-box:** In this scenario, all the VMs that are part of the cluster reside on the same ESX host. As you might have guessed, this immediately creates a single point of failure: the ESX host.

▶ **Cluster-across-boxes:** In this scenario, the cluster nodes (VMs that are members of the cluster) reside on multiple ESX hosts, thereby creating an ideal cluster environment by eliminating a single point of failure scenario. Shared storage is a prerequisite in this scenario whereby each of the nodes that make up the cluster can access the same storage so that if one VM fails, the other can continue to function and access the same data.

▶ **Physical-to-virtual cluster:** In this scenario, one member of the cluster is a virtual machine, whereas the other member is a physical machine. Shared storage is a prerequisite in this scenario.

At the time of this writing, the only VMware-supported clustering service is Microsoft Clustering Services (MSCS). You can consult the VMware white paper titles "Setup for Microsoft Cluster Service" on the topic located at http://www.vmware.com/pdf/vi3_35/esx_3/vi3_35_25_u1_mscs.pdf.

> **EXAM ALERT**
>
> Because there are probably many third-party software vendors that advertise support for clustering inside ESX VMs, it is likely that the VCP exam will challenge your knowledge on the official VMware stand on supported clustering services with VMs.

Exam Prep Questions

1. What are the two VMware HA cluster-wide settings that you can configure? (Select all that apply.)

   ○ **A.** Host Failures

   ○ **B.** DRS

   ○ **C.** Admission Control

   ○ **D.** Fault Tolerance

2. When does the phenomenon of split-brain occur?

   ◯ **A.** When ESX has lost access to its shared storage

   ◯ **B.** When ESX has stopped receiving a heartbeat from its VMs

   ◯ **C.** When ESX has stopped receiving a heartbeat from the other nodes in the cluster

   ◯ **D.** When ESX cannot resolve DNS

3. Which incoming TCP and UDP ports are used for heartbeats and state synchronization? (Select all that apply.)

   ◯ **A.** TCP 8042 - 8045

   ◯ **B.** UDP 8042 - 8045

   ◯ **C.** TCP 8012 - 8015

   ◯ **D.** UDP 8012 - 8015

4. What are the two types of virtual machine backups? (Select all that apply.)

   ◯ **A.** Differential

   ◯ **B.** File-level

   ◯ **C.** Shadow-copy

   ◯ **D.** Image-level

5. Which outgoing TCP and UDP ports are used for heartbeats and state synchronization? (Select all that apply.)

   ◯ **A.** TCP 2150 - 2250

   ◯ **B.** UDP 2150 - 2250

   ◯ **C.** TCP 2050 - 2250

   ◯ **D.** UDP 2050 - 2250

6. True or false: It is a recommended and crucial task that you back up the Service Console to preserve the ESX host configuration.

   ◯ **A.** True

   ◯ **B.** False

7. How often does an ESX server that is part of an HA cluster send out a heartbeat to the rest of the hosts in the same cluster? (Select all that apply.)

   ○ **A.** 15 seconds

   ○ **B.** 15,000 milliseconds

   ○ **C.** 5 seconds

   ○ **D.** 20 milliseconds

8. True or false: VMware Consolidated Backup supports file-level backup for all guest operating systems.

   ○ **A.** True

   ○ **B.** False

9. True or false: VMware HA is a fault-tolerance system that allows a VM to have zero downtime in the event that its parent host should fail.

   ○ **A.** True

   ○ **B.** False

10. Which of the following is not a supported VM cluster in ESX?

   ○ **A.** Cluster-in-a-box

   ○ **B.** Cluster-across-boxes

   ○ **C.** ESX-host-cluster

   ○ **D.** Physical-to-virtual cluster

Answers to Exam Prep Questions

1. Answers **A** and **C** are correct. The two settings that you can configure cluster-wide for VMware HA are Host Failures and Admission Control; therefore, answers B and D are incorrect.

2. Answer **C** is correct. This phenomenon occurs when an ESX host stops receiving a heartbeat from other members of the HA cluster and it cannot ping its SC gateway address; therefore, answers A, B, and D are incorrect.

3. Answers **A** and **B** are correct. The incoming TCP and UDP ports are 8042 and 8045; therefore, answers C and D are incorrect.

4. Answers **B** and **D** are correct. The two types of VM level backups are file-level and image-level backups; therefore, answers A and C are incorrect.

5. Answers **C** and **D** are correct. The outgoing TCP and UDP ports are 2050 and 2250; therefore, answers A and B are incorrect.

6. Answer **B**, False, is correct. Although backing up the Service Console is an option, it is really not required because most of the ESX host configuration is stored in the VirtualCenter database. The Service Console files rarely change, and those that do don't merit a backup. It is thereby easier to reinstall ESX than it is worth backing up the SC.

7. Answers **A** and **B** are correct. ESX hosts that are members of the same HA cluster inform each other that they are still alive via a heartbeat that they broadcast every 15 seconds or 15,000 milliseconds; therefore, answers C and D are incorrect.

8. Answer **B**, False, is correct. VMware Consolidated Backup supports only file-level backups on Windows-based systems and image-level backups for all guest operating systems.

9. Answer **B**, False, is correct. VMware HA is not a fault-tolerance system, and consequently, in the event of a host failure, the VMs running on that host also fail.

10. Answer **C** is correct. There is no such thing as an ESX-host-cluster other than the VirtualCenter features of DRS and HA; therefore, answers A, B, and D are incorrect.

Practice Exam 1

Hints and Pointers

Other than years of hands-on experience, the best way to prepare for the VMware VCP-310 test is to take practice (or sample) exams. VMware also requires all VCP candidates to take an authorized, instructor-led course leading up to the exam. According to VMware:

> The accepted courses are: "Install and Configure"; "Deploy, Secure, and Analyze"; and "Fast Track". If you are a current VCP, there are no course prerequisites.

It is critical that you learn to approach VMware's certification tests thinking the way VMware wants you to. If you have taken hundreds of certification tests from other vendors, you may have a tendency to answer the way other vendors deem correct. That might or might not be correct on a VMware exam. Therefore, take these practice tests and start thinking like a VMware Certified Professional.

This book contains two sample tests, in addition to the practice questions provided at the end of each chapter. You can find the answers and explanations to these questions following this practice exam. These practice questions are simply that—practice questions to get you ready for the form, fashion, and types of questions you will encounter on the exam. None are live exam questions.

After you go through these practice questions a few times, you should have a good idea what topics you need to brush up on. There are other practice tests on the market, which may or may not help you. The purpose of the practice questions in this book is to reinforce important, testable concepts, facts, and objectives. The answers and explanations should guide you in filling in voids in your current knowledge base. By all means, supplement your study using the content and Exam Alerts in this book with a thorough review of the VMware Authorized Courseware and the online documents available on the VMware website.

Most of the questions are single-answer or multiple-answer multiple-choice questions with a few accompanied by exhibits. As you prepare, you should get at least 85% of the answers correct on each practice exam before moving on. Remember, you can, with proper preparation, successfully pass the VCP-310 exam. And this Exam Cram will help you.

I encourage you, as you prepare, to check the following websites for updates to the exam and the exam process:

▶ http://mylearn.vmware.com/portals/certification/faqs.cfm?ui=www#1871

▶ http://mylearn1.vmware.com/portals/certification/

▶ http://mylearn.vmware.com/lcms/mL_faq/1714/VCP3.5Blueprint.PDF

All the best in your journey to the VCP!

Practice Exam 1

1. You are considering the VI3 suite as a server virtualization solution for your growing enterprise. You are mainly interested in a feature that lets you move a virtual machine from one server to another without having to power it off. Which product in the VI3 suite interests you?

   ○ **A.** DRS

   ○ **B.** HA

   ○ **C.** VMotion

   ○ **D.** VCB

2. Which of the following VirtualCenter 2.5 tasks does a Virtual Machine User have permissions to do by default?

   ○ **A.** Create a Task

   ○ **B.** Create a Virtual Machine

   ○ **C.** Add a New Disk

   ○ **D.** Remove a Disk

3. You want to create an HA cluster using VMware. Which of the following is a requirement to accomplish this?

- ○ **A.** DNS name resolution must be configured for all hosts in an HA cluster.
- ○ **B.** All hosts in an HA cluster must have identical DNS hostnames.
- ○ **C.** All hosts in an HA cluster must have identical IP addresses.
- ○ **D.** All hosts in an HA cluster must be able to resolve hostnames using IP addresses.

4. Which of the following services are provided by the Service Console? (Choose two.)

- ○ **A.** VIC
- ○ **B.** Web Server
- ○ **C.** Firewall
- ○ **D.** CPU Scheduling

5. You want to deploy VirtualCenter 2.5 in your enterprise. Which is considered a minimum requirement for successfully accomplishing this?

- ○ **A.** 1GB RAM
- ○ **B.** 256MB disk space
- ○ **C.** 10/100 network adapter
- ○ **D.** RHEL 3 Update 6

6. You are configuring your Service Console firewall. Which port controls transmissions from the iSCSI client?

- ○ **A.** 22
- ○ **B.** 902
- ○ **C.** 8000
- ○ **D.** 3260

7. While configuring the Service Console firewall, you notice that port 27000 is open. What does that control?

- ○ **A.** SSH client
- ○ **B.** HTTP transmissions
- ○ **C.** Transmissions from the ESX Server to the License Server
- ○ **D.** Remote Console traffic

8. Which of the following is a limitation of an ESX Server 3.5 host?

- ○ **A.** 512 virtual switch port groups
- ○ **B.** 64 vSwitches
- ○ **C.** 2048 ports
- ○ **D.** 512 ports per vSwitch

9. You are installing ESX Server 3.5. What is the default size assigned to the /BOOT partition?

- ○ **A.** 5GB
- ○ **B.** 544MB
- ○ **C.** 100MB
- ○ **D.** 2GB

10. You want to deploy a VMware Consolidated Backup solution on your network. Which of the following are true statements of VCB? (Choose three.)

- ○ **A.** Entire virtual machines can be backed up using VCB.
- ○ **B.** Entire virtual machines can be backed up only using a third-party backup solution.
- ○ **C.** A single VMDK can be backed up using VCB.
- ○ **D.** A single VMDK can be backed up using only a third-party backup solution.
- ○ **E.** Single guest files can be backed up using VCB.
- ○ **F.** Single guest files can be backed up only using a third-party backup solution.

11. Which of the following is considered an ESX Server component in the VI3 suite?

- ○ **A.** VMotion
- ○ **B.** Virtual SMP
- ○ **C.** HA
- ○ **D.** DRS

12. Which of the following are ways of licensing an ESX Server 3.5 host? (Choose two.)

   ○ **A.** Server based

   ○ **B.** Network based

   ○ **C.** Directory based

   ○ **D.** Host based

13. What are the two ways that a VI3 license key is constructed?

   ○ **A.** Per seat

   ○ **B.** Per server

   ○ **C.** Per processor

   ○ **D.** Per instance

14. Your VI3 enterprise environment is using a centralized License Server. You have three ESX Server 3.5 hosts. The License Server fails. How long a grace period is available during which all hosts will continue to function without interruption?

   ○ **A.** 10 days

   ○ **B.** 14 days

   ○ **C.** 60 days

   ○ **D.** 90 days

15. You have installed a single instance of VirtualCenter 2.5 in your enterprise. According to VMware, what is the maximum number of ESX Server 3.5 hosts you can manage with this configuration?

   ○ **A.** 200

   ○ **B.** 20

   ○ **C.** 2000

   ○ **D.** 20,000

   ○ **E.** 100

16. Your VI3 enterprise environment uses a centralized License Server. You have three ESX Server 3.5 hosts. The License Server fails and you are not able to restore it within the default period allowed. Which features are available after this default period? (Choose two.)

   - ○ **A.** VMotion a virtual machine between two hosts
   - ○ **B.** Power on a virtual machine
   - ○ **C.** Turning on an ESX Server 3.5 host
   - ○ **D.** Deleting a virtual machine

17. In VirtualCenter 2.5, you are configuring a new virtual machine CPU usage alarm. On the Triggers tab, what are the two possible conditions that this trigger type can have?

   - ○ **A.** Is Above
   - ○ **B.** Is Below
   - ○ **C.** Is Equal To
   - ○ **D.** Is Not Equal To

18. In VirtualCenter 2.5, you are configuring a new alarm. What variables can you configure on the Triggers tab? (Choose two.)

   - ○ **A.** Warning
   - ○ **B.** Tolerance
   - ○ **C.** Frequency
   - ○ **D.** Alert

19. You are configuring an ESX Server 3.5 host alarm in VirtualCenter 2.5. What are two configurable actions that can occur? (Choose two.)

   - ○ **A.** Suspend the host
   - ○ **B.** Send an email
   - ○ **C.** Reset the host
   - ○ **D.** Run script

20. You have opted to deploy a virtualization solution in your enterprise using the VI3 suite. Which product do you need to install if you want to connect to a VirtualCenter Server or an ESX Server from a Windows workstation?

    ○ **A.** HA

    ○ **B.** VCB

    ○ **C.** VMotion

    ○ **D.** VIC

21. Which of the following is *not* a built-in role found in the Service Console and in VirtualCenter 2.5?

    ○ **A.** Read-Write

    ○ **B.** Administrator

    ○ **C.** No Access

    ○ **D.** Read-Only

22. What is the maximum number of ESX Server 3.5 hosts that can be present in a cluster?

    ○ **A.** 14

    ○ **B.** 24

    ○ **C.** 28

    ○ **D.** 32

23. You want to monitor one of your ESX Server 3.5 nodes in your VI3 environment. You decide to create an alarm. When you try to configure the alarm, you can select the type of alarm you want to create. Which of the following is an available option on the General tab?

    ○ **A.** Monitor a Cluster

    ○ **B.** Monitor a Server

    ○ **C.** Monitor a Network

    ○ **D.** Monitor a Host

24. Which of the following statements correctly describes a resource pool in a VI3 environment?

    ○ **A.** A container created in Hosts and Clusters view is used to limit the host CPU and memory utilization for a group of virtual machines.

    ○ **B.** A container created in Hosts and Clusters view is used to limit the disk space allocated for a group of virtual machines.

    ○ **C.** A container created in Hosts and Clusters view is used to limit the disk space allocated for a group of hosts.

    ○ **D.** A container created in Hosts and Clusters view is used to allocate throughput for a group of hosts.

25. Which of the following are attributes of a resource pool? (Choose two.)

    ○ **A.** Sessions

    ○ **B.** Throughput

    ○ **C.** Shares

    ○ **D.** Reservations

26. You have added your ESX Server 3.5 host to VirtualCenter 2.5. What Service Console account is created when you do this, so that VirtualCenter can accomplish tasks on the ESX Server?

    ○ **A.** vpxuser

    ○ **B.** root

    ○ **C.** Administrator

    ○ **D.** VirtualMachineAdministrator

27. You have given Alex sufficient permissions to administer the ESX Server 3.5 host. You want her to be able to manage all virtual machines on the host except for the Windows Vista machine. You do not want her to have any permission to this VM. What is the easiest way to accomplish this?

    ○ **A.** Delete her account.

    ○ **B.** Rename her account.

    ○ **C.** Configure an IRF.

    ○ **D.** Assign her the No Access Role at the Vista VM.

28. You want to connect to the VirtualCenter 2.5 Web Access interface. Which of the following can you use to accomplish this?

   ○ **A.** IE 6.0

   ○ **B.** Firefox 1.0.3

   ○ **C.** Netscape Navigator 6.0

   ○ **D.** Opera 8.0

29. Which edition of ESX Server 3.5 gives you access to the VMotion feature?

   ○ **A.** Enterprise only

   ○ **B.** Foundation only

   ○ **C.** Standard only

   ○ **D.** Enterprise and Standard

   ○ **E.** Enterprise, Standard, and Foundation

30. Which authentication protocol is used by iSCSI in a VI3 environment?

   ○ **A.** IPSEC

   ○ **B.** PAP

   ○ **C.** CHAP

   ○ **D.** MSCHAPv2

31. Your CIO has informed you that you will be introducing the VI3 product suite into your enterprise. Which product in the VI3 suite provides the virtualization layer on which virtual machines run?

   ○ **A.** DRS

   ○ **B.** ESX Server 3.5

   ○ **C.** VC

   ○ **D.** SMP

32. Which of the following is a correct representation of an iSCSI Target ID using the following data:

Date=August 2008

Domain=pearson.com

Alternate Name=VM1A

Host Name=PracticeTest

- ○ **A.** iqn.2008-08.com.pearson:VM1A
- ○ **B.** iqn.pearson.com.VM1A.PracticeTest
- ○ **C.** iscsi. 2008-08.com.pearson:VM1A
- ○ **D.** iscsi.pearson.com.VM1A.PracticeTest

33. You want to create a Windows Server 2003 virtual machine on your ESX Server 3.5 host. What is the maximum disk size that can be assigned to this VM if you want to use a virtual SCSI disk?

- ○ **A.** 2GB
- ○ **B.** 32GB
- ○ **C.** 2TB
- ○ **D.** 2EB

34. You have created a Windows Vista virtual machine. Which file contains virtual hard disk information for this VM?

- ○ **A.** .vmx
- ○ **B.** .vmdk
- ○ **C.** .vswp
- ○ **D.** .vmsd

35. Which of the following VI3 products is licensed using the per processor basis? (Choose all that apply.)

- ○ **A.** ESX Server 3.5 Host
- ○ **B.** VMotion
- ○ **C.** DRS
- ○ **D.** HA

36. Which RAID level should you incorporate into your VI3 environment if you want to use mirrored arrays?

- ○ **A.** RAID 0
- ○ **B.** RAID 1
- ○ **C.** RAID 4
- ○ **D.** RAID 5

37. You want to come up with a LUN design that works with your VI3 environment. What VMware design schemes are available? (Choose two.)

- ○ **A.** Dynamic
- ○ **B.** Static
- ○ **C.** Adaptive
- ○ **D.** Predictive

38. You want to run the VCB Proxy for your backup solution. On which platform will this utility run?

- ○ **A.** Windows physical machine
- ○ **B.** Windows virtual machine
- ○ **C.** Linux physical machine
- ○ **D.** Linux virtual machine

39. What resources can you monitor on a performance graph of an ESX Server 3.5 host? (Choose two.)

- ○ **A.** Ports
- ○ **B.** Users
- ○ **C.** CPU
- ○ **D.** RAM

40. You have just installed an ESX Server 3.5 host. Which of the following statements is true concerning postinstallation access to this host?

- ○ **A.** By default, root has full SSH access to the host.
- ○ **B.** By default, root is denied full access to the host using VIC.
- ○ **C.** By default, root is denied full access to the host by means of SSH.
- ○ **D.** By default, root has limited access to the host using VIC.
- ○ **E.** By default, root has limited access to the host using SSH.

41. Where would you find the `PermitRootLogin` parameter in a VI3 environment?

- ○ **A.** On an ESX Server 3.5 host in the `/etc/login/login.config` file
- ○ **B.** On a VirtualCenter 2.5 server in the `/etc/login/login.config` file
- ○ **C.** On an ESX Server 3.5 host in the `/etc/ssh/sshd_config` file
- ○ **D.** On a VirtualCenter 2.5 server in the `/etc/ssh/sshd_config` file

42. You have just installed an ESX Server 3.5 host. What is the default amount of memory allocated to the Service Console?

- ○ **A.** Depends on the hardware used
- ○ **B.** 272MB
- ○ **C.** 722MB
- ○ **D.** 277MB
- ○ **E.** 800MB

43. Your ESX Server 3.5 host physically has two quad-core processors installed in it. You want to license this host on a per processor basis. How many licenses do you need to purchase?

- ○ **A.** 1
- ○ **B.** 2
- ○ **C.** 4
- ○ **D.** 6
- ○ **E.** 8

44. You have three ESX Server 3.5 hosts with four quad-core CPUs in each. Additionally, you want to install VMotion on two of these servers. On a per processor basis, how many licenses do you need to purchase and install to satisfy all licensing requirements?

- ○ **A.** 4
- ○ **B.** 6
- ○ **C.** 8
- ○ **D.** 12
- ○ **E.** 20

45. What is the minimum number of ports an ESX Server 3.5 vSwitch can have?

   ○ **A.** There is no minimum.

   ○ **B.** 4

   ○ **C.** 8

   ○ **D.** 16

   ○ **E.** 32

46. Which of the following statements correctly reflect similarities between a physical switch and a virtual switch? (Choose two.)

   ○ **A.** They both support STP.

   ○ **B.** Just like physical switches can be connected to one another, virtual switches can be connected to one another.

   ○ **C.** They both forward frames to one or more ports.

   ○ **D.** They both have MAC tables that they maintain.

47. You want to provide communication between virtual machines on a single ESX Server 3.5 host. You do not want these machines to have access to other networks. Which type of virtual switch configuration should you use to accomplish this?

   ○ **A.** Loopback Virtual Switch

   ○ **B.** Internal Virtual Switch

   ○ **C.** Single Adapter Virtual Switch

   ○ **D.** Multiadapter Virtual Switch

48. You are configuring a virtual switch policy. Which tab should you select if you want to configure the average bandwidth?

   ○ **A.** General

   ○ **B.** Security

   ○ **C.** Traffic Shaping

   ○ **D.** NIC Teaming

49. You have recently deployed several ESX Server 3.5 hosts. You have applied Update 1 to both ESX hosts. Using these hosts, which of the following is a true statement concerning a Fiber Channel SAN?

    ◯ **A.** Its maximum transmission rate between two nodes is 1.5GB/sec.

    ◯ **B.** Its maximum transmission rate between two nodes is 2MB/sec.

    ◯ **C.** Its maximum transmission rate between two nodes is 4MB/sec.

    ◯ **D.** Its maximum transmission rate between two nodes is 4GB/sec.

50. Which of the following are considered industry accepted topologies for a Fiber Channel SAN? (Choose two.)

    ◯ **A.** Point-to-Point

    ◯ **B.** Multipoint-to-Point

    ◯ **C.** Multipoint-to-Multipoint

    ◯ **D.** Point-to-Multipoint

    ◯ **E.** Arbitrated Loop

    ◯ **F.** Switched Fabric

    ◯ **G.** Mesh Loop

51. You want to install VirtualCenter Server 2.5 in your VI3 environment. You want to experience the fewest number of glitches possible during the installation. Based on VMware's recommendations, which of the following statements should you follow?

    ◯ **A.** Install the Database Server after the VirtualCenter Server.

    ◯ **B.** Install the VirtualCenter Server after the Database Server.

    ◯ **C.** Install the VIC before any other component.

    ◯ **D.** Install the License Server immediately after the VirtualCenter Server is installed.

52. You are creating a cluster in a VI3 environment. Which of the following are correct statements concerning how you can configure the cluster? (Choose three.)

    ◯ **A.** You can enable it to be Low Availability only.

    ◯ **B.** You can enable it to be High Availability only.

    ◯ **C.** You can enable it to be a Distributed Resource Scheduler only.

    ◯ **D.** You can enable it to be both Low Availability and a Distributed Resource Scheduler resource pool.

○ **E.** You can enable it to be both a Low Availability and a High Availability resource pool.

○ **F.** You can enable it to be both a High Availability and a Distributed Resource Scheduler resource pool.

53. Which of the following is *not* a type of port group that can be configured on a virtual switch?

○ **A.** Service Console

○ **B.** Root

○ **C.** VMkernel

○ **D.** Virtual Machine

54. In a VI3 environment, what is a way to quickly generate similarly configured virtual machines?

○ **A.** Copy

○ **B.** Duplicate

○ **C.** Replica

○ **D.** Template

55. You are interested in installing the VMware Converter Enterprise in your VI3 environment. Which of the following will *not* be a good environment for this add-on product?

○ **A.** SuSE Linux Enterprise Server 10 SP1 physical machine

○ **B.** Windows 2000 Server virtual machine

○ **C.** Windows Vista 64-bit virtual machine

○ **D.** Windows Server 2008 32-bit physical machine

56. You are interested in installing the VMware Converter Enterprise in your VI3 environment. Which of the following is *not* a cloning method used by VMware Converter Enterprise?

○ **A.** Cold cloning

○ **B.** Warm cloning

○ **C.** Hot cloning

○ **D.** Remote cloning

○ **E.** Local cloning

57. When you are using VMotion, which is a true statement concerning CPU requirements?

    ○ **A.** VMotion works across CPU vendors.

    ○ **B.** VMotion works across CPU families.

    ○ **C.** VMotion works across CPUs with different multimedia instructions.

    ○ **D.** VMotion works across CPUs with different numbers of cores.

58. Which of the following statements is true concerning the creation of a virtual machine?

    ○ **A.** You can create a VM with a maximum of 2 SCSI adapters.

    ○ **B.** You can create a VM with a maximum of 60 SCSI hard drives.

    ○ **C.** You can create a VM with a maximum of 4 floppy disks.

    ○ **D.** You can create a VM with a maximum of 4 parallel ports.

59. What is another name for vmmemctl in a VI3 environment?

    ○ **A.** SAN Driver

    ○ **B.** DRS Driver

    ○ **C.** Balloon-Driver

    ○ **D.** VMotion Driver

60. You are installing a new Windows Vista VM in your VI3 environment. You want to install VMware Tools after the VM is installed. Which of the following are benefits of installing VMware Tools? (Choose three.)

    ○ **A.** Improved startup performance

    ○ **B.** Improved video capabilities

    ○ **C.** Improved memory management

    ○ **D.** Improved mouse capabilities

61. You want to create a SuSE Linux virtual machine on your ESX Server 3.5 host. What is the maximum number of vCPUs that this VM can be assigned?

    ○ **A.** 1

    ○ **B.** 2

    ○ **C.** 3

    ○ **D.** 4

62. You have chosen to use a RAID 5 solution for your VI3 environment. You have four 1TB drives that you want to use for this configuration. In this configuration, how much practical storage space is available?

○ **A.** 1TB

○ **B.** 2TB

○ **C.** 3TB

○ **D.** 4TB

63. Which of the following features are supported if you decide to implement an NFS storage solution in your VI3 environment? (Choose all that apply.)

○ **A.** Format VMFS

○ **B.** Boot and ESX Server

○ **C.** Raw Device Mapping

○ **D.** VMotion

○ **E.** DRS

○ **F.** HA

64. You begin creating a new alarm in VirtualCenter 2.5. On the Alarm Settings screen on the General tab, which trigger, by default, is given the highest priority?

○ **A.** Red

○ **B.** Yellow

○ **C.** Green

○ **D.** None

65. In the following address, used in a Fiber Channel SAN, what LUN is being accessed?

vmhba0:1:33:2

○ **A.** 0

○ **B.** 1

○ **C.** 2

○ **D.** 33

66. What is another name for the address assigned to the host bus adapter in a Fiber Channel SAN?

- ○ **A.** Fiber Channel Name
- ○ **B.** MAC Address
- ○ **C.** World Wide Name
- ○ **D.** World Wide MAC

67. What are two types of zoning used in a Fiber Channel SAN? (Choose two.)

- ○ **A.** Hard
- ○ **B.** Soft
- ○ **C.** Static
- ○ **D.** Dynamic
- ○ **E.** Defined
- ○ **F.** Undefined

68. What is the maximum number of vSwitches that an ESX Server 3.5 host can have?

- ○ **A.** 32
- ○ **B.** 64
- ○ **C.** 127
- ○ **D.** 255

69. What is the maximum number of LUNs that an ESX Server 3.5 host will process by default when it is powered on?

- ○ **A.** 32
- ○ **B.** 64
- ○ **C.** 128
- ○ **D.** 256

70. You want to create a resource pool in VirtualCenter. By default, which of the following roles have the permissions necessary to accomplish this task? (Choose three.)

○ **A.** Datacenter Administrator

○ **B.** Virtual Machine Administrator

○ **C.** Virtual Machine Power User

○ **D.** Virtual Machine User

○ **E.** Resource Pool Administrator

71. You want to deploy VMotion and HA in your VMware Enterprise Environment. You already have two ESX Server 3.5 hosts deployed. Which licensing model do you need to use to successfully deploy these features?

○ **A.** Network based

○ **B.** Host based

○ **C.** Server based

○ **D.** Directory based

72. What is the maximum number of virtual CPUs per host that an ESX Server 3.5 can have if no updates have been applied?

○ **A.** 32

○ **B.** 64

○ **C.** 128

○ **D.** 256

73. Which HA cluster component on an ESX Server 3.5 host keeps a record of the other hosts in the cluster?

○ **A.** AAM

○ **B.** VMap

○ **C.** vpxa

○ **D.** IQN

74. You are installing ESX Server 3.5. What is the default size assigned to the partition used for a core dump?

- ○ **A.** 5GB
- ○ **B.** 544MB
- ○ **C.** 2GB
- ○ **D.** 100MB

75. What are three reasons why a company would elect to deploy a VI3 solution in their enterprise? (Choose three.)

- ○ **A.** Multiple operating systems can be reliably run on a single server device.
- ○ **B.** Increase server utilization.
- ○ **C.** Decrease server utilization.
- ○ **D.** Multiple machines can be managed from a single point.
- ○ **E.** Hardware requirements are increased by a 10:1 ratio.

13

Answers to Practice Exam 1

1. C
2. A
3. A
4. B, C
5. C
6. D
7. C
8. A
9. C
10. A, C, E
11. B
12. A, D
13. C, D
14. B
15. A
16. C, D
17. A, B
18. A, D

19. B, D
20. D
21. A
22. D
23. D
24. A
25. C, D
26. A
27. D
28. A
29. A
30. C
31. B
32. A
33. C
34. B
35. A, B, C, D
36. B

37. C, D
38. A
39. C, D
40. C
41. C
42. B
43. B
44. E
45. C
46. C, D
47. B
48. C
49. D
50. A, F
51. B
52. B, C, F
53. B
54. D

55. A	**62.** C	**69.** D
56. B	**63.** D, E, F	**70.** A, B, E
57. D	**64.** A	**71.** C
58. B	**65.** D	**72.** C
59. C	**66.** C	**73.** A
60. B, C, D	**67.** A, B	**74.** D
61. D	**68.** C	**75.** A, B, D

Answers to Exam Questions

1. **C.** One of the product features of the VI3 suite is VMotion, which lets you move a virtual machine from one server to another without having to power it off. VMotion is a feature of the ESX Server 3.5 and the VirtualCenter. DRS, the Distributed Resource Scheduler, is a feature of the VI3 suite that provides for the automatic distribution of resources across ESX hosts in a cluster. Virtual machines are migrated from an ESX host that is low on resources to another ESX host that has ample resources. Answer A is incorrect. HA, VMware High Availability, is a feature that enables virtual machines to be automatically restarted during an ESX Server failure. VMs that are on a clustered server that fails are rapidly restarted on another host in the cluster. Answer B is incorrect. VCB, VMware Consolidate Backup, is a feature of the VI3 suite that provides a centralized solution for backing up virtual machines using a centralized proxy server. Answer D is incorrect.

2. **A.** There are a number of default roles created during a VirtualCenter 2.5 installation. These roles provide an administrative way to efficiently assign one or more privileges to a user or group. One of the default roles is a Virtual Machine User. One privilege that a user assigned to the role of Virtual Machine User has by default is Create a Task. The other responses are not default privileges of the Virtual Machine User, so Answers B, C, and D are incorrect. They are default privileges of other VirtualCenter 2.5 roles.

3. **A.** There are several requirements for setting up an HA cluster in a VI3 environment. One of the key requirements is that DNS resolution of all hostnames must be configured. Hosts must be able to resolve other hosts using a configured DNS solution. Hosts cannot have the same IP address or DNS name in a cluster, so Answers B and C are incorrect. Answer D is incorrect because it does not take into account that DNS must be configured for resolution.

4. **B and C.** The ESX Server and the virtual machines that are guests of the server are managed by the Service Console. The Service Console on an ESX Server is the equivalent of a server operating system. Two services provided by the Service Console are

firewall and an Apache Tomcat Web Server. CPU scheduling is managed by the VMkernel, so answer D is incorrect. The VIC, or Virtual Infrastructure Client, allows you to connect to an ESX Server from a Windows station. Answer A is incorrect.

5. **C.** One of the requirements for installing the VirtualCenter 2.5 is a 10/100 Network Adapter. That being said, VMware recommends a gigabit adapter for a VirtualCenter 2.5 implementation. Answers A, B, and D are incorrect because they are not minimum requirements.

6. **D.** Several key ports that are important when configuring a firewall on an ESX Server include port 3260, which controls transmissions from the iSCSI client. Port 22 controls transmission to the SSH client, so Answer A is incorrect. Port 902 controls transmission to the VirtualCenter agent, so Answer B is incorrect. Port 8000 controls incoming transmissions from VMotion, so Answer C is incorrect.

7. **C.** Several key ports that are important when configuring a firewall on an ESX Server include port 27000, which controls transmissions from the ESX Server to the license server. Answers A, B, and D are incorrect because they are controlled by ports other than port 27000.

8. **A.** When creating and configuring a virtual network with vSwitches, you need to understand that ESX Server hosts have some limitations. These include the following:

   ▶ No more than 4096 ports

   ▶ No more than 1016 ports per vSwitch

   ▶ No more than 512 virtual switch port groups

   ▶ No more than 127 vSwitches

   Consequently, answer A is correct and answers B, C, and D are incorrect.

9. **C.** The default size assigned to the /BOOT partition during an ESX Server 3.5 installation is 100MB. Answers A, B, and D are incorrect because they are not the default size assigned.

10. **A, C, E.** Three benefits of using a VCB solution on an enterprise network are entire virtual machines can be backed up, single VMDK files can be backed up, and single guest files can be backed up using VCB. Answers B, D, and F are incorrect because VCB can be used to back up these three, when integrated with third-party solutions.

11. **B.** The two major components of the VI3 suite are the ESX Server and the VirtualCenter. The features that come with the suite are categorized under these two components. One of the features of the ESX Server is Virtual SMP. The other options are features of VirtualCenter and are incorrect. Answers A, C, and D are incorrect.

12. **A, D.** When you are installing an ESX Server 3.5 host, four licensing options are available. They are License Server-Server Based, Host License File-Host Based, Evaluation Mode, and Serial Number, which is actually not a true option of a 3.5 host but rather an ESX Server 3.xi host. There are no options for Network Based or Directory Based licensing of an ESX Server 3.5 host. Answers B and C are incorrect.

13. **C, D.** When a license is purchased for the VI3 suite, it can be built on either a per processor or per instance basis. In the VI3 suite there are no per seat or per server licensing options. Answers A and B are incorrect. A license built on the per processor basis activates a feature based on the number of processors on the host. A license built on the per instance basis activates an instance of a feature no matter how many processors are on the host.

14. **B.** In the VI3 suite, there is a 14-day grace period, by default, should a centralized license server fail, during which all hosts continue to function without interruption. Answers A, C, and D are incorrect because they are not the VI3 grace period as defined by VMware.

15. **A.** In the VI3 suite, a single instance of VirtualCenter 2.5 can manage up to 200 ESX Server 3.5 hosts. Earlier versions of VirtualCenter and the VI suite could handle a maximum of 100 hosts, but with the release of VC 2.5 and the VI3 suite, 200 hosts can be managed. Answers B, C, D, and E are incorrect.

16. **C, D.** In the VI3 suite, a grace period exists during which all hosts continue to function without interruption should a centralized license server fail. Certain features are available during this grace period, and some are available after the grace period if you are not able to restore the license server in the allotted time period. Some features that are available after the grace period, if the license server has not been restored in time, include turning on an ESX Server 3.5 host and deleting a VM from the inventory. Some features that are not available are powering on a VM and VMotioning a VM between two hosts. Answers A and B are incorrect.

17. **A, B.** In the VI3 suite, alarms are used when monitoring resource usage and the state of defined systems. These alarms can alert an administrator to a condition that needs attention. Based on the configuration of the alarm, an automated follow-up action can be initialized. When configuring a virtual machine CPU usage alarm, you can configure two options on the Triggers tab. Because this is a usage alarm, those options are Is Above, or Is Below. Answers C and D are incorrect; they are not options available for a Usage alarm.

18. **A, D.** In the VI3 suite, alarms are used when monitoring resource usage and the state of defined systems. These alarms can alert an administrator to a condition that needs attention. Based on the configuration of the alarm, an automated follow-up action can be initialized. One of the tabs that requires configuration when creating an alarm is the Triggers tab. On this tab, you can define the type of trigger, its conditions, and the thresholds for warning and alert. Tolerance and frequency are configured elsewhere when setting up an alarm. Answers B and C are therefore incorrect.

19. **B, D.** In the VI3 suite, alarms are used when monitoring resource usage and the state of defined systems. These alarms can alert an administrator to a condition that needs attention. Based on the configuration of the alarm, an automated follow-up action can be initialized. When a host is being monitored, such as in this question, a notification email can be sent, a notification trap can be sent, and a script can be run. Answers A and C are incorrect because these are not possible follow-up actions that can be initialized.

20. D. VMware Infrastructure Client, also known as VIC, lets you connect to a VirtualCenter Server or an ESX Server from a Windows workstation. VIC is a 32-bit Windows application. One of the product features of the VI3 suite is VMotion, which lets you move a virtual machine from one server to another without having to power it off. VMotion is a feature of the ESX Server 3.5 and the VirtualCenter. HA, VMware High Availability, is a feature that enables virtual machines to be automatically restarted during an ESX Server failure. VMs that are on a clustered server that fails are rapidly restarted on another host in the cluster. VCB, VMware Consolidate Backup, is a feature of the VI3 suite that provides a centralized solution for backing up virtual machines using a centralized proxy server. Answers A, B, and C are incorrect.

21. A. A number of default roles are used to secure an ESX Server 3.5 host. These roles provide an administrative way to efficiently assign one or more privileges to a user or group. The default roles available on a host's Service Console are Administrator, No Access, and Read-only. There is no Read-Write role available for an ESX Server 3.5 host. A custom role can be created, but one is not available by default. Answers B, C, and D are default roles and are therefore incorrect.

22. D. The maximum number of ESX Server 3.5 hosts that can be present in a cluster is 32. Answers A, B, and C are incorrect because they do not reflect the correct maximum as documented by VMware.

23. D. In the VI3 suite, alarms are used when monitoring resource usage and the state of defined systems. These alarms can alert an administrator to a condition that needs attention. Based on the configuration of the alarm, an automated follow-up action can be initialized. One of the first configuration steps is to select the type of alarm you are creating. This is done on the General tab. The two options are Monitor a Host for ESX Server 3.5 Hosts and Monitor a Virtual Machine. The correct response is D. Answers A, B, and C are incorrect because they are not options on this tab.

24. A. A resource pool in a VI3 environment is a container created in Hosts and Clusters view used to limit the host CPU and memory utilization for a group of virtual machines. Answers B, C, and D are not the correct definition of a resource pool in a VI3 environment.

25. C, D. A resource pool in a VI3 environment is a container created in Hosts and Clusters view used to limit the host CPU and memory utilization for a group of virtual machines. The attributes of a resource pool that can be configured are Shares, Reservations, Expandable reservations, and Limits. Answers A and B are not configurable attributes of a resource pool.

26. A. The only user who has full permissions to a newly installed ESX Server 3.5 host is the root user. However, when you add this host to VirtualCenter 2.5, an additional user account is created on the host and is made a member of the Administrator role on the host. This user is the vpxuser account. This user account provides the VirtualCenter with access to the ESX host. Answers B, C, and D are incorrect; they are not the account created on an ESX host when it joins a VirtualCenter.

27. **D.** Roles provide an administrative way to efficiently assign one or more privileges to a user or group. When a user is assigned to a role higher in the hierarchy, the permissions he or she receives through the role flow down to objects lower in the hierarchy. Some call this inheritance. If you do not want a user to have permissions to an object lower down in the hierarchy, you can assign the user to another role at that object. In this question, the solution is to assign Alex to the No Access role at the Vista VM. She will keep her permissions above this VM but have no permission at this VM. Answers A, B, and C do not provide a solution that is workable in this situation.

28. **A.** To access the Web Access interface on a VirtualCenter Server, you need a Windows or Linux computer, an IP address, and a Web browser. The required Web browsers are IE 6.0 or later on a Windows computer, Netscape Navigator 7.0 or later, Mozilla 1.x or later, and Firefox 1.0.7 or later. The only browser in this question that matches one of these browsers is A. Answers B, C, and D are incorrect because they do not satisfy the requirements.

29. **A.** Three ESX Server 3.5 editions are available: Enterprise, Standard, and Foundation. The VMotion feature is available only on the Enterprise edition. Answers B, C, D, and E are incorrect because they do not correctly represent the editions on which VMotion is available.

30. **C.** The authentication protocol used by iSCSI in a VI3 environment is the CHAP protocol—the Challenge Handshake Authentication Protocol. This protocol is used by iSCSI initiators and targets. The other protocols are not used for authentication by iSCSI in a VI3 environment. Answers A, B, and D are therefore incorrect.

31. **B.** In the VI3 suite of products, the ESX Server 3.5 provides the virtualization layer on which virtual machines run. DRS, the Distributed Resource Scheduler, is a feature of the VI3 suite that provides for the automatic distribution of resources across ESX hosts in a cluster. Virtual machines are migrated from an ESX host that is low on resources to another ESX host that has ample resources. Answer A is incorrect. VC, the VirtualCenter 2.5, is a Windows-based management tool for managing all enterprise ESX Servers. Answer C is incorrect. SMP, VMware's Virtual Symmetric Multi-Processing, is a VMware solution for providing multiple virtual CPUs to virtual machines. Answer D is incorrect.

32. **A.** The correct representation of an iSCSI node ID generically is iqn.year-month.<domain name reversed>:<alternate name>. When you use the date supplied in the question, the correct ID is iqn.2008-08.com.pearson:VM1A. The other choices do not follow the naming schema used for an iSCSI node ID. Therefore, Answers B, C, and D are incorrect.

33. **C.** When creating and configuring a new virtual machine in a VI3 enterprise, you must know both the hardware requirements for a VM and the maximum hardware that you can configure for a VM. If you are using a SCSI disk(s) for a VM, the maximum disk space allowed for a virtual hard drive is 2TB. Answers A, B, and D are incorrect because they do not reflect the correct maximum allowed disk space.

34. B. When a virtual machine is created, a number of files are created that serve specific purposes. They include the file that stores virtual hard disk information and has a .vmdk extension. The other extensions listed represent files that store virtual hard disk information for the VM. Answers A, C, and D are incorrect.

35. A, B, C, D. When a license is purchased for the VI3 suite, it can be built on either a per processor or per instance basis. A license built on the per processor basis activates a feature based on the number of processors on the host. A license built on the per instance basis activates an instance of a feature no matter how many processors are on the host. VI3 products available on a per processor basis are the ESX Server, VirtualCenter Agent, VMotion, Storage VMotion, Consolidate Backup, DRS, HA, and DPM. All choices are correct.

36. B. RAID, Redundant Array of Independent (Inexpensive) Disks, is often used in a VI3 environment as the platform from which LUNs are defined. A number of RAID levels are common. One of the most common is RAID 1, which provides disk mirroring (mirrored arrays) and disk duplexing, a type of fault tolerance. The other answers A, C, and D do not provide disk mirroring or duplexing.

37. C, D. A logical arrangement of disk space that is allocated from multiple physical disks is a LUN, a Logical Unit Number. VMware uses two schemes: an adaptive scheme and a predictive scheme. VMware does not use the terms *dynamic* or *static* for defining a LUN design. Answers A and B are incorrect.

38. A. A VCB Proxy used in a VI3 environment as part of the backup solution is run on a Windows physical machine. Answers B, C, and D are not platforms compatible with the VCB Proxy and are therefore incorrect.

39. C, D. When the Performance tab is selected for a host in VirtualCenter 2.5, the resources that you can select are CPU, Disk Space, Memory, Network, and System. There are no options for Ports or Users. Answers A and B are incorrect.

40. C. When an ESX Server 3.5 host is initially installed, root has full access to the server using VIC but has no access to the server using SSH. For security reasons, SSH access is denied to root. This access can be changed but should be done so under advisement because of the security issues it raises. Answers A, B, D, and E are incorrect statements of fact.

41. C. The PermitRootLogin is found on an ESX Server 3.5 host in the /etc/ssh/sshd_config file. The other answers—A, B, and D—are incorrect because they do not correctly point to the location where you can find the PermitRootLogin parameter.

42. B. The default amount of memory allocated to the Service Console when an ESX Server 3.5 host is installed is 272MB. Answers A, C, and D are incorrect; they do not reflect the default memory allocated to the Service Console.

43. B. A license built on the per processor basis activates a feature based on the number of processors on the host. According to VMware, a dual-core or quad-core processor counts as a single processor despite the fact that multiple processing units exist on each of these chips. Based on that fact, because two processors are installed, two licenses are required. Answers A, C, D, and E are incorrect because they do not reflect the needed number of licenses.

44. **E.** A license built on the per processor basis activates a feature based on the number of processors on the host. According to VMware, a dual-core or quad-core processor counts as a single processor despite the fact that multiple processing units exist on each of these chips. In this question, you need 12 licenses just for the ESX Servers, and you need 8 licenses for the installation of VMotion on two of the servers. The total number of licenses required is 20. Answers A, B, C, and D are incorrect.

45. **C.** The minimum number of ports that an ESX Server 3.5 vSwitch can have is eight. The other responses are not correct. Answers A, B, D, and E are not representative of the minimum number of ports that a vSwitch has.

46. **C, D.** Physical switches and virtual switches have some characteristics that are similar. For example, they both forward frames to one or more ports, and they both have MAC tables that they maintain. They both do not support STP; you cannot connect vSwitches to one another. Therefore, Answers A and B are incorrect.

47. **B.** In a VI3 environment, the three types of virtual switches are internal, single adapter, and multi-adapter types. An internal virtual switch provides communication between virtual machines on a single ESX Server 3.5 host without access to other external networks. There are no loopback switches. Answers A, C, and D are incorrect because they do not accomplish what is called for in the question.

48. **C.** When you are configuring a virtual switch policy, four tabs are available: General, Security, Traffic Shaping, and NIC Teaming. Average Bandwidth is configured on the Traffic Shaping tab. Answers A, B, and D are incorrect because average bandwidth is not configured on these tabs.

49. **D.** Fiber Channel SANs are typically rated by their transmission rate. Currently, the highest throughput Fiber Channel SAN is 4GB/sec if you are using ESX Server 3.5 Hosts with Update 1 applied. If you have applied Update 2, the throughput, according to VMware, goes up to 8GB/sec. Answers A, B, and C are incorrect because they do not reflect the maximum data transmission rate between two nodes.

50. **A, F.** Two industry-accepted topologies for a Fiber Channel SAN are Point-to-Point and Switched Fabric. The other responses are not Fiber Channel topologies or are not supported by VMware. Answers B, C, D, E, and G are incorrect.

51. **B.** When you are doing an installation of VirtualCenter 2.5 in an enterprise, the correct order of component installation is critical if you want to avoid as many issues as possible. The order recommended by VMware is 1-Database Server, 2-License Server, 3-VC Server, and finally 4-VIC. Based on this order, answer B is correct. The VC Server should be installed after the Database Server is installed. Answers A, C, and D are incorrect because they do not reflect an order recommended by VMware.

52. B, C, and F. When you create a cluster, you can enable it to be High Availability only, Distributed Resource Scheduler only, or both High Availability and Distributed Resource Scheduler. There is no Low Availability option in a VI3 environment. Answers A, D, and E are incorrect.

53. B. Three types of port groups can be configured on a virtual switch in a VI3 environment. They are Service Console, VMkernel, and virtual machine. There is no Root port group on a vSwitch. Answers A, C, and D are incorrect because they are configurable port groups.

54. D. In a VI3 environment, the new and improved way to provision or generate similarly configured virtual machines is to use a template. In some environments, you do this with images, copies, and duplicates, but in VI3, you do this with templates. Answers A, B, and C are incorrect.

55. A. The VMware Converter Enterprise is a Windows application. It does not run on Linux platform. It can run on a 32-bit or 64-bit Windows OS as a physical machine or as a virtual machine. This includes Windows 2000 Server and Windows Server 2008. Answers B, C, and D are incorrect because this is not a Windows platform.

56. B. The VMware Converter Enterprise is a Windows application capable of cloning a physical or virtual disk to a new virtual disk. Converter Enterprise can perform hot cloning, cold cloning, remote cloning, and local cloning. It does not perform warm cloning. Answer B is incorrect.

57. D. A main consideration for using VMotion in a VI3 environment is the CPUs that are in the source and destination hosts. The CPUs in the source and destination hosts must be from the same vendor and family. Also, the CPUs must not have different multimedia instructions. There can be a different number of cores and cache sizes. Answers A, B, and C are incorrect because they violate the CPU requirements for VMotion.

58. B. When creating and configuring a new virtual machine in a VI3 enterprise, you must know both the hardware requirements for a VM and the maximum hardware that you can configure for a VM. A virtual machine in this environment can have a maximum of 4 parallel ports, 4 SCSI adapters with up to 15 devices on each, for a total of 60 devices (hard drives), 2 floppy drives, and 4 serial ports. Answers A, C, and D are incorrect because they exceed the defined maximums.

59. C. Another name for vmmemctl in a VI3 environment is the balloon-driver. Its function is to dynamically reclaim memory in VMs when an ESX system is experiencing physical memory strain. Based on memory needs, the balloon-driver can be inflated or deflated. Answers A, B, and D are not available options.

60. B, C, and D. VMware Tools is a software add-on that is installed after a VM's operating system has been installed and is up and running. VMware Tools improves a VM's operability and performance. Some of the benefits of VMware Tools are it improves mouse performance, video capability, and memory management. It does not improve startup performance because the guest OS has to be up and running for the VMware Tools to be active. Answer A is incorrect.

61. D. When creating and configuring a new virtual machine in a VI3 enterprise, you must know both the hardware requirements for a VM and the maximum hardware that you can configure for a VM. A virtual machine in this environment can have a maximum of four CPUs. A VM in the VI3 environment can have one, two, or four vCPUs. Answers A, B, and C are incorrect because they do not correctly reflect the correct number of vCPUs that a VM can have.

62. C. RAID, Redundant Array of Independent (Inexpensive) Disks, is often used in a VI3 environment as the platform from which LUNs are defined. A number of RAID levels are common. One of the most common is RAID 5, which provides Disk Striping with parity. In a RAID 5 environment, you typically have three or more drives that are in the array. In this environment, data is written across all drives as is parity data. In essence, the practical storage capacity of a RAID 5 array is the equivalent of N-1 drives. In this question, that means you have 3TB of practical storage. The equivalent of one drive is written as parity across all drives in the array. Answers A, B, and D are incorrect because they do not accurately reflect the practical storage capacity.

63. D, E, F. In a VI3 suite, an NFS storage solution supports DRS, HA, and VMotion. It does not support Raw Device Mapping, formatting VMFS, or booting an ESX Server. Answers A, B, and C are therefore incorrect.

64. A. In the VI3 suite, alarms are used when monitoring resource usage and the state of defined systems. These alarms can alert an administrator to a condition that needs attention. Based on the configuration of the alarm, an automated follow-up action can be initialized. When you are defining the type of alarm, an available option is to define the trigger priority, the order in which alarms are triggered. Alerts are red, warnings are yellow, and safe/normal operating state is green. The trigger priority can either be defined as red first or green first. The default setting is red, or alerts have top priority. Answers B, C, and D are incorrect because they do not reflect the default trigger priority setting.

65. D. In the address vmhba0:1:33:2, host bus adapter 0 is accessing partition 2 on LUN 33 using storage processor 1. Answers A, B, and C are incorrect.

66. C. Another name for the address assigned to the host bus adapter in a Fiber Channel SAN is the WWN, or World Wide Name. It is also referred to as the World Wide Port Name. Its function is similar to the MAC address assigned to a router port or network adapter. Answers A, B, and D are incorrect.

67. A, B. In a Fiber Channel SAN, zoning is used to create a logical group of physical devices to facilitate communication between them. Two main types of zoning are used in a Fiber Channel SAN: hard and soft. Answers C, D, E, and F are incorrect because they are not types of zones used in an FC SAN.

68. C. An ESX Server 3.5 host can have a maximum of 127 vSwitches. Answers A, B, and D are incorrect. They do not correctly reflect the maximum number of vSwitches that can be configured on an ESX Server 3.5 host.

69. D. When an ESX Server 3.5 host is powered on, it, by default, processes the first 256 LUNs that are present and to which it is given access. Answers A, B, and C are not correct.

70. A, B, E. In a default installation of VirtualCenter 2.5, numerous roles are created automatically. Each role has a default set of defined permissions. Based on the task required, some of these roles can accomplish the task, whereas others cannot. The roles that have the default permissions to create a resource pool are the Datacenter Administrator, Virtual Machine Administrator, and a Resource Pool Administrator. Answers C and D are incorrect; they do not have necessary permissions to create a resource pool.

71. C. When you are installing an ESX Server 3.5 host, four licensing options are available. They are License Server-Server Based, Host License File-Host Based, Evaluation Mode, and Serial Number, which is actually not a true option of a 3.5 host but rather an ESX Server 3.xi host. A Host Based License works great for a small network environment. For enterprises, VMware recommends a Server Based License Model. If you want to deploy enterprise features such as HA, DRS, and VMotion, you need to use the Server Based License Model, which uses a centralized license server to house licenses. Answers A, B, and D are incorrect for this scenario. Answers A and D are not even possible choices; they are choices used in security deployments of other products.

72. C. When you are planning an ESX Server 3.5 installation and deployment, it is important to know some of the maximums that you can configure. One important one is the maximum number of virtual CPUs you can have per host. The maximum is 128 if no updates have been applied to the host. If Update 2 has been applied, the maximum is 192. Answer C is correct, and answers A, B, and D are incorrect.

73. A. When an ESX host is added to an HA cluster, several components are installed on the host. They include the AAM (Automated Availability Manager), VMap, and the vpxa. AAM is the engine for HA, and the vpxa service manages components of the HA cluster. Communication between the AAM and vpxa is managed by VMap. The AAM keeps a record of the other hosts in the cluster. Answers B and C are incorrect. Answer D is a term associated with iSCSI addressing.

74. D. The default size assigned to the partition used for a core dump, the vmkcore partition, during an ESX Server 3.5 installation is 100MB. Answers A, B, and C are incorrect because they are not the default size assigned.

75. A, B, D. There are a host of benefits for deploying a VI3 enterprise solution that can be delineated, depending on which VMware reference you cite. Three benefits are multiple operating systems can be reliably run on a single server device; server utilization will be increased; and multiple machines, including virtual machines, can be centrally managed. Answers C and E are not benefits of a VI3 solution.

14

Practice Exam 2

Hints and Pointers

Other than years of hands-on experience, the best way to prepare for the VMware VCP-310 test is to take practice (or sample) exams. VMware also requires all VCP candidates to take an authorized, instructor-led course leading up to the exam. According to VMware:

> The accepted courses are: "Install and Configure"; "Deploy, Secure, and Analyze"; and "Fast Track". If you are a current VCP, there are no course prerequisites.

It is critical that you learn to approach VMware's certification tests thinking the way VMware wants you to. If you have taken hundreds of certification tests from other vendors, you may have a tendency to answer the way other vendors deem correct. That might or might not be correct on a VMware exam. Therefore, take these practice tests and start thinking like a VMware Certified Professional.

This book contains two sample tests, in addition to the practice questions provided at the end of each chapter. You can find the answers and explanations to these questions following this practice exam. These practice questions are simply that—practice questions to get you ready for the form, fashion, and types of questions you will encounter on the exam. None are live exam questions.

After you go through these practice questions a few times, you should have a good idea what topics you need to brush up on. There are other practice tests on the market, which may or may not help you. The purpose of the practice questions in this book is to reinforce important, testable concepts, facts, and objectives. The answers and explanations should guide you in filling in voids in your current knowledge base. By all means, supplement your study using the content and Exam Alerts in this book with a thorough review of the VMware Authorized Courseware and the online documents available on the VMware website.

Most of the questions are single-answer or multiple-answer multiple-choice questions with a few accompanied by exhibits. As you prepare, you should get at least 85% of the answers correct on each practice exam before moving on. Remember, you can, with proper preparation, successfully pass the VCP-310 exam. And this Exam Cram will help you.

I encourage you, as you prepare, to check the following websites for updates to the exam and the exam process:

▶ http://mylearn.vmware.com/portals/certification/faqs.cfm?ui=www#1871

▶ http://mylearn1.vmware.com/portals/certification/

▶ http://mylearn.vmware.com/lcms/mL_faq/1714/VCP3.5Blueprint.PDF

All the best in your journey to the VCP!

Practice Exam 2

1. You have connected to the VirtualCenter Server to perform a management task on one of your ESX Servers. You need to identify the Service Console port on this server. What label is given to this port in VirtualCenter interface?

   ○ **A.** vswif0

   ○ **B.** vSwitch

   ○ **C.** VMotion

   ○ **D.** VMkernel

2. You are installing an ESX Server 3.5. What is the default size assigned to the swap partition?

   ○ **A.** 100MB

   ○ **B.** Varies

   ○ **C.** 2000MB

   ○ **D.** 544MB

3. On an ESX Server 3.5, which partition is written to when the system crashes?

   ○ **A.** /

   ○ **B.** Swap

   ○ **C.** VMFS3

   ○ **D.** vmkcore

4. You want to remove an alarm in VirtualCenter. By default, which of the following roles have the permissions necessary to accomplish this task? (Choose three.)

- ○ **A.** Datacenter Administrator
- ○ **B.** Virtual Machine Administrator
- ○ **C.** Virtual Machine Power User
- ○ **D.** Virtual Machine User
- ○ **E.** Resource Pool Administrator

5. Which of the following VirtualCenter 2.5 tasks does a Resource Pool Administrator have permissions to do by default?

- ○ **A.** Modify a Role
- ○ **B.** Create a Resource Pool
- ○ **C.** Create a Cluster
- ○ **D.** Create a Virtual Machine

6. You have opted to add an ESX Server 3.5 host to your current HA cluster. Which of the following is installed on this host when you bring it into the cluster? (Choose two.)

- ○ **A.** VMap
- ○ **B.** vpxa
- ○ **C.** esxtop
- ○ **D.** IQN

7. In a VI3 environment, two virtual machines are contending for available resources. What determines how much resource will be available to each VM?

- ○ **A.** DTP
- ○ **B.** Traffic shaping
- ○ **C.** Resource pool
- ○ **D.** Resource share

8. Which of the following statements are true regarding the installation of VMware's Web Access utility? (Choose two.)

   ○ **A.** Web Access is automatically installed when ESX Server is installed.

   ○ **B.** Web Access is an optional feature when ESX Server is installed.

   ○ **C.** On a VirtualCenter Server, Web Access is automatically installed when VirtualCenter is installed.

   ○ **D.** On a VirtualCenter Server, Web Access can be installed from the VirtualCenter Server Windows setup package.

9. You have licensed your ESX Server 3.5 host using a Host Based Licensing model. The license file is going to be configured through the VIC. You need to locate the license file in the file system hierarchy. Where is this file located?

   ○ **A.** `/etc/vmware/vmware.lic`

   ○ **B.** `/etc/vmware.lic`

   ○ **C.** `c:\vmware\vmware.lic`

   ○ **D.** `c:\vmware.lic`

10. Your VI3 enterprise environment uses a centralized license server. You have three ESX Server 3.5 hosts. The license server fails and you are not able to restore it within the default grace period. Which features are not available after the grace period? (Choose two.)

   ○ **A.** Relaunching virtual machines that are located on a failed host on a DRS cluster

   ○ **B.** Launching a virtual machine

   ○ **C.** Turning on an ESX Server 3.5 host

   ○ **D.** Deleting a virtual machine

11. You have installed a single instance of VirtualCenter 2.5 in your enterprise. According to VMware, what is the maximum number of virtual machines that you can manage with this configuration?

   ○ **A.** 200

   ○ **B.** 2,000

   ○ **C.** 20,000

   ○ **D.** 200,000

12. You need to create a virtual machine using Windows Server 2003. Of the following requirements for this VM, which one will prevent the installation from being successful?

4GB RAM

4 NICS

4 DVD-ROM drives

4 processors

- ○ **A.** 4GB RAM
- ○ **B.** 4 NICS
- ○ **C.** 4 DVD-ROM drives
- ○ **D.** 4 processors

13. In VirtualCenter 2.5, you want to create a new alarm. What are the two types of alarms that you can create? (Choose two.)

- ○ **A.** Host based
- ○ **B.** Virtual machine based
- ○ **C.** Server based
- ○ **D.** Network based

14. You are configuring a new virtual machine state alarm. On the Triggers tab in VirtualCenter 2.5, what are the two possible conditions that this trigger type can have?

- ○ **A.** Is Above
- ○ **B.** Is Below
- ○ **C.** Is Equal To
- ○ **D.** Is Not Equal To

15. In VirtualCenter 2.5, you are configuring an alarm for a Windows XP SP2 virtual machine. This type of alarm can generate which two actions? (Choose two.)

- ○ **A.** Power off the virtual machine
- ○ **B.** Reduce RAM usage
- ○ **C.** Send a notification trap
- ○ **D.** Reduce CPU usage

16. Which of the following is a limitation of an ESX Server 3.5 host?

    ○ **A.** 1016 ports

    ○ **B.** 1016 vSwitches

    ○ **C.** 1016 virtual switch port groups

    ○ **D.** 1016 ports per vSwitch

17. Which of the following are built-in Service Console roles? (Choose two.)

    ○ **A.** No Access

    ○ **B.** Read-Only

    ○ **C.** Virtual Machine Administrator

    ○ **D.** Virtual Machine User

18. Which of the following databases is supported by VirtualCenter 2.5?

    ○ **A.** Oracle 8

    ○ **B.** Windows SQL Server 2000

    ○ **C.** Windows SQL Server 2005

    ○ **D.** Windows SQL Server 2005 Enterprise SP1

19. You want to create a Windows Server 2003 virtual machine. Which of the following configurations will prevent you from creating this VM?

    ○ **A.** 1 CPU

    ○ **B.** 2 CPUs

    ○ **C.** 3 CPUs

    ○ **D.** 4 CPUs

20. You have installed a new standalone ESX Server 3.5 host. Who is the only user that exists on this new server who has full permissions to administer it?

    ○ **A.** Administrator

    ○ **B.** Admin

    ○ **C.** The user who installed the server

    ○ **D.** The root user

21. You are installing the ESX Server 3.5. During the installation, which component is installed and is considered the ESX Server operating system?

   ○ **A.** Service Console

   ○ **B.** VC

   ○ **C.** VIC

   ○ **D.** SMP

22. Which of the following are functions of the VMkernel on an ESX Server 3.5? (Choose two.)

   ○ **A.** Convert a physical machine to a virtual machine

   ○ **B.** CPU scheduling

   ○ **C.** SSH

   ○ **D.** Manage memory

23. You have created a Windows XP SP2 virtual machine. Which file should you check if you want to view the virtual machine configuration file?

   ○ **A.** .vmx

   ○ **B.** .vmdk

   ○ **C.** .vswp

   ○ **D.** .vmsd

24. You have created a Windows XP SP2 virtual machine. You want to log in to this VM after booting. You need to send the Alt+Ctrl+Del keystroke combination to this VM to initiate the process. This does not work as you expected. You do not want to use a menu option. Which of the following keystroke combinations should you use to accomplish this in the VM?

   ○ **A.** Alt+Esc

   ○ **B.** Ctrl+Esc

   ○ **C.** Shift+Ctrl+Del

   ○ **D.** Alt+Ctrl+Ins

25. Which RAID level offers no fault tolerance?

   ○ **A.** RAID 0

   ○ **B.** RAID 1

   ○ **C.** RAID 4

   ○ **D.** RAID 5

26. On your VI3 enterprise environment, your license server has experienced a major failure. Within the available grace period, which of the following tasks are classified as restricted operations by VMware? (Choose two.)

   ○ **A.** Running a virtual machine

   ○ **B.** Connecting to an ESX Server 3.5 host

   ○ **C.** Removing a license key

   ○ **D.** Adding an ESX Server 3.5 host

27. You have chosen to use RAID 1 for your VI3 environment. You want to use two 1TB drives for this configuration. In this configuration, how much practical storage space is available?

   ○ **A.** 500MB

   ○ **B.** 1TB

   ○ **C.** 2TB

   ○ **D.** 4TB

28. What is a logical arrangement of disk space that is allocated from multiple physical disks?

   ○ **A.** LUN

   ○ **B.** DAS

   ○ **C.** NAS

   ○ **D.** SAN

29. Which of the following is considered a Virtual Center component in the VI3 Suite?

   ○ **A.** Virtual SMP

   ○ **B.** VCB

   ○ **C.** ESX Server

   ○ **D.** HA

30. You have chosen to implement the VMware Adaptive Scheme for LUN design. What are the benefits of using this method when designing your LUN strategy? (Choose two.)

   ○ **A.** There is less need for an SAN Administrator.

   ○ **B.** Microsoft clusters are supported.

   ○ **C.** Snapshot management is facilitated.

   ○ **D.** Share allocation is more flexible.

31. You want to deploy VirtualCenter 2.5 in your network. Which of the following platforms meets the minimum requirements for this deployment?

   ○ **A.** Windows XP Home

   ○ **B.** Windows 2000 Server SP2

   ○ **C.** SuSE Linux Enterprise Server 10 SP1

   ○ **D.** Windows Server 2003 SP1

32. You want to create a performance graph for your ESX Server 3.5 host. When you select the Performance tab, what is shown in the default view?

   ○ **A.** CPU consumption

   ○ **B.** Disk space usage

   ○ **C.** RAM usage

   ○ **D.** Network utilization

33. When viewed from the Service Console, what is the default number of ports created with a virtual switch?

   ○ **A.** 16

   ○ **B.** 32

   ○ **C.** 48

   ○ **D.** 64

34. You have just installed an ESX Server 3.5 host. What is the maximum amount of memory you can allocate to the Service Console?

- ○ **A.** There is no maximum.
- ○ **B.** 277MB
- ○ **C.** 272MB
- ○ **D.** 800MB
- ○ **E.** 1GB
- ○ **F.** 2TB

35. You have purchased eight ESX Server licenses. Based on a per processor model, which of the following do you have ample licenses for? (Choose all that apply.)

- ○ **A.** 8 ESX Server 3.5 hosts each with 2 quad-core processors
- ○ **B.** 4 ESX Server 3.5 hosts each with 2 single-core processors
- ○ **C.** 2 ESX Server 3.5 hosts each with 4 single-core processors
- ○ **D.** 1 ESX Server 3.5 host with 2 quad-core processors

36. Your ESX Server 3.5 host is licensed using the Server Based Licensing Model. The license file is going to be configured through the VIC. You need to locate the license file in the file system hierarchy. Where is this file located?

- ○ **A.** On the host at `/etc/vmware/vmware.lic`
- ○ **B.** On the host at `C:\Program Files\VMWare\vmware.lic`
- ○ **C.** On the license server at `/etc/vmware/vmware.lic`
- ○ **D.** On the license server at `C:\Program Files\VMWare\VMWare License Server\Licenses`

37. Which of the following is *not* a type of virtual switch in a VI3 environment?

- ○ **A.** Loopback Virtual Switch
- ○ **B.** Internal Virtual Switch
- ○ **C.** Single Adapter Virtual Switch
- ○ **D.** Multiadapter Virtual Switch

38. Which type of virtual switch configuration should you deploy in a VI3 environment if you want NIC teaming?

- ○ **A.** Internal Virtual Switches only

- ○ **B.** Internal Virtual Switches and Single Adapter Virtual Switches

- ○ **C.** Single Adapter Virtual Switches only

- ○ **D.** Multiadapter Virtual Switches only

39. You are configuring a NIC team by using the NIC Teaming tab. Which of the following is a true statement?

- ○ **A.** By default, the NIC team is configured to use a Rolling Failover policy of NO.

- ○ **B.** By default, the NIC team is configured to use a Rolling Failover policy of YES.

- ○ **C.** By default, the NIC team is configured to use a Load Balancing policy of NO.

- ○ **D.** By default, the NIC team is configured to use a Load Balancing policy of YES.

40. One of your coworkers wants to install the VIC to access an ESX Server 3.5. On which of the following platforms can he successfully install VIC?

- ○ **A.** 32-bit Windows XP

- ○ **B.** 64-bit Windows Vista

- ○ **C.** SLED 10

- ○ **D.** 32-bit Ubuntu 8.04

41. You are configuring the Service Console firewall. Which port controls authentication traffic from the VirtualCenter to an ESX Server 3.5?

- ○ **A.** 902

- ○ **B.** 22

- ○ **C.** 443

- ○ **D.** 27000

42. You are configuring an ESX Server 3.5 host. What is the maximum number of vSwitches that you can configure on this host?

○ **A.** 64

○ **B.** 127

○ **C.** 255

○ **D.** 1016

43. You are configuring a virtual network using the VI3 product suite. One of the virtual machines that you need to configure is Windows XP SP2. This virtual machine will be a guest on an ESX Server 3.5. VMware Tools will be installed. The high performance network interface that you need to configure inside this guest is known as a

_____.

○ **A.** NIC team

○ **B.** vmxnet adapter

○ **C.** virtual switch

○ **D.** VMkernel port

44. Which of the following is *not* a storage option available to an ESX Server 3.5 host in a VI3 environment?

○ **A.** Removable Disk Storage

○ **B.** Fiber Channel Storage

○ **C.** iSCSI Storage

○ **D.** Network Attached Storage

○ **E.** Local Storage

45. You are trying to select the best, most efficient, and reliable storage area network solution for your VI3 environment. Based on your needs, which solution should you select?

○ **A.** iSCSI

○ **B.** NAS

○ **C.** Fiber Channel

○ **D.** Local

46. Which of the following VI3 products is licensed using the per instance method?

◯ **A.** Consolidated Backup

◯ **B.** VirtualCenter

◯ **C.** ESX Server 3.5 Host

◯ **D.** VirtualCenter Agent

47. The process of hiding specific LUNs from ESX Server 3.5 hosts is called

_____.

◯ **A.** LUN masking

◯ **B.** LUN zoning

◯ **C.** LUN defense

◯ **D.** LUN abatement

48. Which of the following statements is true in relationship to a Fiber Channel SAN in a VI3 environment?

◯ **A.** ESX Server 3.5 supports a maximum of 2 host bus adapters per system and a maximum of 15 devices or targets per HBA.

◯ **B.** ESX Server 3.5 supports a maximum of 4 host bus adapters per system and a maximum of 15 devices or targets per HBA.

◯ **C.** ESX Server 3.5 supports a maximum of 8 host bus adapters per system and a maximum of 15 devices or targets per HBA.

◯ **D.** ESX Server 3.5 supports a maximum of 16 host bus adapters per system and a maximum of 15 devices or targets per HBA.

49. In your VI3 environment, you have established a SAN using multipathing. What are the two types of multipathing available in this environment? (Choose two.)

◯ **A.** Fixed

◯ **B.** Flexible

◯ **C.** MRU

◯ **D.** LRU

50. You have downloaded a copy of ESX Server 3.5 for evaluation. You are not sure that it will meet your needs, so you do not purchase a license file for the installation. How long of an evaluation period do you have according to the VMware Licensing Agreement before you have to purchase a full license?

   ○ **A.** 30 days

   ○ **B.** 60 days

   ○ **C.** 90 days

   ○ **D.** 120 days

51. You are preparing to do an installation of VirtualCenter 2.5 in your enterprise. You want to avoid as many issues as possible. For you to accomplish this, which of the following correctly reflects the order in which you should install the components?

   ○ **A.** 1-VIC, 2-License Server, 3-VC Server, 4-Database Server

   ○ **B.** 1-VC Server, 2-VIC, 3-License Server, 4-Database Server

   ○ **C.** 1-License Server, 2-VIC, 3-Database Server, 4-VC Server

   ○ **D.** 1-Database Server, 2-License Server, 3-VC Server, 4-VIC

52. What is the maximum number of hosts that can be supported by a resource pool?

   ○ **A.** 32

   ○ **B.** 64

   ○ **C.** 128

   ○ **D.** Unlimited

53. By default, the balloon driver on an ESX system is configured to consume _____ of the memory of a virtual machine.

   ○ **A.** 25%

   ○ **B.** 50%

   ○ **C.** 65%

   ○ **D.** 75%

   ○ **E.** 85%

54. You have installed VirtualCenter 2.5 in your VI3 environment. You want to view the system logs. Which file holds the system logs?

○ **A.** vpxd-index

○ **B.** vpxd-logs

○ **C.** system-logs

○ **D.** system-events

55. In VI3, what are two ways to create a template? (Choose two.)

○ **A.** Copy to a Template

○ **B.** Clone to a Template

○ **C.** Export to a Template

○ **D.** Convert to a Template

56. You decide to create an alarm in VirtualCenter 2.5. When you try to configure the alarm, you select the Triggers tab. On that tab, you have to select the type of trigger this alarm will monitor. Which of the following is a type of trigger found on this tab? (Choose two.)

○ **A.** State

○ **B.** Dynamic

○ **C.** Usage

○ **D.** Static

57. You are considering using VMware Converter Enterprise. What can you do with Converter Enterprise? (Choose two.)

○ **A.** Convert a physical machine to a virtual machine

○ **B.** Convert a virtual machine to a physical machine

○ **C.** Move a VM from one host to another

○ **D.** Export an ESX VM to another format

58. You are considering using VMware Converter Enterprise. What do you need to have in place to accomplish this? (Choose three.)

○ **A.** Server

○ **B.** Agent

○ **C.** Client plug-in

○ **D.** 128GB RAM

59. Which of the following is a prerequisite for the source and destination hosts if you are going to use VMotion?

- ○ **A.** Access to the same virtual networks
- ○ **B.** 10/100 network
- ○ **C.** Physical switches that are labeled the same
- ○ **D.** Compatible CPUs

60. You have begun using VMotion. During the process, the wizard displays a message. Which of the following conditions will prevent the migration from completing successfully?

- ○ **A.** A VM has a snapshot.
- ○ **B.** A VM is connected to an internal vSwitch on the source host.
- ○ **C.** A VM is configured for a removable DVD-ROM but is not connected to it.
- ○ **D.** A heartbeat cannot be detected from the VM that is going to be migrated.

61. You are assigning shares to a VM. Which of the following CPU share settings is reflected by the calculation 1000 * (# of vCPUs)?

- ○ **A.** High
- ○ **B.** Normal
- ○ **C.** Low
- ○ **D.** Custom

62. You have DRS in your VI3 environment. Which of the following would you select if you want two VMs to be kept together on the same host?

- ○ **A.** Affinity
- ○ **B.** Availability
- ○ **C.** Anti-Availability
- ○ **D.** Anti-Affinity

63. You are creating a new alarm for a Windows XP Professional SP2 VM in VirtualCenter 2.5. On the Actions tab, which state change is *not* an available option for initiating an action?

- ○ **A.** Green to Yellow
- ○ **B.** Yellow to Red
- ○ **C.** Red to Green
- ○ **D.** Red to Yellow

64. You are creating a resource pool in VirtualCenter 2.5. What two entities can you config- ure when you create a resource pool? (Choose two.)

- ○ **A.** Network resources
- ○ **B.** I/O resources
- ○ **C.** CPU resources
- ○ **D.** Memory resources

65. What is the maximum number of LUNs that an ESX Server 3.5 host will process by default during the installation?

- ○ **A.** 32
- ○ **B.** 64
- ○ **C.** 128
- ○ **D.** 256

66. In a Fiber Channel SAN, how many bits are assigned to the host bus adapter address?

- ○ **A.** 16
- ○ **B.** 32
- ○ **C.** 48
- ○ **D.** 64

67. Which industry-accepted topologies for a Fiber Channel SAN is the most common and offers the most functionality?

- ○ **A.** Point-to-Point
- ○ **B.** Multipoint-to-Point
- ○ **C.** Multipoint-to-Multipoint
- ○ **D.** Point-to-Multipoint
- ○ **E.** Arbitrated Loop
- ○ **F.** Switched Fabric
- ○ **G.** Mesh Loop

68. Which of the following statements correctly reflect differences between a physical switch and a virtual switch? (Choose two.)

- ○ **A.** Unlike physical switches, virtual switches do not support STP.
- ○ **B.** Unlike physical switches, virtual switches are not able to avoid unnecessary deliveries.
- ○ **C.** Unlike physical switches, virtual switches do not check each frame's MAC address destination when it is received.
- ○ **D.** Unlike physical switches, virtual switches' forwarding data table is unique to each switch.

69. After installing an ESX Server 3.5 host, you want to provide SSH access to root user. Which of the following are ways to accomplish this? (Choose two.)

- ○ **A.** Create a user account on the server that root can use for access.
- ○ **B.** The root user cannot be given SSH access to the server.
- ○ **C.** Modify the `PermitRootLogin` parameter from Yes to No.
- ○ **D.** Modify the `PermitRootLogin` parameter from No to Yes.

70. Which of the following is a correct representation of an iSCSI node using the following generic data fields?

Date

Domain

Alternate Name

Host Name

- ○ **A.** iscsi:Host Name: Domain name:year-month:<alternate name>
- ○ **B.** iqn:Host Name: Domain name:year-month:<alternate name>
- ○ **C.** iscsi:year-month:<domain name reversed>:<alternate name>
- ○ **D.** iqn.year-month.<domain name reversed>:<alternate name>
- ○ **E.** eth0.year-month.<domain name reversed>:<alternate name>
- ○ **F.** scsi0.year-month.<domain name reversed>:<alternate name>

71. In VirtualCenter 2.5, you are configuring a new alarm. What variables can you configure on the Reporting tab? (Choose two.)

- ○ **A.** Threshold
- ○ **B.** Tolerance
- ○ **C.** Frequency
- ○ **D.** Rate

72. You want to create a resource pool. Where can you create one? (Choose two.)

- ○ **A.** Standalone host
- ○ **B.** DRS cluster
- ○ **C.** Standalone VM
- ○ **D.** VirtualCenter Server

73. What is the maximum amount of RAM that can be used on ESX Server 3.5?

- ○ **A.** 64GB
- ○ **B.** 128GB
- ○ **C.** 256GB
- ○ **D.** 1024GB

74. Which edition of ESX Server 3.5 gives you access to VMware HA feature?

- ○ **A.** Enterprise only
- ○ **B.** Foundation only
- ○ **C.** Standard only
- ○ **D.** Enterprise and Standard
- ○ **E.** Enterprise, Standard, and Foundation

75. Which of the following is required if you want to connect to a VirtualCenter 2.5 Web Access interface from a SuSE Linux 10.1 desktop? (Choose two.)

- ○ **A.** IE 7
- ○ **B.** An IP address
- ○ **C.** Firefox 1.0.7
- ○ **D.** Safari 3.1.2
- ○ **E.** A domain name

15

Answers to Practice Exam 2

1. A	19. C	37. A
2. D	20. D	38. D
3. D	21. A	39. A
4. A, B, E	22. B, D	40. A
5. B	23. A	41. A
6. A, B	24. D	42. B
7. D	25. A	43. B
8. A, D	26. C, D	44. A
9. A	27. B	45. C
10. A, B	28. A	46. B
11. B	29. D	47. A
12. C	30. A, C	48. D
13. A, B	31. D	49. A, C
14. C, D	32. A	50. B
15. A, C	33. D	51. D
16. D	34. D	52. A
17. A, B	35. B, C, D	53. C
18. D	36. D	54. A

55. B, D	**62.** A	**69.** A, D
56. A, C	**63.** C	**70.** D
57. A, D	**64.** C, D	**71.** B, C
58. A, B, C	**65.** C	**72.** A, B
59. D	**66.** D	**73.** C
60. B	**67.** F	**74.** D
61. B	**68.** A, D	**75.** B, C

Answers to Exam Questions

1. **A.** The label given to the Service Console port in the VirtualCenter 2.5 interface is vswif0. Answers B, C, and D are labels used in VirtualCenter 2.5 for interfaces other than the Service Console.

2. **D.** The default size assigned to the swap partition during an ESX Server 3.5 installation is 544MB. Answers A, B, and C are incorrect because they are not the default size assigned.

3. **D.** On an ESX Server 3.5, the partition written to when the system crashes is the vmk-core partition. Another term for this process is a *core dump*. Answers A, B, and C are incorrect. The / partition (the root partition of the operating system), the SWAP partition, and the VMFS3 partition are not written to during a core dump.

4. **A, B, E.** In a default installation of VirtualCenter 2.5, numerous roles are created automatically. Each role has a default set of defined permissions. Based on the task required, some of these roles can accomplish the task, whereas others cannot. The roles that have the default permissions to remove an alarm are the Datacenter Administrator, Virtual Machine Administrator, and Resource Pool Administrator. Answers C and D are incorrect. They do not have necessary permissions to remove an alarm.

5. **B.** A number of default roles are created during a VirtualCenter 2.5 installation. These roles provide an administrative way to efficiently assign one or more privileges to a user or group. One of the default roles is the Resource Pool Administrator. One privilege that a user assigned to the role of Resource Pool Administrator has by default is Create a Resource Pool. The other responses are not default privileges of the Resource Pool Administrator, so answers A, C, and D are incorrect. They are default privileges of other VirtualMachine 2.5 roles.

6. **A, B.** When an ESX host is added to an HA cluster, several components are installed on the host. They include the AAM (Automated Availability Manager), VMap, and the vpxa. AAM is the engine for HA, and the vpxa service manages components of the HA cluster. Communication between the AAM and vpxa is managed by VMap. Esxtop and IQN are not HA components. They are used in other aspects of the VI3 enterprise. Therefore, answers C and D are incorrect.

7. **D.** In VI3, a resource share is a way to prioritize which virtual machines have access to available resources, such as memory and CPU. When two virtual machines are contending for available resources, the share value determines how much resource is available to each VM. Answers A, B, and C are not correct because they are not a VI3 way to prioritize resources. They are used in a VI3 environment but with other features. A resource pool is a container created in Hosts and Clusters view used to limit the host CPU and memory utilization for a group of virtual machines.

8. **A, D.** VI3's Web Access utility is automatically installed when ESX Server is installed and can be installed from the VirtualCenter Server Windows setup package as an optional feature when you are installing the VirtualCenter Server. Answers B and C are incorrect because they do not correctly describe the Web Access installation options.

9. **A.** One of the licensing models available when you are installing an ESX Server 3.5 host is the Host Based Model. In this model, each individual host is licensed separately. When you are licensing a host in this way, the license is uploaded to the host and configured using the VIC. The license can be found on the server at `/etc/vmware/vmware.lic`. Answers B, C, and D are incorrect because they do not reflect the correct location of a Host Based License file on an ESX Server 3.5 host.

10. **A, B.** In the VI3 suite, a grace period exists during which all hosts will continue to function without interruption should a centralized license server fail. Certain features are available during this grace period, and some are available after the grace period if you are not able to restore the license server in the allotted time period. Some features are not available after the grace period if the license server has not been restored in time, including starting up a virtual machine and restarting virtual machines that are located on a failed host on a DRS cluster. Answers C and D are incorrect because these features are available after the grace period if the license server cannot be restarted in time.

11. **B.** According to VMware, you can manage up to 2000 virtual machines from a single instance of VirtualCenter 2.5. Answers A, C, and D are incorrect because they do not correctly reflect the maximums defined by VMware.

12. **C.** When creating and configuring a new virtual machine in a VI3 enterprise, you must know both the hardware requirements for a VM and the maximum hardware that you can configure for a VM. A virtual machine in this environment can have a maximum of four CPUs, 16GB RAM, four NICs, and two CD/DVD-ROM drives. Because this VM requires four DVD-ROM drives, it causes the creation and configuration to fail. Answers A, B, and D are not requirements that exceed the maximum hardware requirements for a VM.

13. A, B. In the VI3 suite, alarms are used when monitoring resource usage and the state of defined systems. These alarms can alert an administrator to a condition that needs attention. Based on the configuration of the alarm, an automated follow-up action can be initialized. There are two generic alarm types; they are an alarm that monitors a host and one that monitors a virtual machine. Answers C and D are incorrect because they are not alarm types that can be configured.

14. C, D. In the VI3 suite, alarms are used when monitoring resource usage and the state of defined systems. These alarms can alert an administrator to a condition that needs attention. Based on the configuration of the alarm, an automated follow-up action can be initialized. When configuring a virtual machine state alarm, you can configure two options on the Triggers tab. Because this is a state alarm, those options are Is Equal To or Is Not Equal To. Answers A and B are incorrect; they are not options available for a state alarm.

15. A, C. In the VI3 suite, alarms are used when monitoring resource usage and the state of defined systems. These alarms can alert an administrator to a condition that needs attention. Based on the configuration of the alarm, an automated follow-up action can be initialized. When a virtual machine is being monitored, such as in this question, a notification email can be sent, a notification trap can be sent, a script can be run, a VM can be powered on or off, and a VM can be suspended or reset. Answers B and D are incorrect because they are not follow-up actions that can configure an alarm for a virtual machine.

16. D. When creating and configuring a virtual network with vSwitches, you need to understand that ESX Server hosts have some limitations. They include the following:

▶ No more than 4096 ports

▶ No more than 1016 ports per vSwitch

▶ No more than 512 virtual switch port groups

▶ No more than 127 vSwitches

Consequently, answer D is correct and answers A, B, and C are incorrect.

17. A, B. A number of default roles created during an ESX Server 3.5 host installation are designed to assist in securing the host. These roles provide an administrative way to efficiently assign one or more privileges to a user or group. The default roles are Administrator, No Access, and Read-only. A Virtual Center 2.5 installation uses these same three roles with a host of others, including Virtual Machine Administrator and Virtual Machine User. Answers C and D are incorrect.

18. D. When you are installing VirtualCenter 2.5, it is important to have a database server that complies with the requirements of VC. VirtualCenter 2.5 supports the following databases: Microsoft SQL Server 2005 Express; Microsoft SQL Server 2000 Standard SP4 and Enterprise; Microsoft SQL Server 2005 Enterprise SP1, SP2, and Express; and Oracle 9iR2 or Oracle 10gR1 or R2. The only selection that meets one of these requirements is D. The other answers, A, B, and C, are not supported databases.

19. C. A virtual machine in a VI3 environment can have one, two, or four virtual CPUs. It cannot have three virtual CPUs. Answers A, B, and C are possible and therefore incorrect.

20. D. The only user who has full permissions to a newly installed ESX Server 3.5 host is the root user. Administrator is a role that you can assign users or groups postinstallation. Admin and the user who installed the host do not have any permission to the host by default. Answers A, B, and C are incorrect.

21. A. The ESX Server and the virtual machines that are guests of the server are managed by the Service Console. The Service Console on an ESX Server is the equivalent of a server operating system. The VC, or VirtualCenter, is a Windows-based management tool for managing all enterprise ESX Servers. Answer B is incorrect. VMware's Virtual Infrastructure Client, also known as VIC, lets you connect to a VirtualCenter Server or an ESX Server from a Windows workstation. VIC is a 32-bit Windows application. Answer C is incorrect. SMP, VMware's Virtual Symmetric Multi-Processing, is a VMware solution for providing multiple virtual CPUs to virtual machines. Answer D is incorrect.

22. B and D. When an ESX Server 3.5 is installed, two interacting components are installed. They are the Service Console and the VMkernel. The VMkernel provides the virtualization layer on bare metal hardware. The Service Console manages access to the physical hardware by installed virtual machines. Three functions of the VMkernel are virtual switch processing of data, scheduling CPU time, and management of memory. Answers A and C are incorrect. The VMkernel does not manage SSH or convert a physical machine to a virtual machine.

23. A. When a virtual machine is created, a number of files are created that serve specific purposes. They include the configuration file, which has a `.vmx` extension. The other extensions listed represent files that are not configuration files for a VM. Answers B, C, and D are incorrect.

24. D. The Alt+Ctrl+Del keystroke sequence can be sent to a VM using either a menu option or by using the Alt+Ctrl+Ins keystroke combination. This initiates the login process on a Windows VM. Answers A, B, and C do not accomplish this.

25. A. RAID, Redundant Array of Independent (Inexpensive) Disks, is often used in a VI3 environment as the platform from which LUNs are defined. A number of RAID levels are common. One of the most common is RAID 0, which provides disk striping but no fault tolerance. The other answers—B, C, and D—provide a level of fault tolerance and so are incorrect.

26. C, D. In the VI3 suite, a grace period exists during which all hosts will continue to function without interruption should a centralized license server fail. Certain features are available during this grace period, and some are available after the grace period if you are not able to restore the license server in the allotted time period. After the grace period, some capabilities are classified by VMware as restricted operations, if a license server is not restored. They include adding and removing a license key, adding and removing a host from a cluster, and adding an ESX Server 3.5 host. Answers A and B are not classified as restricted operations because they are tasks that can be performed during the grace period.

27. **B.** RAID, Redundant Array of Independent (Inexpensive) Disks, is often used in a VI3 environment as the platform from which LUNs are defined. A number of RAID levels are common. One of the most common is RAID 1, which provides disk mirroring (mirrored arrays) and disk duplexing. In a RAID 1 environment, you typically have two drives that are mirrored. With these two mirrored drives, your practical storage is 50% of the total amount of disk space. In this question, that means that you have 1TB of practical storage. Answers A, C, and D are incorrect because they do not accurately reflect the practical storage capacity.

28. **A.** A logical arrangement of disk space that is allocated from multiple physical disks is a LUN, a Logical Unit Number. Answers B, C, and D are not correct because they do not meet the definition.

29. **D.** The two major components of the VI3 suite are the ESX Server and the VirtualCenter. The features that come with the suite are categorized under these two components. One of the features of the Virtual Center is HA. The other answers are features of the ESX Server. Therefore, answers A, B, and C are incorrect.

30. **A, C.** A logical arrangement of disk space that is allocated from multiple physical disks is a LUN, a Logical Unit Number. VMware defines one of two schemes as an Adaptive Scheme. The benefits of the Adaptive Scheme are there is less need for an SAN Administrator, virtual disks can be easily resized, snapshot management is facilitated, and volume management is easier. The other options in answers B and D are incorrect because they are not benefits of the Adaptive Scheme.

31. **D.** VC, the VirtualCenter 2.5, is a Windows-based management tool for managing all enterprise ESX Servers. There are several minimum requirements for installing the VC. The minimum platform requirement includes Windows Server 2003 SP1, Windows Server 2003 R2, Windows XP Pro SP2, and Windows 2000 Server with SP4. Answer D is the only correct response. Windows XP Home is not supported. Answers A, B, and C are incorrect; they do not meet the minimum platform requirements for installing the VirtualCenter 2.5.

32. **A.** When the Performance tab is selected for a host or VM in VirtualCenter 2.5, the default view displayed is CPU consumption. The other choices are configurable options that can be displayed but are not the displayed in the default view. Answers B, C, and D are therefore incorrect.

33. **D.** The default number of ports created with a virtual switch is 64. Only 56 ports are shown in the interface, and only 56 are available. Eight of the ports not shown are reserved for the VMkernel. Answers A, B, and C are not correct because they do not reflect the correct number of ports assigned by default to vSwitch.

34. D. The maximum amount of memory that you can allocate to the Service Console on an ESX Server 3.5 host is 800MB. Answers A, B, C, E, and F are incorrect.

35. B, C, D. A license built on the per processor basis activates a feature based on the number of processors on the host. According to VMware, a dual-core or quad-core processor counts as a single processor despite the fact that multiple processing units exist on each of these chips. Because, in this question, 8 licenses exist on a per processor basis, answers B, C, and D are correct because these configurations have a need for 8 or fewer licenses because 8 or fewer processors are installed. Answer A is incorrect because 16 processors are installed.

36. D. One of the licensing models available when installing an ESX Server 3.5 host is the Server Based Model. In this model, licenses are centrally managed through a license server, and when a host needs a license, it looks to the license server, which allocates the necessary license from a license pool. The licenses stored on a license server are found in the file system at `C:\Program Files\VMWare\VMWare License Server\Licenses`. Answer A is correct if the Host Based Model for licensing is used. Answers B and C are incorrect for either Host Based or Server Based licensing.

37. A. In a VI3 environment, the three types of virtual switches are Internal, Single Adapter, and Multiadapter types. There are no Loopback Switches. Answers B, C, and D are incorrect because they are types of switches.

38. D. In a VI3 environment, the three types of virtual switches are Internal, Single Adapter, and Multiadapter types. Another name for Multiadapter virtual switches is NIC teaming. In NIC teaming, two or more physical NICs support a virtual switch. Answers A, B, and C are not NIC teaming configurations.

39. A. By configuring a NIC team using the NIC Teaming tab, you configure the NIC team to use a Rolling Failover policy of NO. With this setting, the NIC team provides a failover policy and a failback policy. Answers B, C, and D are not true statements and are incorrect.

40. A. VMware's Virtual Infrastructure Client, also known as VIC, lets you connect to a VirtualCenter Server or an ESX Server from a Windows workstation. VIC is a 32-bit Windows application. Only answer A is correct. Answer B is a 64-bit Windows operating system. Answers C and D are Linux operating systems. Answers B, C, and D are therefore incorrect.

41. A. Several key ports are important when configuring a firewall on an ESX Server; they include Port 902, which authenticates traffic from the VirtualCenter to an ESX Server 3.5. Port 22 controls transmission to the SSH client, so Answer B is incorrect. Port 443 controls secure web browser transmissions, so Answer C is incorrect. Port 27000 is a license server port that is used when the VirtualCenter is incorporated into the Enterprise, so Answer D is incorrect.

42. **B.** When creating and configuring a virtual network with vSwitches, you need to understand that ESX Server hosts have some limitations. They include the following:

- No more than 4096 ports

- No more than 1016 ports per vSwitch

- No more than 512 virtual switch port groups

- No more than 127 vSwitches

Consequently, answer B is correct and answers A, C, and D are incorrect.

43. **B.** A vmxnet adapter is a high-performance network interface that is configured inside an ESX Server 3.5 virtual machine, such as a Windows XP SP2 guest that has VMware Tools installed. A NIC team is a single communication channel that is logical in nature. It is made up of multiple physical ports. Answer A is incorrect. A virtual switch is a switch found in the VMkernel used for managing virtual machine traffic. Answer C is incorrect. The VMkernel port is a special virtual switch port that is used for features such as VMotion. It is configured with an IP address. Answer D is incorrect.

44. **A.** Four generic storage options are available to an ESX Server 3.5 host in a VI3 environment. They are Local Storage, iSCSI Storage, Fiber Channel Storage, and Network Attached Storage. Removable Disk Storage is not an option defined by VMware. Answers B, C, D, and E are incorrect because they are available options.

45. **C.** The best, most efficient, and reliable storage area network solution for a VI3 environment is Fiber Channel. iSCSI and NAS are competitive, but they are still not rated as better, more efficient, and reliable than Fiber Channel. Local Storage in its purest form is not a storage area network.

46. **B.** When a license is purchased for the VI3 suite, it can be built on either a per processor or per instance basis. A license built on the per processor basis activates a feature based on the number of processors on the host. A license built on the per instance basis activates an instance of a feature no matter how many processors are on the host. VI3 products available on a per processor basis are the ESX Server, VirtualCenter Agent, VMotion, Storage VMotion, Consolidate Backup, DRS, HA, and DPM. The only VI3 product available on a per instance basis is the VirtualCenter 2.5. Answers A, C, and D are features licensed on a per processor basis.

47. **A.** The process of hiding specific LUNs from ESX Server 3.5 hosts is called LUN masking. LUN zoning is a different process used in Fiber Channel networks to facilitate communication. Answers B, C, and D are incorrect because either they are used for a different reason in a SAN or are not terms used in SAN configuration.

48. **D.** ESX Server 3.5 supports a maximum of 16 host bus adapters per system and a maximum of 15 devices or targets per HBA in relationship to a Fiber Channel SAN solution in a VI3 environment. Answers A, B, and C are not true statements.

49. A, C. In a VI3 environment, a SAN using multipathing has two types of multipathing available: Fixed and MRU (Most Recently Used). There is no Flexible or LRU multipathing types. Therefore, Answers B and D are incorrect.

50. B. When you download a copy of ESX Server 3.5 for evaluation, you have the option of evaluating the software before purchasing a full license. You have access to all the features during the evaluation period. After the evaluation period is up, you must purchase a license if you want to continue running the server. The evaluation time frame is 60 days. In software sales, this is called a *Time Bombed* version of the software. Answers A, C, and D are incorrect. Many other software products give you 30, 90, or 120 days to evaluate the product. VMware gives you 60 days.

51. D. When you are doing an installation of VirtualCenter 2.5 in an enterprise, the correct order of component installation is critical if you want to avoid as many issues as possible. The order recommended by VMware is 1-Database Server, 2-License Server, 3-VC Server, and finally 4-VIC. Answers A, B, and C do not reflect the order recommended by VMware to avoid installation issues.

52. A. The maximum number of hosts that can be supported by a resource pool in a VI3 environment is 32. Answers B, C, and D are incorrect because they do not reflect the correct maximum.

53. C. By default, the balloon driver on an ESX system is configured to consume 65% of the memory of a virtual machine. Answers A, B, D, and E are incorrect.

54. A. In VirtualCenter 2.5, the system logs are held in the vpxd-index file. Answers B, C, and D are not files that hold the system logs for VirtualCenter 2.5 and are therefore not correct.

55. B, D. There are two ways to create a template from a fully configured and installed VM. You can right-click on the VM and select either Clone to a Template or Convert to a Template. There are no options named Copy to a Template or Export to a Template. Therefore, answers A and C are incorrect.

56. A, C. When you are configuring an alarm for an entity or resource in a VI3 environment, one of the configuration steps is to select the type of trigger the alarm will monitor. The two general types of triggers are State and Usage. Based on whether you select a State or Usage trigger, the available conditions change. There are no options for Dynamic or Static trigger types, so answers B and D are incorrect.

57. A, D. VMware Converter Enterprise is a tool that extends the capabilities of VirtualCenter 2.5. With it, you can convert a physical machine to a virtual machine, and a virtual machine to a virtual machine. You can also export an ESX VM to another format. There are also other benefits to using Converter Enterprise. You cannot convert a virtual machine to a physical machine or move a VM from one host to another. That is task that is well managed by VMotion. Answers B and C are incorrect.

58. A, B, and C. There are four prerequisites for installing the VMware Converter Enterprise: Server, CLI, Agent, and Client Plug-in. There is no recommended RAM requirement for this add-on. Answer D is incorrect.

59. D. The prerequisites for the source and destination hosts if you are going to use VMotion include compatible CPUs, gigabit network, access to the same physical networks, and virtual switches that are labeled the same. Answers A, B, and C do not meet the prerequisites and are incorrect.

60. B. After you begin using VMotion, the wizard displays messages, which can be warnings or errors. Warnings address issues you need to consider but do not prevent the process from completing successfully, whereas errors prevent the migration from completing successfully and need to be addressed. The only message that falls under the error category in this question is B—a VM is connected to an internal vSwitch on the source host. The other messages are warnings. Answers A, C, and D are incorrect.

61. B. When you are assigning shares to a VM, four options are available: High, Normal, Low, and Custom. Each option reflects a number of CPU or Memory shares derived by calculation. When you are calculating CPU shares, the Normal option is selected if your calculation is 1000 * (# of vCPUs). Answers A, C, and D are incorrect.

62. A. You have DRS in your VI3 environment. Several DRS rules govern whether two VMs can exist on the same host at the same time. They include Affinity and Anti-Affinity. Affinity requires that two virtual machines be kept together on the same host, and Anti-Affinity requires that two virtual machines be kept on separate servers. Answers B, C, and D are incorrect. Availability and Anti-Availability are not DRS rules.

63. C. In the VI3 suite, alarms are used when monitoring resource usage and the state of defined systems. These alarms can alert an administrator to a condition that needs attention. Based on the configuration of the alarm, an automated follow-up action can be initialized. When a virtual machine is being monitored, such as in this question, several actions can be taken based on one or more state changes. Alerts are red, warnings are yellow, and safe/normal operating state is green. The state changes that trigger an action are Green to Yellow, Yellow to Red, Red to Yellow, and Yellow to Green. There is no option for Red to Green. Answers A, B, and D are options available on the Actions tab.

64. C, D. A resource pool in a VI3 environment is a container created in Hosts and Clusters view used to limit the host CPU and memory utilization for a group of virtual machines. The two entities that you can configure when you create a resource pool are CPU Resources and Memory Resources. You cannot configure I/O Resources or Network Resources. Answers A and B are incorrect.

65. C. When an ESX Server 3.5 host is installed, it, by default, processes the first 128 LUNs that are present and to which it has access. Answers A, B, and D are not correct.

66. D. In a Fiber Channel SAN, the host bus adapter has an address that is made up of 64 bits. Answers A, B, and C are incorrect.

67. F. Three industry-accepted topologies for a Fiber Channel SAN are Point-to-Point, Switched Fabric, and Arbitrated Loop. The industry-accepted topology for a Fiber Channel SAN that is considered the most common and offers the most functionality is the Switched Fabric topology. All other answers are incorrect.

68. A, D. There are differences between physical and virtual switches. They include the following: virtual switches do not support STP, and each virtual switch has a unique forwarding data table. Answers B and C are incorrect because they do not correctly reflect differences between physical and virtual switches.

69. A, D. By default, the root user is not granted SSH access to an ESX Server 3.5 host. There are two ways to overcome this limitation. The first is to create a user account on the server that root can use for SSH access. The second is to modify the `PermitRootLogin` parameter in the appropriate configuration file from No to Yes. Answers B and C are incorrect because they are not ways to grant root SSH access or are false statements.

70. D. The correct representation of an iSCSI node ID generically is iqn.year-month.<domain name reversed>:<alternate name>. The other choices do not follow the naming schema used for an iSCSI node ID. Answers A, B, C, E, and F are incorrect.

71. B, C. In the VI3 suite, alarms are used when monitoring resource usage and the state of defined systems. These alarms can alert an administrator to a condition that needs attention. Based on the configuration of the alarm, an automated follow-up action can be initialized. One of the tabs that requires configuration when you are creating an alarm is the Reporting tab. On this tab, you can define an alarm's Tolerance and Frequency. Tolerance is defined as a percentage, and Frequency is defined in seconds. Answers A and D are not options available on the Reporting tab.

72. A, B. A resource pool in a VI3 environment is a container created in Hosts and Clusters view used to limit the host CPU and memory utilization for a group of virtual machines. A resource pool can be created on a standalone host or on a DRS cluster as a management object. A resource pool cannot be created on a VM or on a VC server. Answers C and D are incorrect.

73. C. When you are planning an ESX Server 3.5 installation and deployment, it is important to know some of the maximums that you can configure. One important one is the maximum RAM you have per host. The maximum is 256GB. Answers A, B, and D are incorrect.

74. D. Three ESX Server 3.5 editions are available: Enterprise, Standard, and Foundation. The VMware HA feature is available only on the Enterprise and Standard editions. Answers A, B, C, and E are incorrect because they do not correctly represent the editions on which VMware HA is available.

75. B, C. To access the Web Access interface on a VirtualCenter Server, you need a Windows or Linux computer, an IP address, and a web browser. The required web browsers are IE 6.0 or later on a Windows computer, Netscape Navigator 7.0 or later, Mozilla 1.x or later, and Firefox 1.0.7 or later. The correct responses are an IP address and Firefox 1.0.7. The other responses do not meet the requirements. Therefore, answers A, D, and E are incorrect.

APPENDIX A

Need to Know More?

McCain, Chris. *Mastering VMware Infrastructure 3*. Sybex. 2008. ISBN 0470183136.

Khnaser, Elias. VMware Infrastructure 3 Training DVD. Elias Khnaser. 2008. URL: http://www.eliaskhnaser.com.

What's on the CD-ROM

The CD-ROM features an innovative practice test engine powered by MeasureUp, giving you yet another effective tool to assess your readiness for the exam.

Multiple Test Modes

MeasureUp practice tests can be used in Study, Certification, or Custom modes.

Study Mode

Tests administered in Study mode allow you to request the correct answer(s) and explanation to each question during the test. These tests are not timed. You can modify the testing environment during the test by selecting the Options button.

You can also specify the objectives or missed questions you want to include in your test, the timer length, and other test properties. You can also modify the testing environment during the test by selecting the Options button.

In Study mode, you receive automatic feedback on all correct and incorrect answers. The detailed answer explanations are a superb learning tool in their own right.

Certification Mode

Tests administered in Certification mode closely simulate the actual testing environment you will encounter when taking a licensure exam and are timed. These tests do not allow you to request the answer(s) and/or explanation to each question until after the exam.

Custom Mode

Custom mode allows you to specify your preferred testing environment. Use this mode to specify the categories you want to include in your test, the timer length, number of questions, and other test properties. You can modify the testing environment during the test by selecting the Options button.

Attention to Exam Objectives

MeasureUp practice tests are designed to appropriately balance the questions over each technical area covered by a specific exam. All concepts from the actual exam are covered thoroughly to ensure that you're prepared for the exam.

Installing the CD

System Requirements:

- ▶ Windows 95, 98, ME, NT4, 2000, or XP
- ▶ 7MB disk space for testing engine
- ▶ An average of 1MB disk space for each individual test
- ▶ Control Panel Regional Settings must be set to English (United States)
- ▶ PC only

To install the CD-ROM, follow these instructions:

1. Close all applications before beginning this installation.

2. Insert the CD into your CD-ROM drive. If the setup starts automatically, go to step 6. If the setup does not start automatically, continue with step 3.

3. From the Start menu, select Run.

4. Click Browse to locate the MeasureUp CD. In the Browse dialog box, from the Look In drop-down list, select the CD-ROM drive.

5. In the Browse dialog box, double-click Setup.exe. In the Run dialog box, click OK to begin the installation.

6. On the Welcome screen, click MeasureUp Practice Questions to begin installation.

7. Follow the Certification Prep Wizard by clicking Next.

8. To agree to the Software License Agreement, click Yes.

9. On the Choose Destination Location screen, click Next to install the software to `C:\Program Files\Certification Preparation`. If you cannot locate MeasureUp Practice Tests on the Start menu, see the section titled "Creating a Shortcut to the MeasureUp Practice Tests," later in this appendix.

10. On the Setup Type screen, select Typical Setup. Click Next to continue.

11. In the Select Program Folder screen, you can name the program folder where your tests will be located. To select the default, click Next and the installation continues.

12. After the installation is complete, verify that Yes, I Want to Restart My Computer Now is selected. If you select No, I Will Restart My Computer Later, you cannot use the program until you restart your computer.

13. Click Finish.

14. After restarting your computer, choose Start, Programs, Certification Preparation, Certification Preparation, MeasureUp Practice Tests.

15. On the MeasureUp Welcome Screen, click Create User Profile.

16. In the User Profile dialog box, complete the mandatory fields and click Create Profile.

17. Select the practice test you want to access and click Start Test.

Creating a Shortcut to the MeasureUp Practice Tests

To create a shortcut to the MeasureUp Practice Tests, follow these steps:

1. Right-click your desktop.

2. From the Shortcut menu, select New, Shortcut.

3. Browse to `C:\Program Files\MeasureUp Practice Tests` and select the `MeasureUpCertification.exe` or `Localware.exe` file.

4. Click OK.

5. Click Next.

6. Rename the shortcut MeasureUp.

7. Click Finish.

After you complete step 7, use the MeasureUp shortcut on your desktop to access the MeasureUp products you ordered.

Technical Support

If you encounter problems with the MeasureUp test engine on the CD-ROM, please contact MeasureUp at (800) 649-1687 or email support@measureup.com. Support hours of operation are 7:30 a.m. to 4:30 p.m. EST. In addition, you can find Frequently Asked Questions (FAQ) in the Support area at www.measure-up.com. If you would like to purchase additional MeasureUp products, call (678) 356-5050 or (800) 649-1687 or visit www.measureup.com.

Glossary

802.1Q VLAN tagging   VLAN tagging allows you to create several port groups on a single vSwitch and assign them a VLAN ID that corresponds to the VLAN ID configured on the switch. These port groups can then route traffic to the specific VLANs.

admission control   This configurable HA option allows you to set a policy to control virtual machine power on tasks. The two valid policies are either to allow or disallow VMs from powering on if they violate availability constraints.

Affinity   This rule implies that virtual machines should be on the same ESX host at all times.

alarms   These thresholds are configured on either a host or a virtual machine that is designed to send the administrator a notification that a certain threshold has been reached.

Anti-Affinity   This rule implies that virtual machines cannot exist on the same ESX host at the same time.

available memory   Available memory is the initial memory that you configure for a virtual machine during its creation.

balloon-driver   This guest operating system device driver is installed as part of the VMware Tools installation. When an ESX system comes under physical memory strain, the VMkernel selects a virtual machine (after taking into consideration each VM's memory shares and reservations) and inflates the device driver inside the guest operating system and consumes all the available memory that is not being used by the operating system. It then releases this acquired memory to the ESX system to ease its memory requirements. When the need for this memory ceases to exist, the device driver is deflated or stopped, and the memory is returned to the guest operating system.

beacon probe   In addition to doing Link Status, this method is similar to a heartbeat; it continuously sends packets between the adapters, and if a heartbeat is missed, it assumes there is an issue and fails over.

block-level transfer   This block of storage is presented to a host as local storage. It is transmitted over the median as a block of data.

cluster   This is the implicit collection of CPU and memory resources across ESX hosts that are members of this cluster to allow for the creation of VMware Distributed Resource Scheduler (DRS) and VMware High Availability (HA) clusters.

cluster-across-boxes   Cluster-across-boxes implies that the node members of the cluster reside on different ESX hosts.

cluster-in-a-box   A cluster-in-a-box is a type of cluster that implies all the cluster's nodes reside on the same ESX host.

cold cloning   Cold cloning is the process of cloning a machine while it is not online.

cold migration   A cold migration is used to move a virtual machine from one ESX host to another while the machine powered off.

Converter Enterprise   This add-on product is used to extend VirtualCenter capabilities. Its primary function is to convert physical or virtual machines into ESX-compatible virtual machines.

Core Services   This is the main module of VirtualCenter, the basic heart of the application that gives way to virtual machine provisioning, Task Scheduler, events logging, and so on.

datacenter   This is the logical repository of hosts and virtual machines.

Distributed Resource Scheduler VMware DRS is an enterprise-level feature that uses VMotion to load-balance an ESX host's CPU and memory resources, thereby maintaining and ensuring that all ESX hosts that are members of this cluster always have a balanced load in terms of CPU and memory.

Distributed Services   This module gives way to features like VMotion, High Availability, and Distributed Resource Scheduler. This is the place where the features that require a separate license stem from.

expandable reservation   This option allows child resource pools to tap into the parent resource pool and harness whatever resources are available to satisfy their own shortage.

Fiber Channel   This type of SAN is a high-speed transport protocol that moves SCSI commands between two nodes at speeds of up to 8GB (as of ESX 3.5 Update 2).

file-level transfer   File-level transfer occurs when the host is presented with a logical pointer to a block of disk; a perfect example of this is a network drive letter in Windows. When transmitting over the network, the data is transferred on a file level.

graphical mode   Graphical mode allows you to install ESX using the full-featured graphical interface wizard.

guided consolidation   Guided consolidation analyzes systems based on their performance metrics and determines whether they are good candidates for virtualization.

hard zoning   Hard zoning is implemented at the Fiber Channel Switch level and prevents physical access to any device that is not a member of the zone, thus making this type of zoning a more secure one.

Hardware Execution Context   An H.E.C. is a thread that is scheduled on a physical processor. The number of H.E.C.s available for scheduling depends on the number of physical cores available in the system.

host-based license file   This license file is uploaded to the ESX host and can be used only by this particular host.

host isolation   ESX host isolation occurs when the host stops receiving a heartbeat from the rest of the hosts in the High Availability cluster. When this situation occurs, it is otherwise known as a "split-brain" network phenomenon.

hot cloning   Hot cloning is the process of cloning a machine while online without taking it offline or affecting its productivity.

hyperthreading   This Intel Corporation technology allows you to schedule multiple threads on the same processor at the same time.

iSCSI software initiator   This feature renders a network interface card in an ESX server as a multifunction NIC, which can then be used to connect to storage devices using TCP/IP over Ethernet.

iSCSI   Internet Small Computer System Interface is an IP-based storage network that is capable of transmitting SCSI commands over your existing Ethernet infrastructure.

license server   This server is the central repository where license files are stored in a pool and assigned to ESX Server hosts as needed.

limit This is the maximum that a virtual machine can consume in terms of CPU, measured in megahertz (MHz) and memory measured in megabytes (MB).

link status This method determines if there is a network connection by whether a connection is detected on the port. If a cable is connected to the port, it reports the connection as active; if not, it fails over.

LUN masking This is the process of obscuring or hiding specific LUNs from being visible to hosts.

map This is a way of graphically understanding the connection topology of hosts and virtual machines to each other and to networks and storage.

NAS Network Attached Storage is a self-sufficient storage system, an entity on its own that can be attached via Ethernet to the traditional network.

NFS Network File System is a network protocol. ESX 3.5 supports NFS3 over TCP.

NIC teaming NIC teaming allows for the grouping of multiple physical NICs on the same vSwitch to provide fault tolerance, redundancy, and load balancing of outgoing IP traffic from the virtual switch.

Notify Switches This option notifies physical switches of changes such as a physical NIC failover or a new physical NIC addition to a NIC team.

per instance A per instance license is based on how many servers in your environment have the software installed on them. Currently, VirtualCenter is the only component that is licensed on a per instance basis.

per processor A per processor license model is constructed based on the number of physical CPU sockets that are available in a system.

permission A permission is assigned to an object in the inventory and grants a user or group the right to perform a certain task that is affiliated with that user's or group's assigned role.

physical-to-virtual cluster In this type of cluster, traditional physical machines and virtual machines make up the cluster's nodes.

port trunking A trunk port is a port on the physical switch that you configure to be aware of other VLANs that exist on other switches; as such, anything that plugs into this port is able to pass IP communications to all the visible VLANs.

privilege This is an allowed action or function; in other words, a privilege allows a user or group to perform a certain task.

promiscuous mode Promiscuous mode, if set to Accept ,would pass all the unicast frames that pass through the virtual switch to a virtual machine connected to that virtual switch. This setting is set to Reject by default to prevent frames destined for a particular VM from being read by other VMs.

reservation This is the minimum that a virtual machine needs in terms of CPU and memory resources to function properly.

resource pool A resource pool allows for the grouping of virtual machines and applies the same resource policy on them. A resource pool can be created for a single ESX host or to a DRS cluster to govern the CPU and memory resources.

role This is a collection of privileges that a user or group is allowed to perform.

root folder This folder is the topmost level of the inventory. It is the highest level, and there is nothing before it.

Route Based on IP Hash When this setting is selected, each packet's source and destination IP addresses are hashed, and an uplink communication link is selected based on that hashing.

Route Based on Originating Port ID This setting configures communications based on the virtual port where the virtual machine is connected on the virtual switch.

Route Based on Source MAC Hash This setting configures communications uplinks based on the MAC address of the virtual machine from which the traffic originated.

server-based license file This license file is uploaded on the license server and allows for the licenses to be pooled and, as such, allows any ESX hosts that point to this license server to gain licenses as long as licenses are available.

Service Console The Service Console is used to manage ESX Server, but is it is also used to help the VMkernel during its boot process. The Service Console operating system is a modified version of Red Hat Linux Enterprise 3 Update 9 (as of ESX 3.5 Update 2).

share A share identifies the frequency and priority a virtual machine will have in terms of accessing time slices on the physical CPU and memory. All VMs are assigned shares; the more shares a virtual machine is assigned, the more priority it has over physical resources.

snapshot This is a moment-in-time capture of a virtual machine's state, including its settings, memory, and disk states.

soft zoning Soft zoning, which is implemented at the Fiber Channel Switch level, is the method of obscuring ports so that they are not visible to devices outside their native zone.

SSH Secure Shell access allows you to remotely access your ESX Server and configure and manage it from a command line.

template   Area template is a pre-configured VM whose sole purpose is to allow for the the quick and easy provisioning of virtual machines. A template is an image of a VM that you intend to use as the basis for deploying other VMs.

text mode   This lightweight installation method has limited graphics, no mouse support, and relies solely on a text-based installation; it is ideal for ESX Server installations over slow networks.

traffic shaping   Traffic shaping allows for greater control over the amount of outgoing bandwidth that is available to virtual machines.

transparent page sharing   This technique of memory optimization detects virtual machines that are accessing the same memory pages, and instead of allocating different copies of that memory space for each VM, it maps all the VMs that are accessing the same memory space to a single memory space.

Users and Groups   Users and Groups are accounts that are allowed to log in to the virtual infrastructure.

Virtual Infrastructure client   This is the centralized client tool that allows you to administer all aspects of your VMware Infrastructure from a graphical user interface. The VI client allows you to create, manage, and monitor your virtual machines and allows you to log in to either your ESX hosts directly or to VirtualCenter.

virtual machine   A VM is a collection of virtual hardware that collectively present a framework that allows a guest operating system to be installed and thus allows for the complete functionality of this guest operating system. A VM is made up of software, specifically a collection of files that can be manipulated like any other files.

Virtual Machine Failure Monitoring
This technology is disabled by default. Its function is to monitor virtual machines, which it queries every 20 seconds via a heartbeat. (Prior to the release of ESX 3.5 Update 2, this technology was experimental.)

VMFS   Virtual Machine File System is a VMware-developed file system designed solely to run virtual machines. VMFS is a light file system and, as such, does not have all the overhead that the other file systems have, making it an ideal environment for virtual machines to run in. The only structure you can create on VMFS volumes is directories to organize the VM files.

VMkernel   Also known as the hypervisor, this software is installed on the bare metal hardware and thus creates the virtualization layer. The VMkernel is the regulator that manages access to the physical hardware.

VMkernel swap   The virtual machine's memory pages are copied into the swap file to allow the VM to continue to function and then relinquish this memory to the

VMkernel. This is a last-resort measure in case the balloon-driver cannot allocate enough memory to satisfy the VMkernel's needs. As with any other system, when heavy paging occurs, the VM's performance will suffer.

VMotion   This feature allows a running virtual machine to be migrated without interruption from one host to another.

VMware Consolidated Backup (VCB) VCB is an alternative method of backing up and restoring virtual machines at the file level or image level. It is based on snapshots and is a backup framework that allows third-party backup software to plug in and back up VMs in a centralized fashion.

VMware DRS   Distributed Resource Scheduler is a VMware cluster technology that allows for the balancing of ESX host CPU and memory resources.

VMware HA   High Availability is a technology that allows you to restart virtual machines on a different ESX host in the event that the original ESX host should experience any problems. HA ensures the VMs are brought back online as quickly as possible.

VMware Infrastructure 3   VMware Infrastructure 3 is a suite of applications that collectively make enterprise class virtualization possible.

VMware SMP   VMware Virtual Symmetric Multi-Processing is the VMware-developed technology that allows virtual machines to have more than one virtual CPU. SMP allows VMs to have up to four CPUs.

VMware Tools   This software package is installed after the guest operating system is up and running; it provides performance and other enhancements to the virtual machine's operability.

vpxuser   vpxuser is added to the Administrators group in ESX after ESX server is joined to VirtualCenter. VirtualCenter uses this user to authenticate itself to the ESX host to send preapproved commands.

Index

W - X - Y - Z

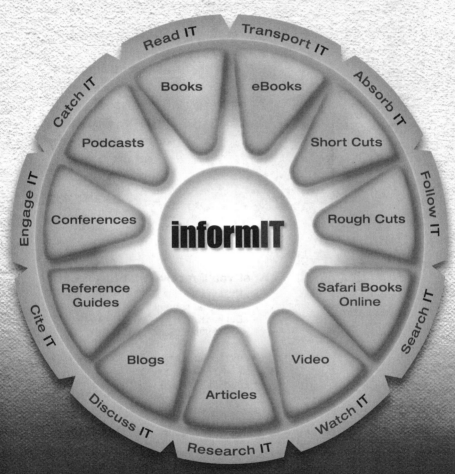

Register this book!

Register this book at
www.quepublishing.com
and
unlock benefits
exclusive to the owners
of this book.

What you'll receive with this book:

- ▶ Hidden content
- ▶ Additional content
- ▶ Book errata
- ▶ New templates, spreadsheets,
  or files to download
- ▶ Increased membership discounts
- ▶ Discount coupons
- ▶ A chance to sign up to receive content updates,
  information on new editions, and more

Book registration is free and only takes a few easy steps.

1. Go to www.quepublishing.com/bookstore/register.asp.
2. Enter the book's ISBN (found above the barcode on the back of your book).
3. You will be prompted to either register for or log-in to Quepublishing.com.
4. Once you have completed your registration or log-in, you will be taken to your "My Registered Books" page.
5. This page will list any benefits associated with each title you register, including links to content and coupon codes.

The benefits of book registration vary with each book, so be sure to register every Que Publishing book you own to see what else you might unlock at Quepublishing.com!

FREE Online Edition

Your purchase of **VCP Exam Cram: VMware Certified Professional** includes access to a free online edition for 45 days through the Safari Books Online subscription service. Nearly every Exam Cram book is available online through Safari Books Online, along with more than 5,000 other technical books and videos from publishers such as Addison-Wesley Professional, Cisco Press, IBM Press, O'Reilly, Prentice Hall, Que, and Sams.

SAFARI BOOKS ONLINE allows you to search for a specific answer, cut and paste code, download chapters, and stay current with emerging technologies.

Activate your FREE Online Edition at www.informit.com/safarifree

> **STEP 1:** Enter the coupon code: SSUQYCB.

> **STEP 2:** New Safari users, complete the brief registration form. Safari subscribers, just log in.

If you have difficulty registering on Safari or accessing the online edition, please e-mail customer-service@safaribooksonline.com